# COWBOY CLOTHING AND GEAR

The Complete Hamley Catalog of 1942

Hamley & Company

DOVER PUBLICATIONS, INC.

New York

## Copyright

Copyright © 1995 by Dover Publications, Inc.
All rights reserved under Pan American and International Copyright Conventions.


## Bibliographical Note

*Cowboy Clothing and Gear: The Complete Hamley Catalog of 1942*, first published by Dover Publications, Inc., in 1995, is an unabridged republication of *Hamley's Cowboy Catalog No. 41*, originally published by Hamley & Company, Pendleton, Oregon, in 1942. A new Introduction has been written specially for this edition.


## Library of Congress Cataloging-in-Publication Data

Hamley & Company.
    Cowboy clothing and gear : the complete Hamley catalog of 1942 / Hamley & Company.
       p.    cm.
    "Unabridged republication of Hamley's cowboy catalog no. 41, originally published by Hamley & Company, Pendleton, Oregon, in 1942"—T.p. verso.
    ISBN 0-486-28841-2 (pbk.)
    1. Cowboys—Collectibles—Catalogs.    2. Cowboys—Costume—Catalogs.
3. Hamley & Company—Catalogs.  I. Title.  II. Series: Hamley's cowboy catalog ; no. 41.
F596.H268   1995
978—dc20

95-21984
CIP


Manufactured in the United States of America
Dover Publications, Inc., 31 East 2nd Street, Mineola, N.Y. 11501

# Introduction

HAMLEY & COMPANY has become famous throughout the world for the quality of its saddles. The Hamley tradition was started by two brothers from Wisconsin, J. J. and Henry Hamley. Armed with two railway tickets, $10.00 in pocket money, $500.00 in credit and a dream, they arrived in Ashton, South Dakota, in 1883 and opened the Hamley Brothers Harness Shop.

For the first two or three years, things went well, but after four or five years of drought, the ranchers could no longer afford to buy anything. In 1880, deeply in debt, the brothers moved to Kendrick, Idaho, where there was a gold-mining boom. Business was good, but other problems arose—part of the town, and the store with it, burned in 1892; brother Henry died in 1894 and a second fire destroyed the business in 1904. In 1905, J. J. Hamley moved again, this time to Pendleton, Oregon, where the company still stands in its original location.

Hamley & Company was run by the Hamley family until 1980. We purchased the business in 1988, and today, backed by more than a hundred years of tradition, Hamley & Company is manufacturing saddles and all related leather items with the same quality and pride that began the company in 1883. Many of the items you will find in the catalog reprinted here are still being sold by Hamley & Company.

We want to thank Dover Publications for selecting one of our great catalogs from the past to reproduce.

Loren & Margaret Wood
HAMLEY & COMPANY

# Hamley's

## COWBOY CATALOG / NO. 41

## HAMLEY & COMPANY
### PENDLETON, OREGON, U. S. A.

[ORIGINAL FRONT COVER]

# *Hamley quality is built in ..*

Long ago we realized that to insure the quality of Hamley saddles we must start with the tree. As a result of this realization the Hamley saddle tree shop was established in Pendleton, where saddle tree and leather craftsmen work out ideas together to make better trees for Hamley saddles. Many improvements in design, construction and new features have resulted from this teamwork.

To the man who spends much of his time in a saddle, its design, quality and craftsmanship are vitally important.

We pledge ourselves to continue to maintain the high standards of excellence which have made the name Hamley stand for "tops" in saddles for over half a century.

*L. H. Hamley*

☆            ☆            ☆            ☆

## SADDLEMAKERS FOR FOUR GENERATIONS

Hamley & Company had its beginning in 1883, when J. J. and Henry Hamley, who had learned the saddlery business from their father, arrived at Ashton, South Dakota, from Wisconsin. Seven years later, in 1890 they moved to Kendrick, Idaho. In 1894, Henry Hamley died. J. J. carried on and in June, 1905, moved to Pendleton, Oregon, where he was active head of the business until his death in 1939.

Through the genius of J. J. Hamley, with the assistance of his sons Lester and John, the business grew from a small saddle shop serving local needs to a nationwide enterprise serving customers in every state in the union and in many foreign countries.

Lester and David Hamley, son and grandson of J. J., representing the third and fourth generation of saddle-making Hamleys, grew up in the business and are now active heads of the company.

*The famous Hamley Circle "H" trademark is the symbol of quality backed by over a half century of building honest value into good saddles and other leather articles. It is the rider's guarantee of saddle satisfaction.*

LESTER H. HAMLEY
*President*

J. DAVID HAMLEY
*Vice President*

RALPH H. SCHWALBE
*Secretary-Treasurer*

# Your Saddle is Tailored from Tree to

Tree making is an art in the Hamley Saddle Tree Shop . . . devoted exclusively to making better trees for Hamley Saddles. Here you see the tree shop foreman carefully fitting the cantle to a new saddle tree.

After a Hamley Saddle tree is built into one strong unit, the seat is hand-shaped to fit like a glove.

The finished tree is covered with select bull hide which shrinks to fit the tree tighter than a drum.

In the Hamley Saddle Shop, expert saddlemakers cut and fit the select leathers for your saddle.

# Finished Saddle by Hamley Craftsmen

Here Clem Hogue, foreman of the Hamley Saddle Shop, marks off a seat pattern for a new saddle.

Hand stamping a Hamley saddle skirt . . . a job for an expert with years of experience and a taste for art.

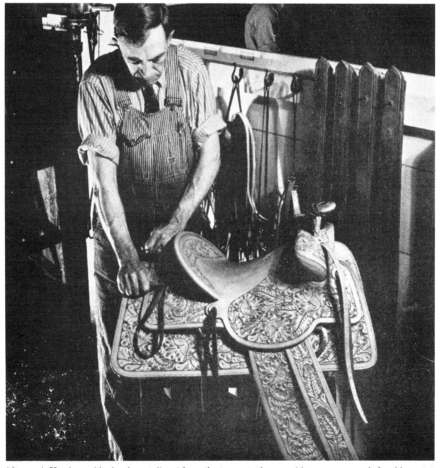

After each Hamley saddle has been tailored from the tree out, the assembly man prepares it for shipment to its new-owner. Satisfied Hamley owners can be found in every state in the union and in many foreign countries.

3

# You're Always Welcome at Hamley's

*In this building on S. E. First St. and Court Ave. in Pendleton, Oregon, you'll find the Hamley store, saddle shop and offices. Pay us a visit when you're in our vicinity.*

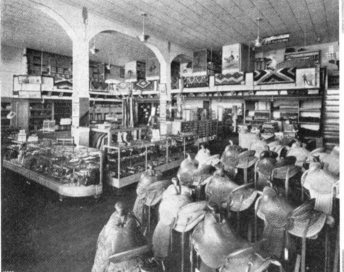

*During Pendleton's famous Round-Up in September each year you'll find this Hamley showroom overflowing with cowboys, ranchers and other folks who like to see and feel the honest quality of real leather articles.*

*Most Hamley customers can't visit our store personally. That is why we have a large staff trained to take care of the thousands of orders received each year from those who appreciate Hamley quality.*

4

# Guarantee

We hereby agree with the holder of this Catalog that we will refund the money for any goods that are not exactly as represented, and we furthermore agree to repay all expenses incurred in any unsatisfactory transaction, including transportation charges both ways, subject to conditions named in Article 4 below.

*F.H.Hamley*

*President, Hamley & Co.*

**1** **OUR TERMS ARE CASH.** No charge for exchange on checks and drafts drawn on United States Banks. At least one-fourth the amount of every order must accompany order. Strictly one price to all. All prices are subject to change without notice. Where prices are reduced, goods will be shipped at the reduced price and the saving returned to you. In case of advance in price, we will advise you before shipping the goods, if you so request. All prices are F.O.B. Pendleton, except where otherwise stated.

**2** **HOW TO SEND MONEY.** The best way is by postal or express money order. We also accept bank drafts and checks drawn by responsible parties. Make all drafts, orders and checks payable to Hamley & Co. *Be sure when sending stamps or currency to register your letter.*

**3** **HOW TO WRITE AN ORDER.** Write distinctly. Especially your *name and full address*. Give post office, county and state. State exact amount of money sent. Use our order forms if possible; we supply them free. Do not cut illustrations from catalog. Simply give number, page, size, price and color when necessary.

**4** **RETURN GOODS AND EXCHANGES.** We will exchange goods if not satisfactory if returned at once and in good condition, with the following exceptions:

Goods made to order to measurement.

Goods not cataloged, which have been procured especially to your order.

No article which has been worn or used in any way, without consent from us.

An article being returned for exchange or refund must be returned by the individual who placed the order for the article.

**5** **IMPORTANT—READ THIS SURE:** Never be afraid to ask questions. This Catalog is supposed to give full information but we are here to serve you, and inquiries regarding qualities, prices, etc., will always be answered promptly. Explain fully what you want and we are sure we can please you. Your satisfaction means our success.

**6** **REFERENCES.** As to our reliability and reputation, we refer you to any Commercial Rating Agency in America. We also refer you to the First National Bank and United States National Bank, Pendleton, Oregon.

## About Prices

All prices in this Catalog are *net*, f.o.b., Pendleton, except where otherwise noted, and subject to reductions or advances at any time, as conditions demand. **Prices are figured down just as close as it is possible to figure and still maintain the quality.**

The quotations on heavy stock saddles include trees as long as 15 inches, and skirts of the right dimensions to balance with the tree. On saddles priced at $80.00 and over, for square skirts, we include skirts as large as 30 x 15 inches. For skirts this large it requires a tree fully 14½ or 15 inches long to make the saddle balance. For a tree as short as 13 inches, skirts should not be over 28 inches long.

## Safe Delivery Guaranteed

All goods shipped by Hamley & Company are insured, for the full value of each shipment, against error, destruction, and unsatisfactory delivery. All orders are carefully packed and protected in every way possible; items which are fragile or easily broken are so labeled—thus they receive careful handling in the mails. We know of instances, however, where post offices burned, destroying all mails; goods were delivered to the wrong person; or where items were carelessly crushed in transit. In such instances new goods are sent to replace.

Hamley orders are guaranteed to reach you in satisfactory condition.

# HAMLEY'S STIRRUP LEATHER FEATURE SOLVES THE "FREE-SWING" PROBLEM

Patent No. 2,207,982

## 100%
### More Freedom!
than with any old-style stirrup leather rigging. Rider sits naturally, comfortably.

Natural position of stirrup leathers is *forward* in every Hamley Saddle made with this Hamley feature!

**Views below from under side of tree**     **Views below from top side of tree**

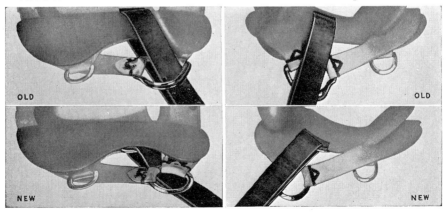

ONLY $5.00 EXTRA IN ANY HAMLEY SADDLE. THIS FEATURE CANNOT BE ADDED TO A SADDLE WHICH IS ALREADY MADE OR STARTED BECAUSE IT IS PART OF THE TREE.

# *The* NORTHWEST
## No. G434

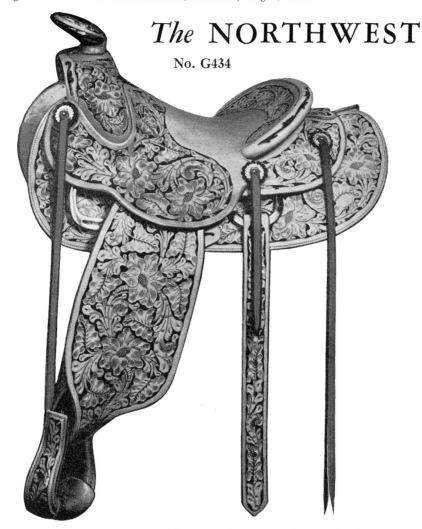

This saddle, created and made by Hamley & Company,
and presented by the Pendleton Round-Up Association,
became the property of Cody Dodson at the 1939 Pendleton Round-Up when he won the Northwest Bucking
Championship.

BECAUSE of the steady increase in the popularity of the Hamley Bernard tree, it was
chosen for this fine prize saddle. This tree has a 13″ swell fork, and the horn is about 3″
high at the front edge, with a 4½″ top. The cantle is 2¾″ high, finished with a Semi-
Cheyenne roll.

The stamping is the same pattern as used on saddle No. F615, but it has a dark
brown dyed background. The scroll on the front of fork and top of cantle binding is hand-
stamped and dyed.

Saddle is mounted with No. 129X sterling silver conchas (1½″ in diameter), horn cap,
and special cantle plate. It comes equipped with front cinch, stamped back cinch and tugs.

The Northwest can be furnished on other trees and with changes
throughout to suit the purchaser. Price as shown and described......... **$175.00**
Without silver cantle plate and horn cap, and with plain background...........**$150.00**

READ ABOUT THE HAMLEY STIRRUP LEATHER
FEATURE ON OPPOSITE PAGE

# Hamley Builds Outstanding
## *Prize Saddles*

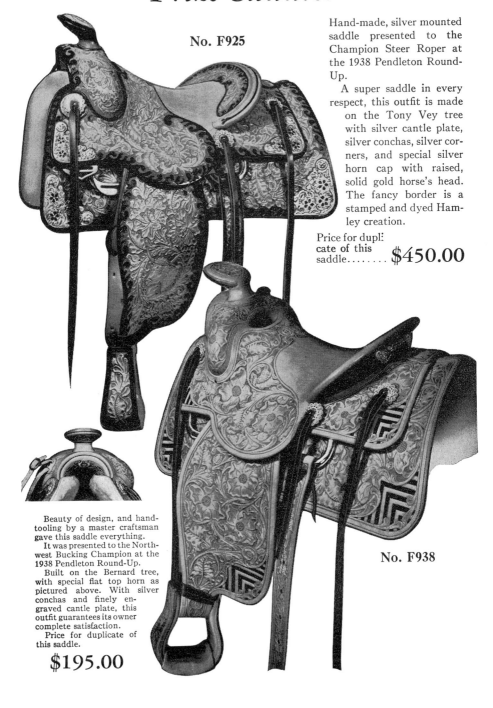

**No. F925**

Hand-made, silver mounted saddle presented to the Champion Steer Roper at the 1938 Pendleton Round-Up.

A super saddle in every respect, this outfit is made on the Tony Vey tree with silver cantle plate, silver conchas, silver corners, and special silver horn cap with raised, solid gold horse's head. The fancy border is a stamped and dyed Hamley creation.

Price for duplicate of this saddle........ **$450.00**

Beauty of design, and hand-tooling by a master craftsman gave this saddle everything.

It was presented to the Northwest Bucking Champion at the 1938 Pendleton Round-Up.

Built on the Bernard tree, with special flat top horn as pictured above. With silver conchas and finely engraved cantle plate, this outfit guarantees its owner complete satisfaction.

Price for duplicate of this saddle.

**$195.00**

**No. F938**

# *The* OREGON

## *. . . good for everything!*

### No. F439

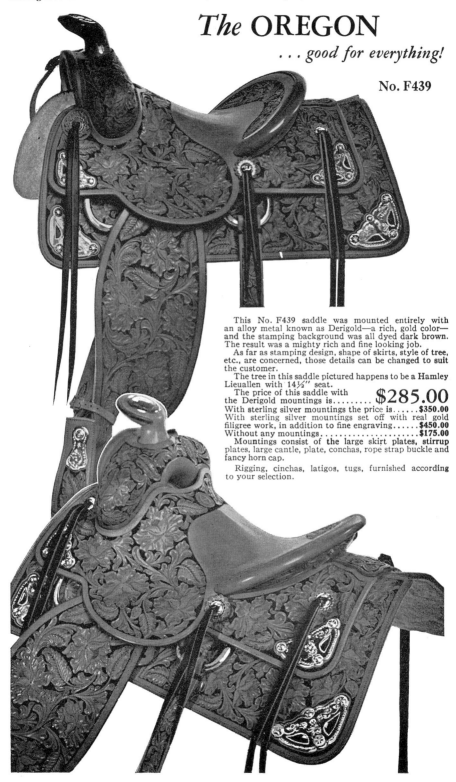

This No. F439 saddle was mounted entirely with an alloy metal known as Derigold—a rich, gold color—and the stamping background was all dyed dark brown. The result was a mighty rich and fine looking job.

As far as stamping design, shape of skirts, style of tree, etc., are concerned, those details can be changed to suit the customer.

The tree in this saddle pictured happens to be a Hamley Lieuallen with 14½" seat.

The price of this saddle with the Derigold mountings is......... **$285.00**

With sterling silver mountings the price is......**$350.00**
With sterling silver mountings set off with real gold filigree work, in addition to fine engraving......**$450.00**
Without any mountings......................**$175.00**

Mountings consist of the large skirt plates, stirrup plates, large cantle, plate, conchas, rope strap buckle and fancy horn cap.

Rigging, cinchas, latigos, tugs, furnished according to your selection.

# *The* TONY VEY

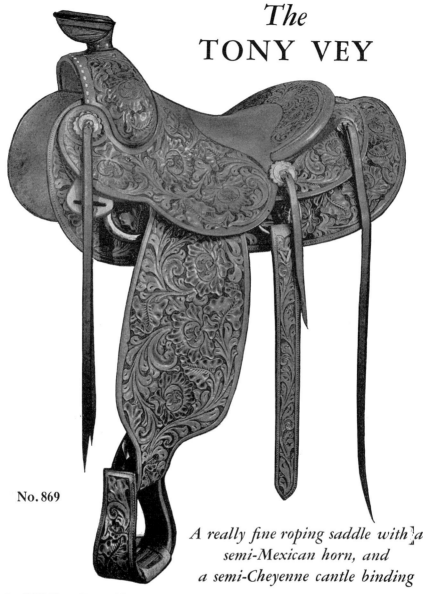

**No. 869**

*A really fine roping saddle with a
semi-Mexican horn, and
a semi-Cheyenne cantle binding*

THIS Tony Vey saddle was so named because it was originally made for Antone (Tony) Vey, one of the successful and highly respected cattlemen of this locality. Tony is himself a fine roper; he knows what a good roping saddle is.

The tree is a Vey Special with low, sloping cantle 1½ inches high; the fork is also low and is 12 inches across. The horn is the semi-Mexican type, and has a 4-inch top.

All materials are selected and the saddle is hand-stamped throughout, even to the rear leather cincha and tug, and the under covering of the fork.

This saddle is finer than most people buy, but for the lover of super-equipment it is a dream come true.

Can be furnished on other trees and with changes throughout to suit the purchaser. Price, as shown and described.............. **$160.00**

**Read about the Hamley Stirrup Leather Feature, Page 6**

# *The* CHEYENNE

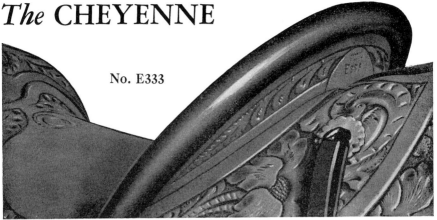

No. E333

## *Semi-Cheyenne Cantle*

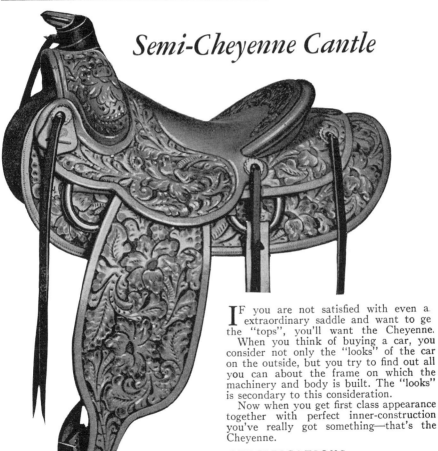

IF you are not satisfied with even a extraordinary saddle and want to ge the "tops", you'll want the Cheyenne.

When you think of buying a car, you consider not only the "looks" of the car on the outside, but you try to find out all you can about the frame on which the machinery and body is built. The "looks" is secondary to this consideration.

Now when you get first class appearance together with perfect inner-construction you've really got something—that's the Cheyenne.

### SPECIFICATIONS

TREE—"Campbell Roper." Fork 14″ across when finished. Cantle 2¾″ high. Horn 3¾″ across top when covered, 2¾″ high, flat top.

WEIGHT—About 39 pounds complete.

SKIRTS—Large round as shown.

RIGGING—Full double, three-quarter double or Hamley Flat Plate single. (If single ring rigging or "E-Z" 'rigging is wanted deduct $3.50 from prices.)

CANTLE-BINDING—Special semi-Cheyenne, extra heavy. (If ordinary hand-sewed binding is wanted deduct $2.50 from price of saddle.)

PRICE—
As shown...... **$125.00**

| | |
|---|---|
| With square skirts | $137.50 |
| As shown, check stamp | 97.50 |
| Square skirts | 105.00 |
| As shown, plain | 95.00 |
| Square skirts | 102.50 |

# *The* ROLLS ROYCE

No.
F621

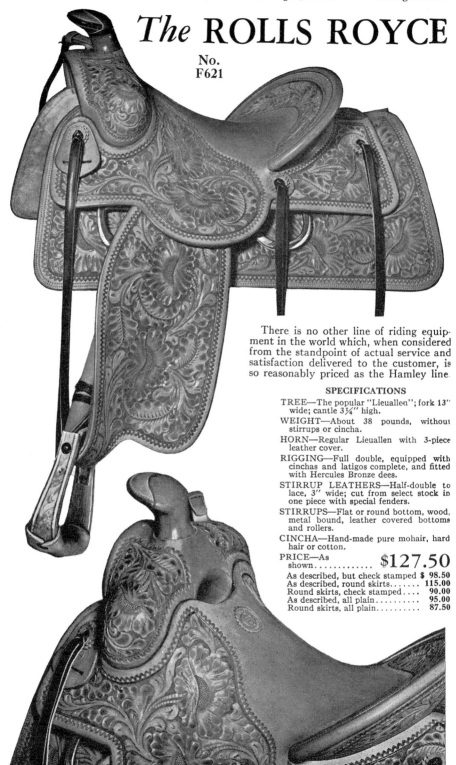

There is no other line of riding equipment in the world which, when considered from the standpoint of actual service and satisfaction delivered to the customer, is so reasonably priced as the Hamley line.

## SPECIFICATIONS

TREE—The popular "Lieuallen"; fork **13"** wide; cantle 3¼" high.

WEIGHT—About 38 pounds, without stirrups or cincha.

HORN—Regular Lieuallen with 3-piece leather cover.

RIGGING—Full double, equipped with cinchas and latigos complete, and fitted with Hercules Bronze dees.

STIRRUP LEATHERS—Half-double to lace, 3" wide; cut from select stock in one piece with special fenders.

STIRRUPS—Flat or round bottom, wood, metal bound, leather covered bottoms and rollers.

CINCHA—Hand-made pure mohair, hard hair or cotton.

PRICE—As shown............ **$127.50**

| | |
|---|---|
| As described, but check stamped | **$ 98.50** |
| As described, round skirts...... | **115.00** |
| Round skirts, check stamped.... | **90.00** |
| As described, all plain.......... | **95.00** |
| Round skirts, all plain.......... | **87.50** |

# *The*  SMOOTHY

## No. G733

## Made on the Lieuallen-Standard Tree

*An unbeatable combination tree*

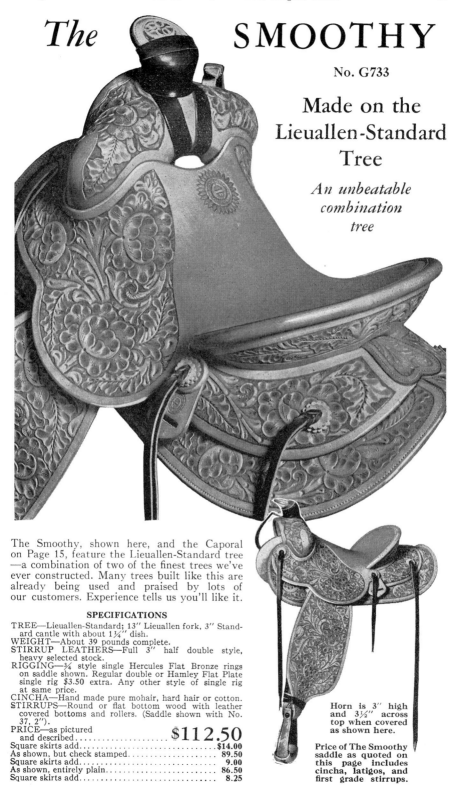

The Smoothy, shown here, and the Caporal on Page 15, feature the Lieuallen-Standard tree —a combination of two of the finest trees we've ever constructed. Many trees built like this are already being used and praised by lots of our customers. Experience tells us you'll like it.

### SPECIFICATIONS

TREE—Lieuallen-Standard; 13″ Lieuallen fork, 3″ Standard cantle with about 1¼″ dish.

WEIGHT—About 39 pounds complete.

STIRRUP LEATHERS—Full 3″ half double style, heavy selected stock.

RIGGING—¾ style single Hercules Flat Bronze rings on saddle shown. Regular double or Hamley Flat Plate single rig $3.50 extra. Any other style of single rig at same price.

CINCHA—Hand made pure mohair, hard hair or cotton.

STIRRUPS—Round or flat bottom wood with leather covered bottoms and rollers. (Saddle shown with No. 37, 2″).

PRICE—as pictured and described . . . . . . . . . . . . . . . . . . . . . **$112.50**

Square skirts add . . . . . . . . . . . . . . . . . . . . . . . . . . . . . .$14.00
As shown, but check stamped . . . . . . . . . . . . . . . . . . . . 89.50
Square skirts add . . . . . . . . . . . . . . . . . . . . . . . . . . . . . . 9.00
As shown, entirely plain . . . . . . . . . . . . . . . . . . . . . . . . 86.50
Square skirts add . . . . . . . . . . . . . . . . . . . . . . . . . . . . . . 8.25

Horn is 3″ high and 3½″ across top when covered as shown here.

Price of The Smoothy saddle as quoted on this page includes cincha, latigos, and first grade stirrups.

# *The* Piquet

**No. D142**

**ANOTHER HAMLEY CUSTOMER AND HIS NEW ROPING SADDLE**

Dear Sirs:

My new Hamley outfit has the admiration of all my friends and myself. It is absolutely the best piece of work I have ever seen; and as easy riding as any saddle I have ever ridden.

It sets so perfectly on my horse that I've hardly needed the rear cincha. I can just tighten up the main cincha and it will hold a calf just swell. You have my sincere appreciation, and you may expect my next order.

Sincerely yours,

GEORGE DE MOSS

Moro, Oregon.

## SPECIFICATIONS

TREE—Hamley "Standard", 13" swell, cantle 3" high with about 1¼" dish, horn 3" high with top 4" across when covered.

WEIGHT—About 38 pounds.

RIGGING—¾ double. Regular double if ordered or ¾ single Patent Flat Plate. If single ring or "E-Z", rigging is wanted, deduct $3.50 from prices quoted.

STIRRUP LEATHERS—Selected heavy, 3" wide, single.

STIRRUPS—Round or flat bottom wood with heavy metal bindings and leather covered bottoms and rollers. No. 37 stirrups with 2½" bottoms are shown in picture.

CINCHAS—Mohair or cotton front with cotton or leather rear.

PRICE—As shown, full hand stamping and double rigging **$118.50**

Same saddle, round skirts. **$107.50**

Square skirts as shown but check stamping . . . . . . . . . . . . **99.50**

Round skirts, check stamping **89.50**

As shown, plain . . . . . . . . . . **96.50**

Round skirts, plain . . . . . . . **86.50**

# *The* CAPORAL

## No. G734

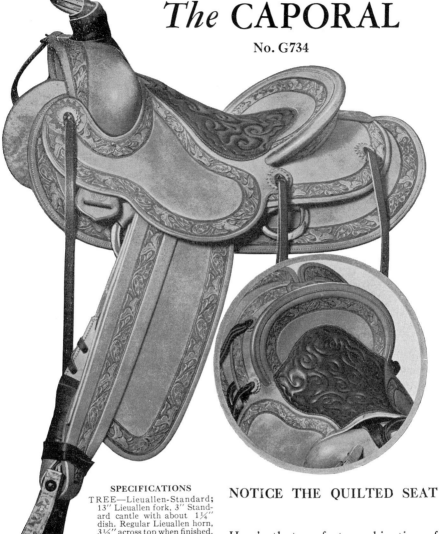

### SPECIFICATIONS

TREE—Lieuallen-Standard; 13″ Lieuallen fork, 3″ Standard cantle with about 1¼″ dish. Regular Lieuallen horn, 3½″ across top when finished, and 3″ high.

WEIGHT—About 39 pounds complete.

STIRRUP LEATHERS—Full 3″ half double style, heavy selected stock.

RIGGING—¾ double style Hercules Fla Bronze rings and dees. Equipped with cinchas and latigos complete.

CINCHAS—Front: mohair, hard hair or cotton; rear: cotton cord, fish cord, web or leather.

SEAT—Quilted to base of cantle. (If plain seat is wanted deduct $3.50 from price quoted).

STIRRUPS—No. 30 or 37 wood, metal bound, with leather covered bottoms and rollers. (See note top of page 65).

PRICE—As pictured and described................ **$103.50**

Square skirts add..........................**$10.00**

As shown, entirely plain................... 89.50

Square skirts add.......................... 8.50

This saddle may be had with a machine embossed flower border instead of the hand-finished border—otherwise as pictured....................**$93.50**

## NOTICE THE QUILTED SEAT

Here's that perfect combination of fine Hamley Saddle Trees again—the Lieuallen-Standard; and on this saddle we have put a new type of border stamping; it's hand-finished, just like those fine Hamley belts that you buy with the fancy silver buckle sets. This is, honestly, one of the prettiest border stampings that we have ever developed—simple, and yet decorative to the $n$th degree.

# *The* DENNY HUNT

### No. H236

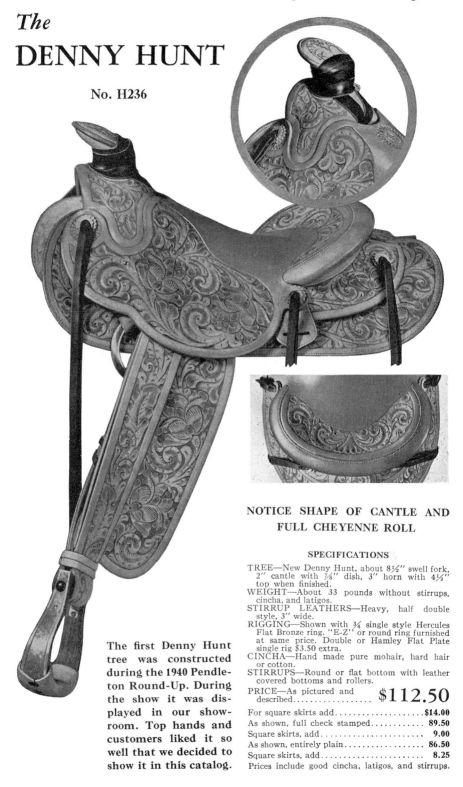

**NOTICE SHAPE OF CANTLE AND FULL CHEYENNE ROLL**

The first Denny Hunt tree was constructed during the 1940 Pendleton Round-Up. During the show it was displayed in our showroom. Top hands and customers liked it so well that we decided to show it in this catalog.

### SPECIFICATIONS

TREE—New Denny Hunt, about 8½″ swell fork, 2″ cantle with ⅞″ dish, 3″ horn with 4½″ top when finished.

WEIGHT—About 33 pounds without stirrups, cincha, and latigos.

STIRRUP LEATHERS—Heavy, half double style, 3″ wide.

RIGGING—Shown with ¾ single style Hercules Flat Bronze ring. "E-Z" or round ring furnished at same price. Double or Hamley Flat Plate single rig $3.50 extra.

CINCHA—Hand made pure mohair, hard hair or cotton.

STIRRUPS—Round or flat bottom with leather covered bottoms and rollers.

PRICE—As pictured and described................. **$112.50**

| | |
|---|---|
| For square skirts add..................... | $14.00 |
| As shown, full check stamped............ | 89.50 |
| Square skirts, add...................... | 9.00 |
| As shown, entirely plain................. | 86.50 |
| Square skirts, add...................... | 8.25 |

Prices include good cincha, latigos, and stirrups.

# *The* LOS BANOS

### No. F615

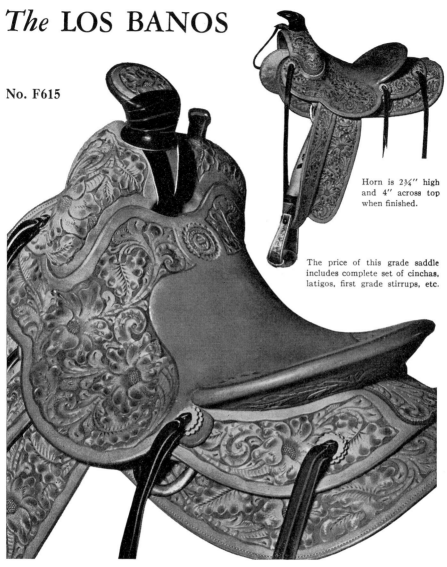

Horn is 2¾″ high and 4″ across top when finished.

The price of this grade saddle includes complete set of cinchas, latigos, first grade stirrups, etc.

## SPECIFICATIONS

TREE—Campbell Roper, 14″ swell fork, 2¾″ cantle.

WEIGHT—About 36 pounds without cinchas or latigos.

RIGGING—¾ double flat ring shown (see two pages immediately following saddle section for other types of rigging, and extra charges).

STIRRUP LEATHERS—Heavy, half double style, 3″ wide.

HORN—Special roper type with 4″ oval top.

PRICE—As pictured and described.............. **$116.50**

| | |
|---|---|
| For square skirts, add................. | **$15.50** |
| As shown here, check stamped........ | **92.50** |
| For square skirts, add................. | **9.00** |
| Round skirts, all plain................. | **89.50** |
| Square skirts, all plain, add........... | **7.50** |

### *Full Mexican Style Horn*

This finely finished horn with 5½″ top and full Mexican belly is made solid as a part of the tree. *Available in The Los Banos, or any other saddle in catalog, only $6.00 extra.*

This style horn only $6.00 extra

# *The* OLD
# COMFY

*Improved Back Saver*

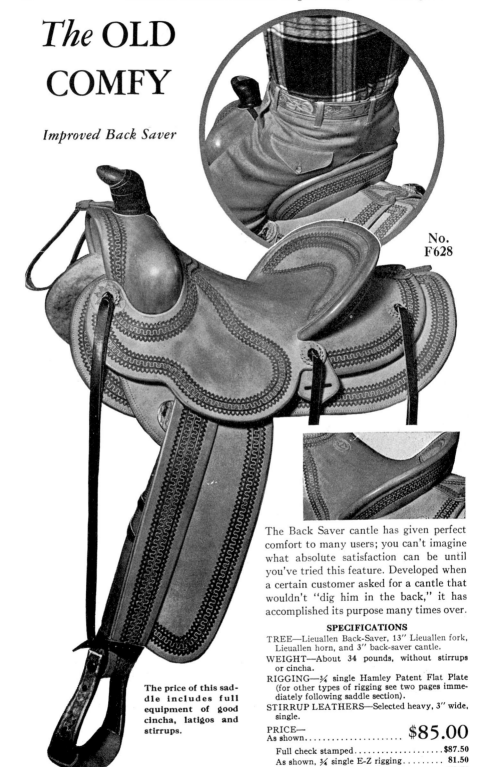

No.
F628

The Back Saver cantle has given perfect comfort to many users; you can't imagine what absolute satisfaction can be until you've tried this feature. Developed when a certain customer asked for a cantle that wouldn't "dig him in the back," it has accomplished its purpose many times over.

**The price of this saddle includes full equipment of good cincha, latigos and stirrups.**

### SPECIFICATIONS

TREE—Lieuallen Back-Saver, 13″ Lieuallen fork, Lieuallen horn, and 3″ back-saver cantle.

WEIGHT—About 34 pounds, without stirrups or cincha.

RIGGING—¾ single Hamley Patent Flat Plate (for other types of rigging see two pages immediately following saddle section).

STIRRUP LEATHERS—Selected heavy, 3″ wide, single.

PRICE—
As shown.................... **$85.00**

Full check stamped....................$87.50
As shown, ¾ single E-Z rigging......... 81.50
Entirely plain........................ 79.50

# *The* BERNARD

### No. F676

*Making
More
Friends
Every
Day!*

Jack Schoewe, pictured above with his Hamley outfit wrote us the following letter after his rig had arrived:

Friend Dave:

I took my saddle from the express company last night and when I unpacked it I sure got a shock—the same kind of a shock that a kid gets on Christmas morning.

To say the saddle pleased me is putting it mildly. Everything I asked for, down to the smallest detail, was painstakingly looked after.

Some of the fellows I know say your prices are too high, but when you consider the workmanship, care, finish, and fitting, to say nothing of the quality of material used, I think yours are the most economical saddles on the market.

Sincerely, JACK SCHOEWE, Milwaukee, Wisconsin.

●

The Bernard tree, created three years ago, and shown in the saddle on this page, has increased in popularity each year; it's ruggedly constructed for work and comfort—has a 13″ swell fork, 2¾″ cantle (slight dish), and a special horn 4½″ across the saddle is finished

### SPECIFICATIONS

TREE—Hamley Bernard.

WEIGHT—As pictured, about 35 pounds.

RIGGING—Equipped with flat bronze or solid nickel dees or "E-Z" rings. Single Flat Plate rigging $3.50 extra, ¾ double "E-Z" or ring rigging $3.50 extra.

The saddle complete as described, including good stirrups, good cincha, latigos, etc. . . . . . . . . . . . **$92.50**

For square skirts add. . . . . .$ 9.00

Price as pictured but with border stamping. . . . . . . . . . . . . . 88.50

For square skirts add. . . . . . . 8.00

# *The* WADE

## No. H233

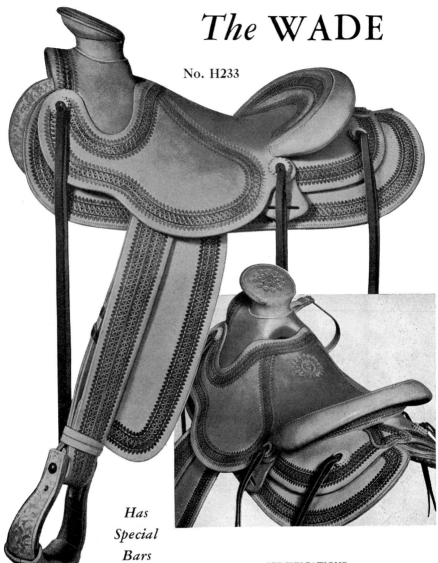

*Has Special Bars*

The bars on this tree have been fashioned from an old saddle brought across the plains by a customer's father. This customer ordered his saddle made with them; shortly several of his friends ordered saddles built the same way. Now, after nearly two years of hard use these men tell us their saddles will fit any horse and stay put uphill and downhill better than any saddle they've ever ridden.

The cantle has a special binding with nearly 1⅞" lip on the outsides, tapered to about 1¼" in the center; it's extra heavy. The horn is not completely round but rather flat on the back side (5½" side to side—5" back to front).

### SPECIFICATIONS

TREE—1940 Wade, slick fork (about 8" swell), 3" back-saver type cantle; special horn 3" high at front, 5½" across top when saddle is finished.

WEIGHT—About 35 pounds without stirrups, cincha, and latigos.

STIRRUP LEATHERS—Heavy half double style, 3" wide.

RIGGING—Shown with Center Fire. Double rigging, or Hamley Flat Plate single rig $3.50 extra. Other single styles same price as quoted.

CINCHA—Hand made pure mohair, hard hair or cotton.

STIRRUPS—Round or flat bottom with leather covered bottoms and rollers.

PRICE—As pictured
and described . . . . . . . . . . . . . . . . . . . . . . . . . . . . . **$98.50**

For square skirts add . . . . . . . . . . . . . . . . . . . . . . . . . . . . . . .$ 9.00
As shown, full check stamped . . . . . . . . . . . . . . . . . . . . . . . . 102.50
Square skirts add . . . . . . . . . . . . . . . . . . . . . . . . . . . . . . . . . . . 10.00
Entirely plain, otherwise as shown . . . . . . . . . . . . . . . . . . . . 96.50
Square skirts add . . . . . . . . . . . . . . . . . . . . . . . . . . . . . . . . . . . 8.50

# *The New* HARNEY

### No. 7983S

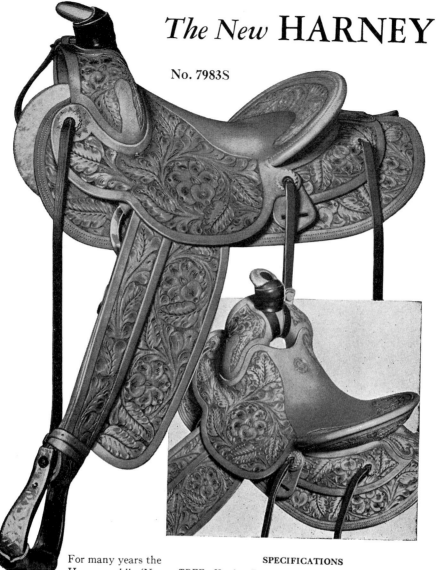

For many years the Harney saddle (No. 7983x) has been featured in the Hamley Catalog, and it has for as many years been a favorite. The *New* Harney (No. 7983S) shown here is the same saddle with two improvements—*a one-piece seat and front jockey*, and *an improved roper horn*, which is just slightly lower than that on the old Harney. The Hamley Roper tree has a reputation, country-wide, for that good old-time reliable service and satisfaction which our grandfathers talk about.

### SPECIFICATIONS

**TREE**—Hamley Roper, 13″ swell fork, 3″ sloping cantle; 3″ horn with 3¼″ top when finished.

**WEIGHT**—About 38 pounds ready for your horse.

**STIRRUP LEATHERS**—Full 3″ half double style, heavy selected stock.

**RIGGING**—Shown with ¾ single style Hercules Flat Bronze ring. "E-Z" or round ring furnished at same price. Double or Hamley Flat Plate single rig $3.50 extra.

**CINCHA**—Hand made pure mohair, hard hair or cotton.

**STIRRUPS**—Round or flat bottom with leather covered bottoms and rollers.

**PRICE**—as pictured and described......................**$103.50**

For square skirts add................................$12.50

As shown, full check stamped........................ 89.50

Square skirts add................................. 9.00

As shown, entirely plain........................... 85.00

Square skirts add................................. 8.25

# *The* OKANOGAN

### *Another Saddle on the Hamley Bernard Tree*

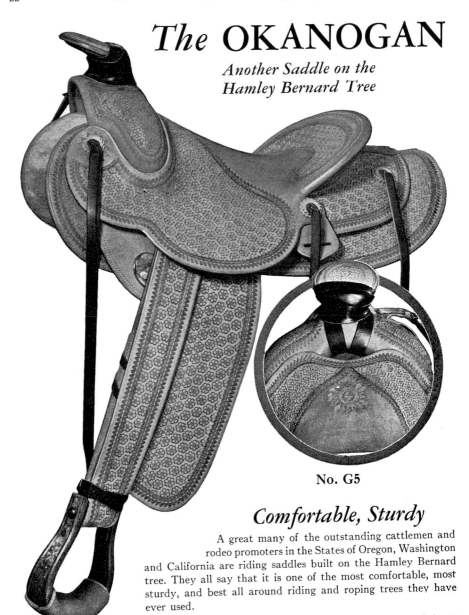

### No. G5

## *Comfortable, Sturdy*

A great many of the outstanding cattlemen and rodeo promoters in the States of Oregon, Washington and California are riding saddles built on the Hamley Bernard tree. They all say that it is one of the most comfortable, most sturdy, and best all around riding and roping trees they have ever used.

**STIRRUPS**—Flat or round bottom, wood, heavy metal bindings, leather covered bottoms and rollers.

**CANTLE-BINDING**—Regular leather, but laid back to improve the line of the saddle as well as the riding comfort.

### SPECIFICATIONS

**TREE**—Hamley Bernard, 13″ swell fork, horn about 3″ high at front edge, with 4½″ top, cantle 2¾″ high.

**WEIGHT**—Complete with cincha and latigos about 37 pounds.

**RIGGING**—¾ single Hamley Patent Flat Plate. Double ring rigging at same price, or if wanted with single ring rigging, deduct $3.50 from price of saddle.

**STIRRUP LEATHERS**—Selected heavy stock, 3″ wide, half-double style.

**PRICE**—As pictured and described **$96.00***

| | |
|---|---:|
| For square skirts add | $ 9.00 |
| As shown, but with border stamping | 92.00* |
| For square skirts, add | 8.00 |
| As shown, entirely plain | 87.50* |
| For square skirts add | 7.75 |

*Deduct $3.50 from prices if single ring rigging is wanted.

## Read about the Hamley Stirrup Leather Feature on Page 6

# The UBANGI
## for Streamlined Efficiency

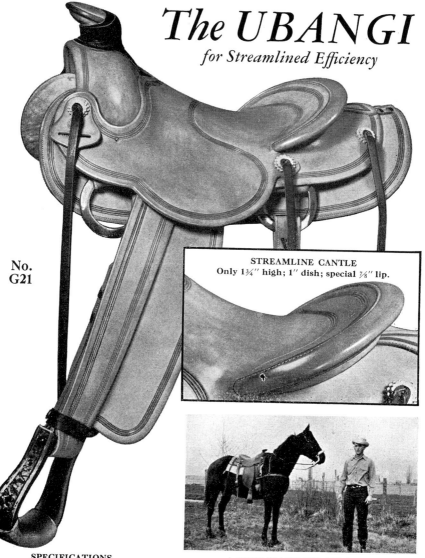

**No. G21**

**STREAMLINE CANTLE**
Only 1¾″ high; 1″ dish; special ⅞″ lip.

**A 100% HAMLEY OUTFIT**

### SPECIFICATIONS

**TREE**—Hamley Professional Roper, 12″ swell fork, 1¾″ cantle, 1″ dish.
**HORN**—Professional Roper, 4¼″ top.
**WEIGHT**—About 31 pounds without latigos and cinchas.
**STIRRUP LEATHERS**—Half-double style, selected heavy, 3″ wide.
**RIGGING**—Full double, equipped with cinchas and latigos complete, and fitted with flat rings in front, and flat dees in rear.
**CINCHAS**—Front: mohair, hard hair or cotton; rear: cotton cord, fish cord, web or leather.
**SKIRTS**—Round, and slightly smaller than regular.
**STIRRUPS**—No. 30 or 37 wood stirrups, metal bound, with leather bottoms and rollers.
**PRICE**—As pictured and described.............. **$86.50**
For square skirts add...............$8.50
**CANTLE**—Streamline cantle with ⅞″ lip. For ordinary cantle binding, deduct $1.50 from price of saddle.

Dear Lester:
I've had my saddle for more than two months now and I like it just fine.
I'm more than glad I added the NEW STIRRUP LEATHER FEATURE to my order; it certainly is a fine improvement and I wouldn't be without it. My saddle needed no breaking in; I feel more comfortable and at ease already than I did in my old one.
I want to thank all of you for the excellent job you did on my new rig.
Sincerely yours,
EHRMAN DAVIS
Union, Oregon.

As Mr. Davis indicates, the only improvement that could be made in this outfit is to include the Hamley Stirrup Leather Rigging as described on page 6. Extra cost for this feature is only $5. If wanted, please be sure to specify in your original order.

# *The* LOW BOY

### No. 6035

The Hamley Low Boy saddle has practically become a fixture in the Hamley line of quality merchandise. Steady customer demand has brought this about.

## *"Can't express it in words"*—

Gentlemen:

I'm not much of a hand at writing, but you asked for it, so here it is.

Now, let's talk about the saddle. When I opened up the bundle and saw the fine clever workmanship you folks put into a saddle, I just had to keep looking at it—spent much as three hours sighting from every angle, and couldn't find a thing that didn't suit me perfectly.

Want to tell you it fits my horse perfect. Have it pretty well broken in now, and it rides so good, well, I just can't express it in words. My saddle and bridle are the talk of the town. Wouldn't part with it for twice what I paid.

When I take my outfit for a ride, we sure tie up traffic.

Yours truly,

HARRY L. BARRETT

Andover, Massachusetts.

### SPECIFICATIONS

TREE—Famous Hamley-Roper Tree, fork 13″ wide, 3″ sloping cantle.

WEIGHT—When made as shown, about 38 pounds.

STIRRUP LEATHERS — Half double style, full 3″, wide, cut from selected heavy saddle leather, skirts square style with round corners.

RIGGING—Full double, equipped with cinchas and latigos complete, and fitted with Hercules bronze dees.

CINCHAS—Front, mohair, hard hair or cotton; rear, cotton cord, fish cord, webb or leather.

STIRRUPS—No. 30 or 37 wood stirrups, metal bound, with leather covered bottoms and rollers.

PRICE—Full hand stamping, and made as pictured and described..... **$123.50**

Round skirts, otherwise as shown **$106.50**

Without stamping, otherwise as pictured....................**$102.50**

(If full double cincha rigging is not wanted, deduct $3.50 from the prices quoted.)

# Hamley's "STANDARD"

### No. 239

**Miss Folsom certainly likes her new Hamley Saddle. Read her letter:**

Dear Sirs:

The saddle you shipped to me arrived in fine shape. I want to thank you ever so much for sending it so promptly. You even sent it a few days ahead of my specified time.

The saddle is truly "A work of art." Just looking at it you can tell that skilled craftsmen have worked on it. It is exactly what I wanted, and I appreciate your filling the order to a "T". I'm immensely pleased with the saddle and every time I put it on a horse, I feel proud to think I own a Hamley saddle like that. It really measures up to every single requirement.

Yours truly,

MARY DALE FOLSOM.

Circle "W" Ranch, Hearst Route, Willits, Calif.

## SPECIFICATIONS

TREE—Hamley Standard with 3" cantle, 1¼" dish; 13" swell fork.

WEIGHT—About 34 pounds as shown.

RIGGING—¾ double with flat ring and flat dee shown (see two pages immediately following saddle section for other types of rigging, and extra charges).

STIRRUP LEATHERS—Selected stock, half double style, 3" wide. (For style like D67, page 26, deduct $3.00).

SKIRTS—California round. (For regular round skirts, deduct $2.00).

STIRRUPS—Round or flat bottom with leather covered bottoms and rollers.

CINCHA—Hard hair, mohair, or cotton front; billeted leather, cotton, or web rear.

PRICE—As pictured and described....... **$112.50**

| | |
|---|---:|
| For square skirts, add............ | **$12.50** |
| As shown, but full check stamped... | 95.00 |
| For square skirts, add............ | 9.00 |
| As shown, but entirely plain ......∴. | 89.50 |
| For square skirts, add............ | 8.00 |
| As shown, but with fenders as on D67, single flat, round or "E-Z" ring rigging, and regular round skirts....... | **$104.00** |

# *The* Majordomo

## No. D67

## FROM HAWAII
## CAME THIS LETTER

Gentlemen:

Some months ago the Hutchinson Sugar Plantation store made a purchase of saddles. I placed my order with them and received my Hamley saddle, and I'm proud of it. I thank you for the service you have given me

We now have five Hamley saddles in our outfit, and we are all Hamley boosters.

I like my Hamley Saddle in every way. Other boys have admired it from the first day I received it. It is hard to say more. It's too much to talk about, and so, I remain a Hamley booster thanking you again for the kind service you have so graciously given me.

Yours truly,
GEORGE R. BECK, JR.
Naalehu, Kauai, Hawaii.

### SPECIFICATIONS

TREE—Hamley Improved Weatherly, 10½" swell. Cantle 2½" high. Horn 3¾" across top when finished.
WEIGHT—About 33 pounds.
STIRRUP LEATHERS—Half double—heavy selected—3" wide.
RIGGING—Centerfire ring in this saddle but may be had with other styles if so ordered.
CINCHA—Mohair, hard hair or cotton.
STIRRUPS—No. 37 or No. 30. See page on which stirrups are pictured
PRICE—Full hand flowered as shown....... **$98.50**
For square skirts add..........**$12.50**

This same saddle may be had with full hand check stamping for $81.75, or entirely plain for $79.75. Add for square skirts check stamp $8.50; plain $7.50.

# *The* NEW ACORN

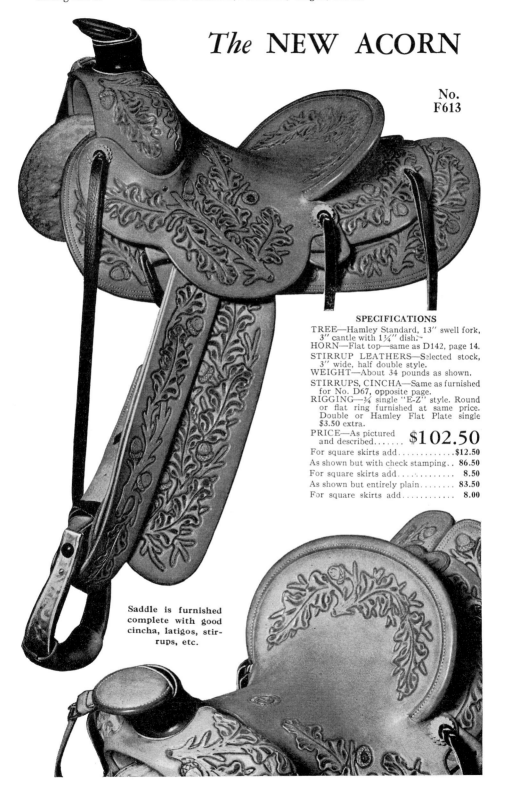

No.
F613

## SPECIFICATIONS

TREE—Hamley Standard, 13″ swell fork, 3″ cantle with 1¼″ dish.

HORN—Flat top—same as D142, page 14.

STIRRUP LEATHERS—Selected stock, 3″ wide, half double style.

WEIGHT—About 34 pounds as shown.

STIRRUPS, CINCHA—Same as furnished for No. D67, opposite page.

RIGGING—¾ single "E-Z" style. Round or flat ring furnished at same price. Double or Hamley Flat Plate single $3.50 extra.

PRICE—As pictured and described...... **$102.50**

For square skirts add............$12.50

As shown but with check stamping.. 86.50

For square skirts add............ 8.50

As shown but entirely plain....... 83.50

For square skirts add............ 8.00

Saddle is furnished complete with good cincha, latigos, stirrups, etc.

# *The* SUNSHINE

## No. G2

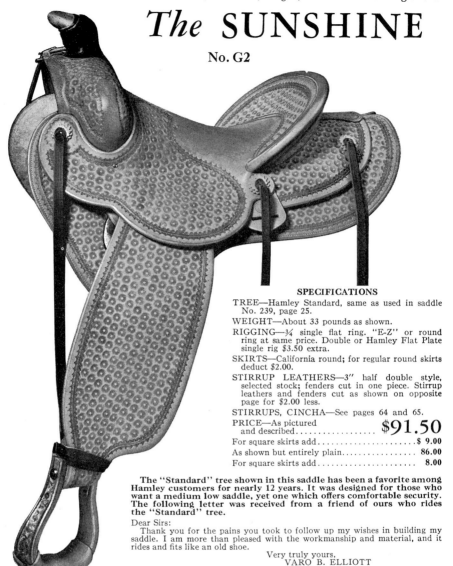

### SPECIFICATIONS

TREE—Hamley Standard, same as used in saddle No. 239, page 25.

WEIGHT—About 33 pounds as shown.

RIGGING—¾ single flat ring. "E-Z" or round ring at same price. Double or Hamley Flat Plate single rig $3.50 extra.

SKIRTS—California round; for regular round skirts deduct $2.00.

STIRRUP LEATHERS—3" half double style, selected stock; fenders cut in one piece. Stirrup leathers and fenders cut as shown on opposite page for $2.00 less.

STIRRUPS, CINCHA—See pages 64 and 65.

PRICE—As pictured
and described.................. **$91.50**

For square skirts add......................$ 9.00

As shown but entirely plain................ 86.00

For square skirts add..................... 8.00

The "Standard" tree shown in this saddle has been a favorite among Hamley customers for nearly 12 years. It was designed for those who want a medium low saddle, yet one which offers comfortable security. The following letter was received from a friend of ours who rides the "Standard" tree.

Dear Sirs:

Thank you for the pains you took to follow up my wishes in building my saddle. I am more than pleased with the workmanship and material, and it rides and fits like an old shoe.

Very truly yours,
VARO B. ELLIOTT
Algonac, Michigan.

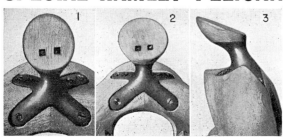

# BUENO SILLA
## No. G725

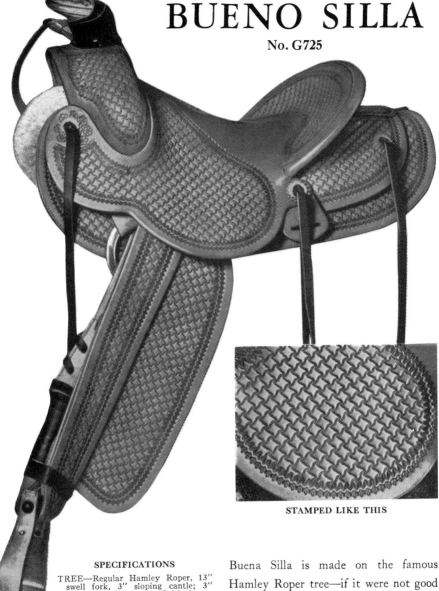

**STAMPED LIKE THIS**

### SPECIFICATIONS

TREE—Regular Hamley Roper, 13″ swell fork, 3″ sloping cantle; 3″ horn with 4″ top when finished.

WEIGHT—About 37 pounds complete.

STIRRUP LEATHERS—Full 3″ half double style, heavy selected stock.

RIGGING—¾ style single Hercules Flat Bronze rings shown. Regular double or Hamley Flat Plate single rig $3.50 extra. Any other style single rig at same price.

CINCHA—Hand made pure mohair, hard hair or cotton.

STIRRUPS—Round or flat bottom with leather covered bottoms and rollers. (Saddle shown with No. 37, 2″).

PRICE—As pictured
and described.................. **$83.50**

With square skirts........................$92.50

All plain, no stamping....................  **79.50**

With square skirts........................  **88.00**

Buena Silla is made on the famous Hamley Roper tree—if it were not good we'd tell you so, as would thousands of riders who are using this tree every day. The Hamley Roper tree appeals to the old-timers because of its comfort and practicability; appeals to the younger generation because it sets nice and low —and appeals to both because of the cooperation it affords between horse and rider when there's hard work to be done.

# "Little Joe"

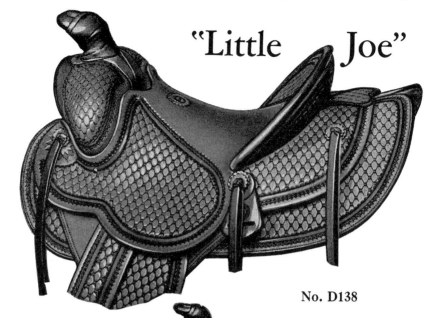

No. D138

## THE EASIEST RIDING SADDLE HE EVER HAD

Dear Sirs:

I am pleased to tell you that the saddle which I recently received from you more than fulfills my expectations.

It is the easiest riding saddle I have ever had, and it certainly fits a horse.

The saddle was *made exactly as I ordered it*, and I am very well satisfied.

Sincerely,
CHARLES RALSTON.
Wise River, Montana

Like a great many other saddles shown in Hamley catalogs during the past 30 years, the "Little Joe" has been a constant favorite among Hamley customers all over the country. In order to maintain a position in the book year in and year out it is necessary that a saddle show a certain amount of increase in sales, or at least hold its own. We are pleased to say that after several years on display, the "Little Joe" still holds its place among the best of them in the Hamley Catalog.

### SPECIFICATIONS

TREE—The comfortable, hard-working "Lieuallen." Fork 13" wide, cantle 3¼" high.

WEIGHT—About 33 pounds.

RIGGING—¾ single style Hamley Patent Flat Plate, or double style ring rigging. If single ring rigging is wanted deduct $3.50.

STIRRUP LEATHERS—3" selected stock, **single** style. Full double $1.50 extra.

STIRRUPS—Flat or round bottom, wood, heavy metal bindings, leather covered bottoms and rollers.

CINCHA—Cotton or mohair. See catalog page on which cinchas are listed.

Price, as pictured..................... **$86.50**

For square skirts add.................... **$ 8.50**

As described, but plain.................. **83.00**

For square skirts add.................... **7.50**

(See note above about "Rigging.")

# The "OK"

## An all around work saddle

### No. F617

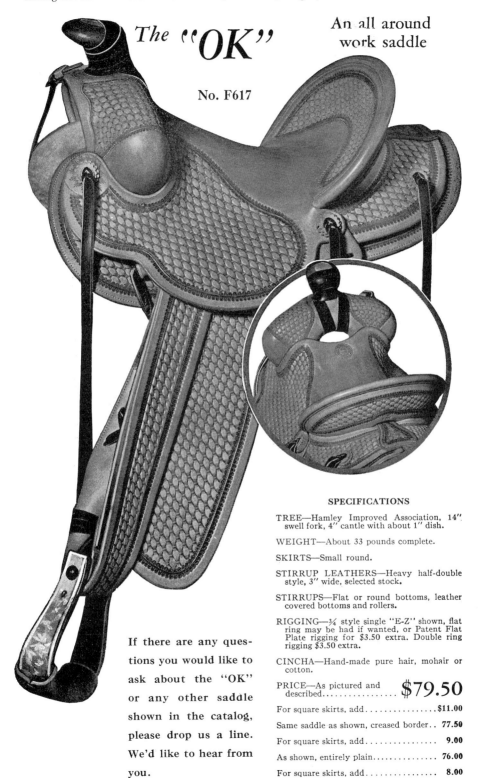

If there are any questions you would like to ask about the "OK" or any other saddle shown in the catalog, please drop us a line. We'd like to hear from you.

### SPECIFICATIONS

TREE—Hamley Improved Association, 14" swell fork, 4" cantle with about 1" dish.

WEIGHT—About 33 pounds complete.

SKIRTS—Small round.

STIRRUP LEATHERS—Heavy half-double style, 3" wide, selected stock.

STIRRUPS—Flat or round bottoms, leather covered bottoms and rollers.

RIGGING—¾ style single "E-Z" shown, flat ring may be had if wanted, or Patent Flat Plate rigging for $3.50 extra. Double ring rigging $3.50 extra.

CINCHA—Hand-made pure hair, mohair or cotton.

PRICE—As pictured and described................. **$79.50**

For square skirts, add...............**$11.00**

Same saddle as shown, creased border.. **77.50**

For square skirts, add............... **9.00**

As shown, entirely plain.............. **76.00**

For square skirts, add............... **8.00**

# *The* Pendleton

Made on
Hamley
Improved
Association
Tree

A top-notch, light weight saddle with small square skirts which, on tree with 14″ seat measure, are 13″ wide and 28″ long. Looks fine on any horse and will be made on other styles of trees when so ordered.

**No. F666**

**SPECIFICATIONS**

TREE—Improved Association, 14″ swell fork; 4″ cantle; 1″ dish.
WEIGHT—About 39 pounds.
RIGGING—Single ring rigging, ¾ or center fire style, or ¾ "E-Z" rigging. Double or ¾ double ring rigging, or single flat plate rigging, $3.50 extra.
STIRRUP LEATHERS—One piece, heavy, half-double style, 3″ wide.

STIRRUPS—Flat or round bottom wood, metal bound and with leather covered bottoms and rollers.
CINCHA—Hand-made mohair, hard hair or cotton.
PRICE—As pictured and described........ **$118.50**
With round skirts................$107.50
Square skirts, check stamped.....  101.50
Round skirts, check stamped......   91.50
Square skirts, entirely plain......   98.50
Round skirts, entirely plain.......   88.50

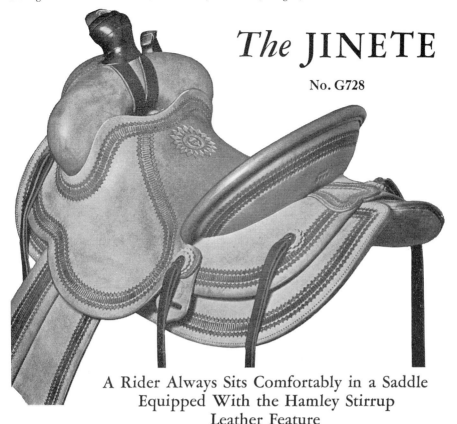

# *The* JINETE

## No. G728

## A Rider Always Sits Comfortably in a Saddle Equipped With the Hamley Stirrup Leather Feature

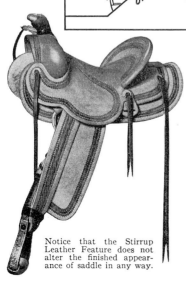

Notice that the Stirrup Leather Feature does not alter the finished appearance of saddle in any way.

### SPECIFICATIONS

TREE—The popular Improved Association; 14″ swell fork, 4″ cantle with about 1″ dish. Horn is rawhide capped and wrapped.

WEIGHT—About 37 pounds complete.

STIRRUP LEATHERS—Full 3″ half double style, heavy selected stock, *with New Stirrup Leather Feature.*

RIGGING—¾ single style using Hercules Flat Bronze rings. Double rigging, or Hamley Flat Plate single rig $3.50 extra.

CINCHA—Hand made pure mohair, hard hair or cotton.

STIRRUPS—Round or flat bottom wood with leather covered bottoms and rollers.

PRICE—As pictured and described.......................... **$89.50**

Square skirts add.............................$ 8.50

As shown, entirely plain........................ 87.50

Square skirts add............................. 8.00

If New Stirrup Leather Feature is not wanted, deduct $5.00.

# "Hamley Association"

## The Original Rodeo Committee Saddle

### Adopted as "Standard Equipment" by every large show in the country.

NOTE: Fenders shown on this saddle are regularly made 15½"x7". If you wish a different size be sure to specify when ordering.

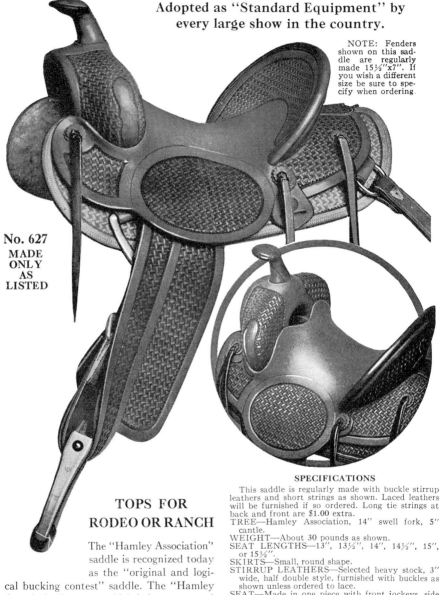

**No. 627**
**MADE**
**ONLY**
**AS**
**LISTED**

## TOPS FOR
## RODEO OR RANCH

The "Hamley Association" saddle is recognized today as the "original and logical bucking contest" saddle. The "Hamley Association" tree on which it is constructed is built right here in our own tree shop and will stand unbelievable abuse. It is a style originated and adopted because of its common-sense practicability for use on the range—for all-around work. Therefore, it is a "fair" tree and tests the skill of the rodeo performer. (See opposite page).

### SPECIFICATIONS

This saddle is regularly made with buckle stirrup leathers and short strings as shown. Laced leathers will be furnished if so ordered. Long tie strings at back and front are $1.00 extra.

TREE—Hamley Association, 14" swell fork, 5" cantle.

WEIGHT—About 30 pounds as shown.

SEAT LENGTHS—13", 13½", 14", 14½", 15", or 15½".

SKIRTS—Small, round shape.

STIRRUP LEATHERS—Selected heavy stock, 3" wide, half double style, furnished with buckles as shown unless ordered to lace.

SEAT—Made in one piece with front jockeys, side jockeys and cantle.

RIGGING—Either "E-Z" or ring style, ¾, with flank attachment fitted with leather cincha. Buckle at each end.

PRICE—

As shown...................... **$77.50**

Without flank cincha......................**$73.50**

### ASSOCIATION "EXTRAS"
### FOR REPAIR

Back Tugs, each postpaid...................**$1.35**

Back "D" with leacher, each.................. .85

Rear Leather Cincha, each.................. 1.85

# HAMLEY ASSOCIATION SADDLES ARE USED AT ALL MAJOR RODEOS

We build special trees in our own tree shop for use in Hamley Association Saddles—trees which will stand up under unbelievable abuse. Whenever you attend a major rodeo in this country, you're safe in betting that the bucking saddles being used, at least in part, bear the Circle H trade mark.

During the past several years Hamley Association saddles in lots of from 3 to 16 have been furnished the following:

McCarty & Elliott, Chugwater, Wyo.
Leo Cremer (Promoter), Shawnut, Mont.
California Rodeo Assn., Salinas, Calif.
Madison Square Garden Rodeo, N. Y.
North Platte, Nebr., Rodeo.
Hayward, Calif. Rodeo.
Texas Cowboy Reunion, Stamford, Tex.
Ft. Worth Fat Stock Show, Ft. Worth, Tex.
Cheyenne Frontier Days, Cheyenne, Wyo.

Pendleton Round-Up, Pendleton, Ore.
Springville, Utah.
Alliance, Nebr., Rodeo.
Muskogee, Okla., Rodeo.
Boston Garden Show.
Victorville, Calif, Rodeo.
Ellensburg, Wash., Rodeo.
Moomaw & Bernard, Tonasket, Wash.
And numerous others.

## TOP HANDS WIN GLORY ON HAMLEY ASSOCIATIONS

Fritz Truan, All-Around Champion Cowboy for 1940 rides a mean one. (Photo by Cal Godshall of Victorville, Calif.)

Doff Aber, winner of the Hamley RAA Prize for 1940, has that determined look. (Photo by Cal Godshall of Victorville, Calif.)

Bill McMacken, two-time All-Around Cowboy at the Pendleton Round-Up, rides this Hamley well. (Photo by Cal Godshall of Victorville, Calif.)

Jack Edmo, second in the Amateur Bucking, 1940 Pendleton Round-Up, riding Weasel. (Bus Howdyshell Photo, courtesy Pendleton Round-Up Assn.)

# *The* Triple X

## XXX

### No. D189

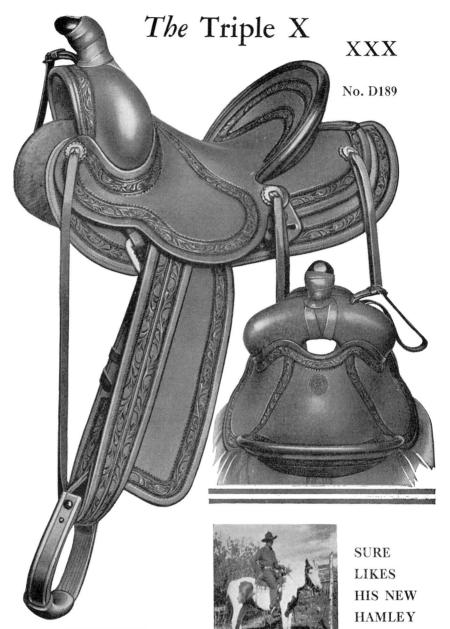

**SURE
LIKES
HIS NEW
HAMLEY**

### SPECIFICATIONS

TREE—Improved Association, 14" swell, 4"
cantle with 1" dish.

WEIGHT—About 34 pounds as shown.

STIRRUP LEATHERS—Selected stock, 3"
wide, half double style.

RIGGING—¾ single "E-Z" shown. Double
or Hamley Flat Plate single $3.50 extra.

STIRRUPS, CINCHA—See pages 64 and 65.

PRICE—
As shown................. **$78.50**

For square skirts add................$ **8.00**

As shown, but no stamping............ **76.00**

Square skirts, no stamping........... **84.50**

Dear Sir:

I've had my new Hamley Saddle for nearly eight months
now, and believe me I'm sure pleased with it in every way
possible. It's the best looking saddle, and the best riding
saddle I ever owned.

You folks can sure do the work; I know now that you
can't go wrong in buying a Hamley Saddle.

Yours truly,

JOHN PASUCHENKO
Grassy Butte, North Dakota.

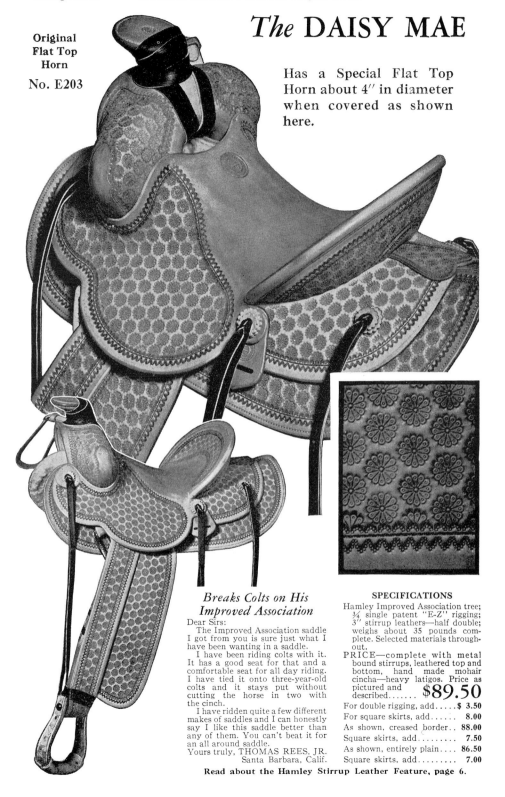

# *The* DAISY MAE

**Original Flat Top Horn**

**No. E203**

Has a Special Flat Top Horn about 4″ in diameter when covered as shown here.

## Breaks Colts on His Improved Association

Dear Sirs:

The Improved Association saddle I got from you is sure just what I have been wanting in a saddle.

I have been riding colts with it. It has a good seat for that and a comfortable seat for all day riding. I have tied it onto three-year-old colts and it stays put without cutting the horse in two with the cinch.

I have ridden quite a few different makes of saddles and I can honestly say I like this saddle better than any of them. You can't beat it for an all around saddle.

Yours truly, THOMAS REES, JR.
Santa Barbara, Calif.

## SPECIFICATIONS

Hamley Improved Association tree; ¾ single patent "E-Z" rigging; 3″ stirrup leathers—half double; weighs about 35 pounds complete. Selected materials throughout.

PRICE—complete with metal bound stirrups, leathered top and bottom, hand made mohair cincha—heavy latigos. Price as pictured and described....... **$89.50**

| | |
|---|---|
| For double rigging, add..... | $ 3.50 |
| For square skirts, add...... | 8.00 |
| As shown, creased border.. | 88.00 |
| Square skirts, add......... | 7.50 |
| As shown, entirely plain.... | 86.50 |
| Square skirts, add......... | 7.00 |

**Read about the Hamley Stirrup Leather Feature, page 6.**

# *The* FIREFLY

## No. F616

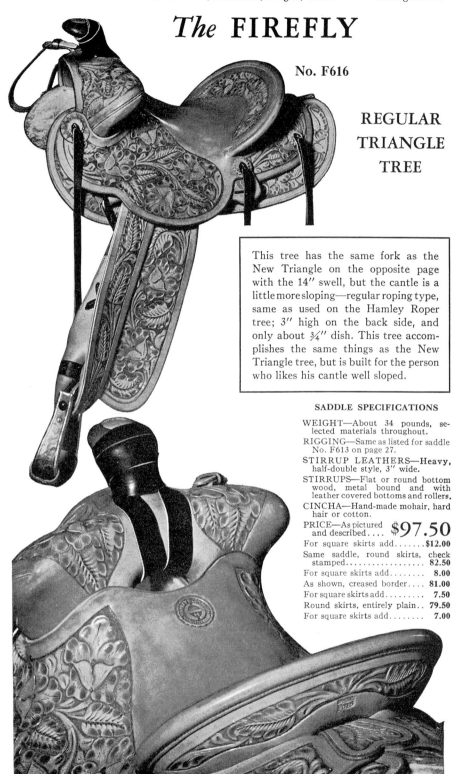

## REGULAR
## TRIANGLE
## TREE

This tree has the same fork as the New Triangle on the opposite page with the 14″ swell, but the cantle is a little more sloping—regular roping type, same as used on the Hamley Roper tree; 3″ high on the back side, and only about ¾″ dish. This tree accomplishes the same things as the New Triangle tree, but is built for the person who likes his cantle well sloped.

### SADDLE SPECIFICATIONS

WEIGHT—About 34 pounds, selected materials throughout.

RIGGING—Same as listed for saddle No. F613 on page 27.

STIRRUP LEATHERS—Heavy, half-double style, 3″ wide.

STIRRUPS—Flat or round bottom wood, metal bound and with leather covered bottoms and rollers.

CINCHA—Hand-made mohair, hard hair or cotton.

PRICE—As pictured and described.... **$97.50**

| | |
|---|---|
| For square skirts add...... | **$12.00** |
| Same saddle, round skirts, check stamped................. | 82.50 |
| For square skirts add........ | 8.00 |
| As shown, creased border.... | 81.00 |
| For square skirts add........ | 7.50 |
| Round skirts, entirely plain.. | 79.50 |
| For square skirts add........ | 7.00 |

*You'll want to know about the Hamley Stirrup Leather Feature on page 6.*

# *The New* "TRIANGLE"

## *. . . a 3-purpose saddle!*

— RIDING
— ROPING
— BUCKING

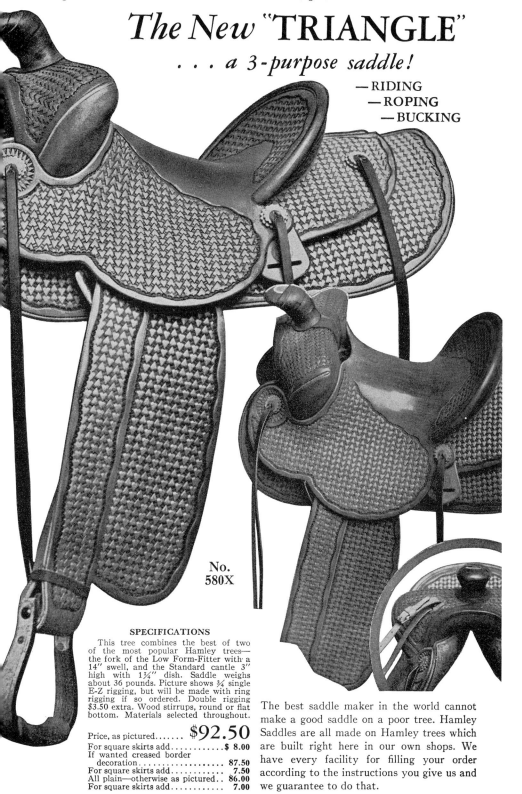

No. 580X

### SPECIFICATIONS

This tree combines the best of two of the most popular Hamley trees— the fork of the Low Form-Fitter with a 14″ swell, and the Standard cantle 3″ high with 1¼″ dish. Saddle weighs about 36 pounds. Picture shows ¾ single E-Z rigging, but will be made with ring rigging if so ordered. Double rigging $3.50 extra. Wood stirrups, round or flat bottom. Materials selected throughout.

Price, as pictured....... **$92.50**
For square skirts add............$ 8.00
If wanted creased border
  decoration................... 87.50
For square skirts add............ 7.50
All plain—otherwise as pictured.. 86.00
For square skirts add............ 7.00

The best saddle maker in the world cannot make a good saddle on a poor tree. Hamley Saddles are all made on Hamley trees which are built right here in our own shops. We have every facility for filling your order according to the instructions you give us and we guarantee to do that.

# *The Famous* "FITZU"

## ONE OF THE MOST POPULAR SADDLES EVER SHOWN IN A HAMLEY COWBOY CATALOG

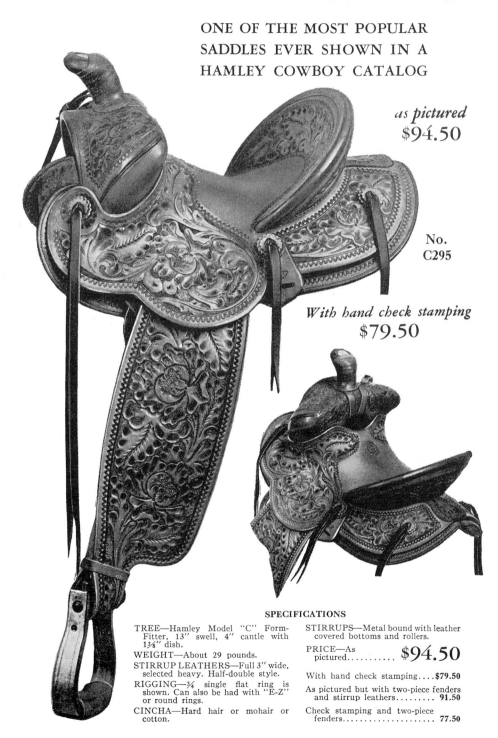

*as pictured*
## $94.50

No.
C295

*With hand check stamping*
## $79.50

### SPECIFICATIONS

TREE—Hamley Model "C" Form-Fitter, 13" swell, 4" cantle with 1⅜" dish.

WEIGHT—About 29 pounds.

STIRRUP LEATHERS—Full 3" wide, selected heavy. Half-double style.

RIGGING—¾ single flat ring is shown. Can also be had with "E-Z" or round rings.

CINCHA—Hard hair or mohair or cotton.

STIRRUPS—Metal bound with leather covered bottoms and rollers.

PRICE—As pictured.......... **$94.50**

With hand check stamping....**$79.50**

As pictured but with two-piece fenders and stirrup leathers........ **91.50**

Check stamping and two-piece fenders.................... **77.50**

# *The* ROANOKE

### No. F665

## SPECIFICATIONS

TREE—Low Model "B" Form-Fitter, 14¾" swell fork, 4" cantle, with 1½" dish.

RIGGING—¾ single "E-Z" but any style single ring rigging may be substituted. Double, or ¾ double, or single Flat Plate rigging $3.50 extra.

HORN—Shown wrapped, but will be leather covered if so ordered.

STIRRUP LEATHERS—Heavy, half-double style 3" wide, selected stock.

STIRRUPS—Flat or round bottom wood, metal bound and with leather covered bottoms and rollers.

CINCHA—Hand-made mohair, hard hair or cotton.

WEIGHT—About 34 pounds.

PRICE—As shown and described.................. **$107.50**

For square skirts add......................$13.00

Full check stamp round skirts.............. 92.50

For square skirts add...................... 9.00

Crease border decoration................... 87.50

For square skirts add...................... 7.50

Hamley Saddles are all made to order for the customers who are to ride them. If you like this saddle but prefer some other tree it will be made that way. Just tell us what you want.

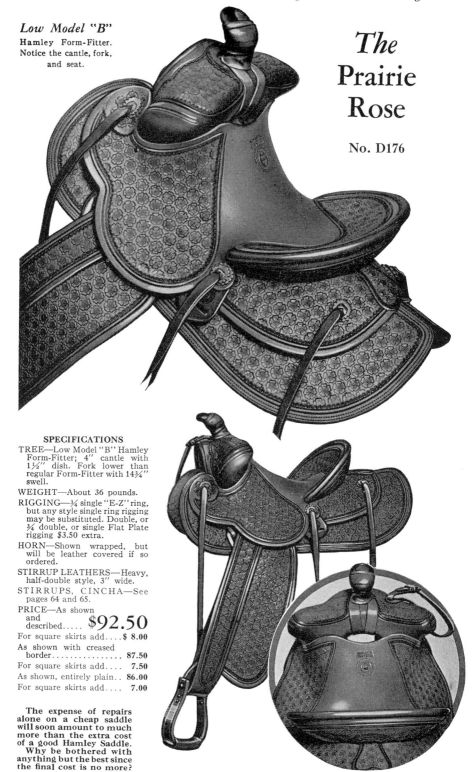

*Low Model "B"*
Hamley Form-Fitter.
Notice the cantle, fork,
and seat.

# The
# Prairie
# Rose

### No. D176

## SPECIFICATIONS

TREE—Low Model "B" Hamley
Form-Fitter; 4″ cantle with
1½″ dish. Fork lower than
regular Form-Fitter with 14¾″
swell.

WEIGHT—About 36 pounds.

RIGGING—¾ single "E-Z" ring,
but any style single ring rigging
may be substituted. Double, or
¾ double, or single Flat Plate
rigging $3.50 extra.

HORN—Shown wrapped, but
will be leather covered if so
ordered.

STIRRUP LEATHERS—Heavy,
half-double style, 3″ wide.

STIRRUPS, CINCHA—See
pages 64 and 65.

PRICE—As shown
and
described..... **$92.50**

For square skirts add....$ 8.00

As shown with creased
border................ 87.50

For square skirts add.... 7.50

As shown, entirely plain.. 86.00

For square skirts add.... 7.00

The expense of repairs
alone on a cheap saddle
will soon amount to much
more than the extra cost
of a good Hamley Saddle.
Why be bothered with
anything but the best since
the final cost is no more?

# *The* "Scobey"

### D171

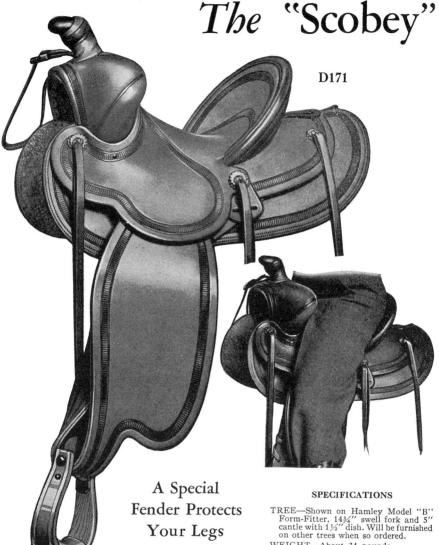

## A Special Fender Protects Your Legs

**HAMLEY ORIGINATED THE "Form-Fitter" AND THE ONLY GENUINE FORM-FITTERS ARE MADE BY HAMLEY AND COMPANY.**

The original Hamley "Form-Fitter" as developed in 1923 had proved itself when in 1932 there were nearly 5,000 in use. Several small changes were made to improve its appearance without altering its accepted characteristics; the outcome was the Hamley Model "B" Form-Fitter shown here.

### SPECIFICATIONS

TREE—Shown on Hamley Model "B" Form-Fitter, 14¾" swell fork and 5" cantle with 1½" dish. Will be furnished on other trees when so ordered.

WEIGHT—About 34 pounds.

STIRRUP LEATHERS—3" full—cut from selected stock in one piece with special fenders.

RIGGING—Center fire flat ring or any standard single rigging. Double rigging $3.50 extra. Single Hamley Flat Plate rigging $3.50 extra.

CINCHA—Mohair, hard hair or cotton.

STIRRUPS—Wood, round or flat bottom, metal bound and with leather covered bottoms and rollers.

PRICE—Round skirts and border decoration as shown . . . . . . . . . . . . . **$89.50**

With square skirts add . . . . . . . . .$ 9.00
Full check stamping, round skirts. 92.50
Full check stamping, square skirts. 9.50

If two-piece fenders and stirrup leathers are wanted deduct $2.50 from prices quoted.

# "7-Up"

This saddle furnished on other trees if so ordered.

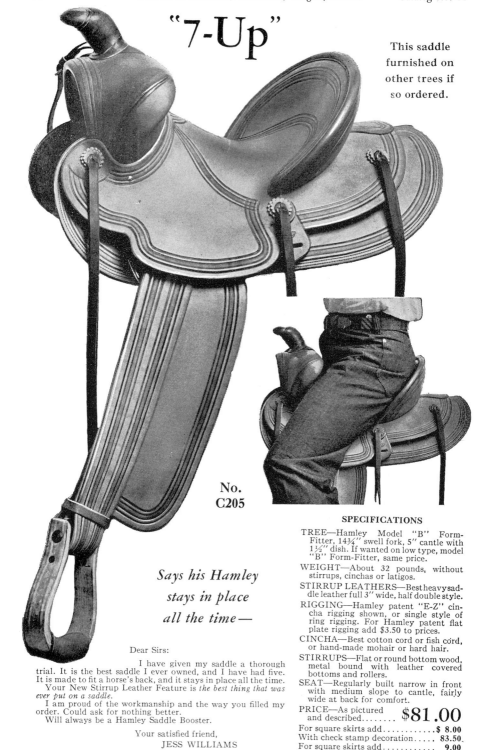

No. C205

*Says his Hamley*
*stays in place*
*all the time —*

Dear Sirs:

    I have given my saddle a thorough trial. It is the best saddle I ever owned, and I have had five. It is made to fit a horse's back, and it stays in place all the time. Your New Stirrup Leather Feature is *the best thing that was ever put on a saddle.*

    I am proud of the workmanship and the way you filled my order. Could ask for nothing better.

    Will always be a Hamley Saddle Booster.

Your satisfied friend,
JESS WILLIAMS
Baker, Oregon.

(See page 6 about Hamley's Stirrup Leather Feature.)

## SPECIFICATIONS

TREE—Hamley Model "B" Form-Fitter, 14¾" swell fork, 5" cantle with 1½" dish. If wanted on low type, model "B" Form-Fitter, same price.

WEIGHT—About 32 pounds, without stirrups, cinchas or latigos.

STIRRUP LEATHERS—Best heavy saddle leather full 3" wide, half double style.

RIGGING—Hamley patent "E-Z" cincha rigging shown, or single style of ring rigging. For Hamley patent flat plate rigging add $3.50 to prices.

CINCHA—Best cotton cord or fish cord, or hand-made mohair or hard hair.

STIRRUPS—Flat or round bottom wood, metal bound with leather covered bottoms and rollers.

SEAT—Regularly built narrow in front with medium slope to cantle, fairly wide at back for comfort.

PRICE—As pictured and described....... **$81.00**

For square skirts add............$ 8.00
With check stamp decoration..... 83.50
For square skirts add...........  9.00
Saddle as pictured except all plain, no stamping................ 79.50
For square skirts add.........`.... 7.50

# FORM FITTER
*Model "C"*

No.
C765

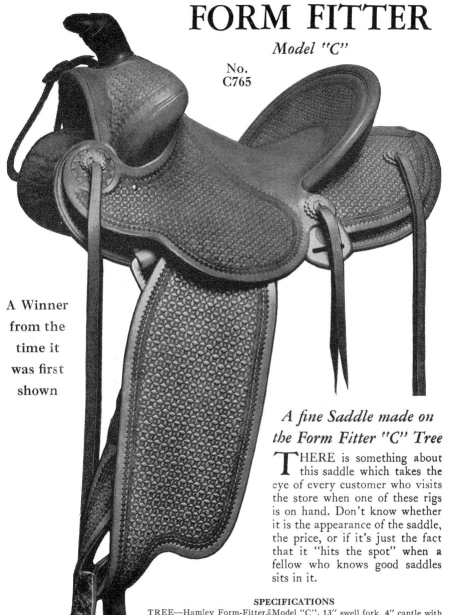

**A Winner
from the
time it
was first
shown**

## A fine Saddle made on the Form Fitter "C" Tree

THERE is something about this saddle which takes the eye of every customer who visits the store when one of these rigs is on hand. Don't know whether it is the appearance of the saddle, the price, or if it's just the fact that it "hits the spot" when a fellow who knows good saddles sits in it.

### SPECIFICATIONS

TREE—Hamley Form-Fitter, Model "C", 13" swell fork, 4" cantle with 1⅜" dish. (Furnished with seat measure from 11" to 14½").

WEIGHT—About 32 pounds.

STIRRUP LEATHERS—Full 3" selected heavy weight, made in one-piece with special shape fenders.

RIGGING—¾ single style patent "E-Z". Also furnished with flat or round bronze rings in rigging. Double rigging $3.50 extra. (Patent flat plate single rigging $3.50 extra).

CINCHA—Hand-made, mohair, or hard hair, or cotton cord, or fish cord.

STIRRUPS—Round or flat bottom wood stirrups with leather covered bottoms and rollers.

HORN—Wrapped as pictured, or leather covered, or sterling white metal.

PRICE—As pictured and described .................... **$79.50**

Same saddle with crease border decoration.....................$77.50
Entirely plain........................................................ 76.00
For square skirts with rounded corners, size 13" x 27" add:
On check stamped saddle.................................................. 6.50
On creased border saddle................................................. 6.00
On plain saddle........................................................... 5.50

**The Hamley Stirrup Leather
Feature is the only thing
that could improve this saddle. See page 6 for details.**

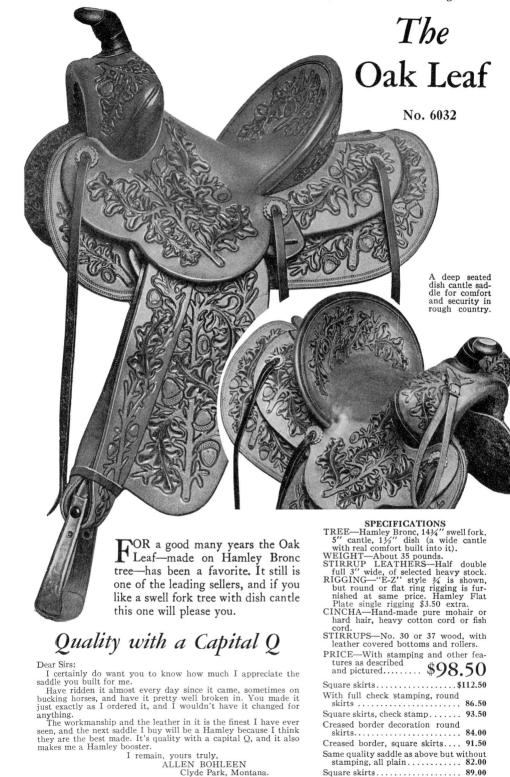

# *The* Oak Leaf

## No. 6032

A deep seated dish cantle saddle for comfort and security in rough country.

FOR a good many years the Oak Leaf—made on Hamley Bronc tree—has been a favorite. It still is one of the leading sellers, and if you like a swell fork tree with dish cantle this one will please you.

## *Quality with a Capital Q*

Dear Sirs:

I certainly do want you to know how much I appreciate the saddle you built for me.

Have ridden it almost every day since it came, sometimes on bucking horses, and have it pretty well broken in. You made it just exactly as I ordered it, and I wouldn't have it changed for anything.

The workmanship and the leather in it is the finest I have ever seen, and the next saddle I buy will be a Hamley because I think they are the best made. It's quality with a capital Q, and it also makes me a Hamley booster.

I remain, yours truly,
ALLEN BOHLEEN
Clyde Park, Montana.

## SPECIFICATIONS

TREE—Hamley Bronc, 14¾″ swell fork, 5″ cantle, 1½″ dish (a wide cantle with real comfort built into it).

WEIGHT—About 35 pounds.

STIRRUP LEATHERS—Half double full 3″ wide, of selected heavy stock.

RIGGING—"E-Z" style ¾ is shown, but round or flat ring rigging is furnished at same price. Hamley Flat Plate single rigging $3.50 extra.

CINCHA—Hand-made pure mohair or hard hair, heavy cotton cord or fish cord.

STIRRUPS—No. 30 or 37 wood, with leather covered bottoms and rollers.

PRICE—With stamping and other features as described and pictured......... **$98.50**

| | |
|---|---|
| Square skirts................. | $112.50 |
| With full check stamping, round skirts...................... | 86.50 |
| Square skirts, check stamp...... | 93.50 |
| Creased border decoration round skirts...................... | 84.00 |
| Creased border, square skirts.... | 91.50 |
| Same quality saddle as above but without stamping, all plain........... | 82.00 |
| Square skirts................. | 89.00 |

# *The* LINE BOSS

## No. H239

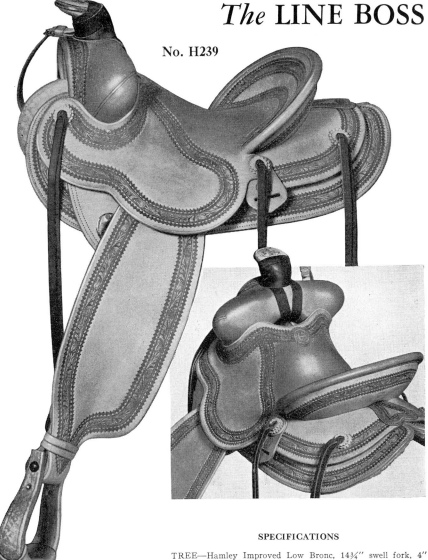

For a good many years we have shown a saddle in the Hamley Catalog called the "Easy Money". Made on the famous Hamley Bronc tree it has become a favorite with thousands. The trend now is to *lower* trees and for that reason we show this Hamley *Improved Low Bronc* tree. Its lines are very similar to the old "Easy Money", but the cantle is 1" lower, and the fork is lowered in proportion.

### SPECIFICATIONS

TREE—Hamley Improved Low Bronc, 14¾" swell fork, 4" cantle, about 1½" dish, horn same as on Lieuallen tree.

WEIGHT—About 33 pounds as shown.

SKIRTS—Medium round shape.

STIRRUP LEATHERS—Selected stock, half double style, 3" wide; cut in one piece with the fenders. (If fenders and stirrup leathers wanted separate, deduct $2.00).

RIGGING—Shown with Hamley Patent Flat Plate; any single or double style ring or dee rigging may be had. **(See prices below.)**

STIRRUPS, CINCHA—See pages 64 and 65.

PRICE—With PATENT FLAT PLATE LEATHER RIGGING AS PICTURED.. **$86.75**

With SINGLE "E-Z", or ROUND, or FLAT RINGS in rigging.......................................**$83.25**

For square skirts add................................ **8.00**

**For information about the Hamley Stirrup Leather Feature see page 6.**

# *The* AMAZON

## No. H240

### The New Lightweight Roper Tree

*Sturdy, yet Easy to Handle*

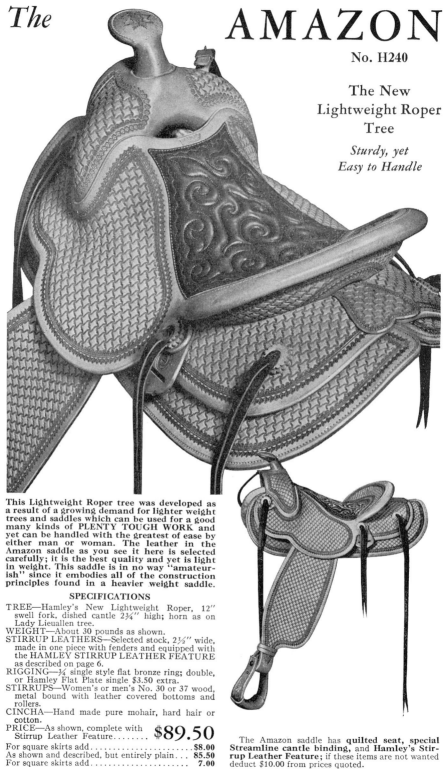

This Lightweight Roper tree was developed as a result of a growing demand for lighter weight trees and saddles which can be used for a good many kinds of PLENTY TOUGH WORK and yet can be handled with the greatest of ease by either man or woman. The leather in the Amazon saddle as you see it here is selected carefully; it is the best quality and yet is light in weight. This saddle is in no way "amateurish" since it embodies all of the construction principles found in a heavier weight saddle.

## SPECIFICATIONS

TREE—Hamley's New Lightweight Roper, 12" swell fork, dished cantle 2¾" high; horn as on Lady Lieuallen tree.

WEIGHT—About 30 pounds as shown.

STIRRUP LEATHERS—Selected stock, 2½" wide, made in one piece with fenders and equipped with the HAMLEY STIRRUP LEATHER FEATURE as described on page 6.

RIGGING—¾ single style flat bronze ring; double, or Hamley Flat Plate single $3.50 extra.

STIRRUPS—Women's or men's No. 30 or 37 wood, metal bound with leather covered bottoms and rollers.

CINCHA—Hand made pure mohair, hard hair or cotton.

PRICE—As shown, complete with Stirrup Leather Feature........ **$89.50**

For square skirts add........................$8.00
As shown and described, but entirely plain... 85.50
For square skirts add..................... 7.00

The Amazon saddle has **quilted seat, special Streamline cantle binding,** and Hamley's **Stirrup Leather Feature;** if these items are not wanted deduct $10.00 from prices quoted.

# *The* LADY LOU

### No. F598

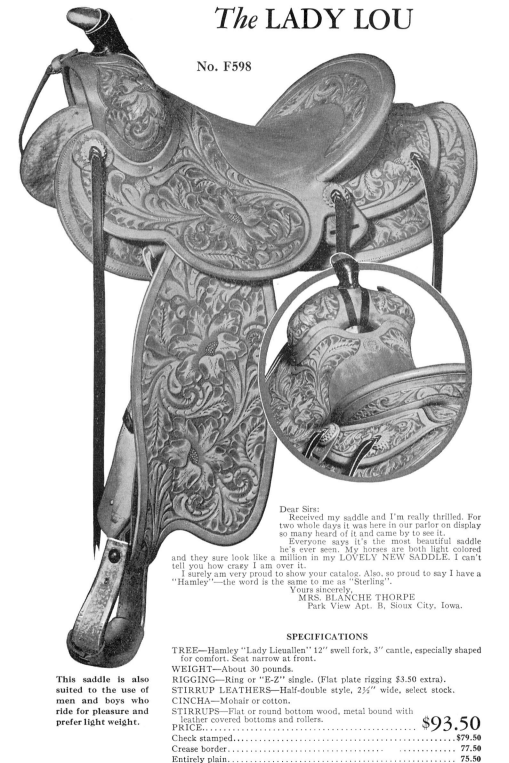

Dear Sirs:
Received my saddle and I'm really thrilled. For two whole days it was here in our parlor on display so many heard of it and came by to see it.
Everyone says it's the most beautiful saddle he's ever seen. My horses are both light colored and they sure look like a million in my LOVELY NEW SADDLE. I can't tell you how crazy I am over it.
I surely am very proud to show your catalog. Also, so proud to say I have a "Hamley"—the word is the same to me as "Sterling".
Yours sincerely,
MRS. BLANCHE THORPE
Park View Apt. B, Sioux City, Iowa.

This saddle is also suited to the use of men and boys who ride for pleasure and prefer light weight.

### SPECIFICATIONS

TREE—Hamley "Lady Lieuallen" 12" swell fork, 3" cantle, especially shaped for comfort. Seat narrow at front.

WEIGHT—About 30 pounds.

RIGGING—Ring or "E-Z" single. (Flat plate rigging $3.50 extra).

STIRRUP LEATHERS—Half-double style, 2½" wide, select stock.

CINCHA—Mohair or cotton.

STIRRUPS—Flat or round bottom wood, metal bound with leather covered bottoms and rollers.

PRICE............................................... **$93.50**

Check stamped.................................................$79.50
Crease border......................................  .............  77.50
Entirely plain.................................................  75.50

# *The* COMBINATION

### No. G28

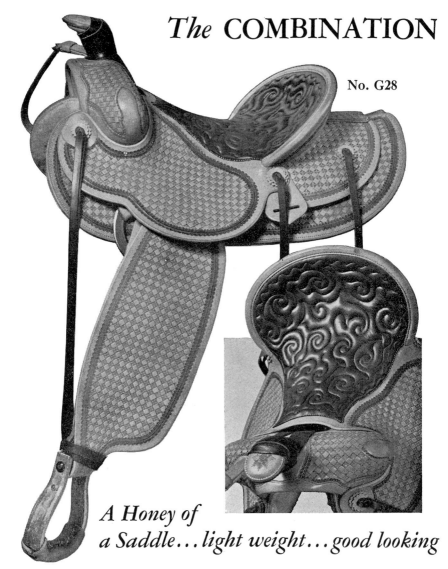

## *A Honey of a Saddle...light weight...good looking*

### SPECIFICATIONS

TREE—Hamley Combination tree, suitable for both men and women. Light weight, especially good for pleasure riding. 13″ swell fork, 3½″ cantle with about 1¼″ dish.

WEIGHT—About 31 pounds.

HORN—Roper type as on the Ubangi, page 23, 3″ high with 3″ top; leather covered and wrapped.

STIRRUP LEATHERS—Half double style, selected stock, 2½″ wide; one piece fenders.

RIGGING—¾ single style, flat ring; equipped with cotton or mohair cincha, and latigos, or tugs.

STIRRUPS—Women's or men's No. 30 or 37 wood stirrups, metal bound, with leather covered bottoms and rollers.

PRICE—As pictured and described............ **$84.00**

Same saddle, all plain.................$82.00

Without quilted seat deduct.......... 4.50

### SHE CHANGED FROM ENGLISH TO WESTERN

Gentlemen:

The saddle has proved very satisfactory and very comfortable. I have always used an English saddle, and had grave doubts about the utility of a Western saddle, but am now convinced that for safety and long distance riding comfort, a Western saddle is the thing.

Sincerely,

MRS. NELSON H. SMITH
Laconia, New Hampshire.

*Have you read about the Hamley Stirrup Leather Feature on page 6?*

# *The* "Lady Lieuallen"

### No. E335

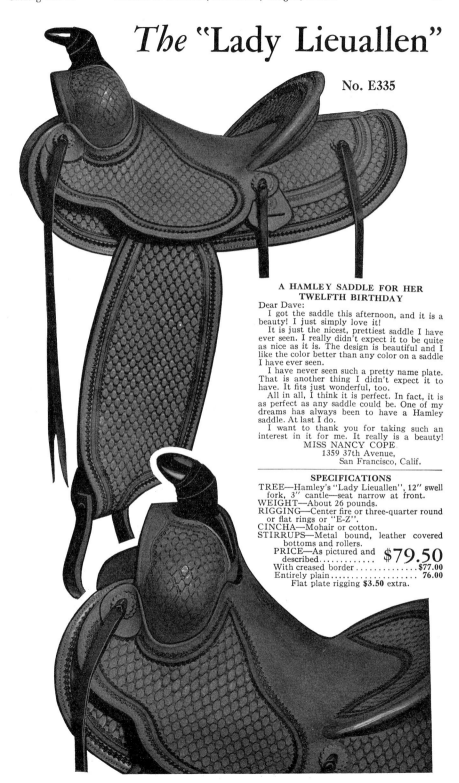

### A HAMLEY SADDLE FOR HER TWELFTH BIRTHDAY

Dear Dave:

I got the saddle this afternoon, and it is a beauty! I just simply love it!

It is just the nicest, prettiest saddle I have ever seen. I really didn't expect it to be quite as nice as it is. The design is beautiful and I like the color better than any color on a saddle I have ever seen.

I have never seen such a pretty name plate. That is another thing I didn't expect it to have. It fits just wonderful, too.

All in all, I think it is perfect. In fact, it is as perfect as any saddle could be. One of my dreams has always been to have a Hamley saddle. At last I do.

I want to thank you for taking such an interest in it for me. It really is a beauty!

MISS NANCY COPE
1359 37th Avenue,
San Francisco, Calif.

### SPECIFICATIONS

TREE—Hamley's "Lady Lieuallen", 12" swell fork, 3" cantle—seat narrow at front.

WEIGHT—About 26 pounds.

RIGGING—Center fire or three-quarter round or flat rings or "E-Z".

CINCHA—Mohair or cotton.

STIRRUPS—Metal bound, leather covered bottoms and rollers.

PRICE—As pictured and described............ **$79.50**
With creased border.............$77.00
Entirely plain.................... 76.00
Flat plate rigging **$3.50** extra.

# Hamley Guest Saddles

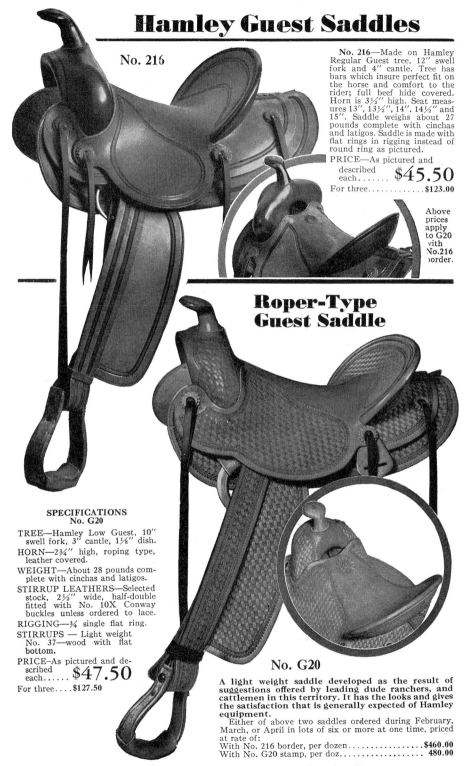

### No. 216

No. 216—Made on Hamley Regular Guest tree, 12″ swell fork and 4″ cantle. Tree has bars which insure perfect fit on the horse and comfort to the rider; full beef hide covered. Horn is 3½″ high. Seat measures 13″, 13½″, 14″, 14½″ and 15″. Saddle weighs about 27 pounds complete with cinchas and latigos. Saddle is made with flat rings in rigging instead of round ring as pictured.

PRICE—As pictured and described each...... **$45.50**

For three............$123.00

Above prices apply to G20 with No.216 border.

## Roper-Type Guest Saddle

### SPECIFICATIONS
### No. G20

TREE—Hamley Low Guest, 10″ swell fork, 3″ cantle, 1⅛″ dish.

HORN—2¾″ high, roping type, leather covered.

WEIGHT—About 28 pounds complete with cinchas and latigos.

STIRRUP LEATHERS—Selected stock, 2½″ wide, half-double fitted with No. 10X Conway buckles unless ordered to lace.

RIGGING—¾ single flat ring.

STIRRUPS — Light weight No. 37—wood with flat bottom.

PRICE—As pictured and described each...... **$47.50**

For three....$127.50

### No. G20

A light weight saddle developed as the result of suggestions offered by leading dude ranchers, and cattlemen in this territory. It has the looks and gives the satisfaction that is generally expected of Hamley equipment.

Either of above two saddles ordered during February, March, or April in lots of six or more at one time, priced at rate of:

With No. 216 border, per dozen................$460.00
With No. G20 stamp, per doz...................  480.00

**See Page 6. Read about the Hamley Stirrup Leather Feature.**

# GENUINE HAMLEY SADDLES FOR BOYS

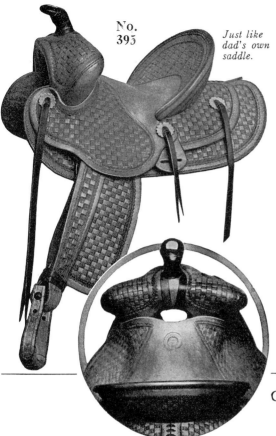

**No. 395**

*Just like dad's own saddle.*

## Boys' Form-Fitter

*You get more comfort and satisfaction out of a genuine Hamley. Besides it is so well made that when you outgrow it, you can probably sell it at a fair price.*

### SPECIFICATIONS

TREE—Junior Form-Fitter, 13" swell fork, 4½" cantle, with 1¾" dish.

WEIGHT—About 20 lbs.

STIRRUP LEATHERS—2" half double style to buckle.

RIGGING—¾ style, round ring.

CINCHA—Cotton fish cord, or cotton cord No. 180.

STIRRUPS—Round or flat bottom, wood.

PRICE—With full check stamping as pictured and other wise as described..... **$43.50**

Entirely plain..................**$42.00**

This saddle is made with seat measure up to 12" and it is also made as small as 10½"

The materials in this saddle are second grade, but it has a strong rigging and good stirrup leathers. The workmanship and finish do not compare with that on our high grade saddles but it is plenty good for the boy or girl who will soon want a larger saddle.

### Give your boy the pleasure of owning a genuine Hamley.

## BOYS' ASSOCIATION

**MORE SELECT QUALITY THROUGHOUT THAN NO. 395**

### No. 295

HERE'S a dandy little saddle "just like dad's." Made just like a big saddle only smaller in proportion. Built on Hamley Boy's Association tree and finished throughout just like a man's high grade saddle. Good light weight materials—hide covered tree, flat top horn. Three-quarter ring rigging, stirrup leathers either to lace or buckle (laced unless otherwise ordered.) Tree sizes 11-in. to 13-in. Each, as shown.................................. **$53.50**

Each, plain......................................... 52.00

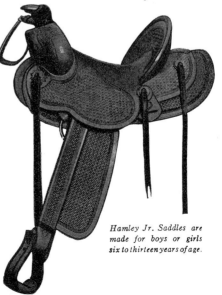

*Hamley Jr. Saddles are made for boys or girls six to thirteen years of age.*

# GOOD SADDLES

### No. F696

## These 4 Hamley "Standardized" Saddles Are REAL VALUES

The four saddles shown on this page and the page opposite are "standardized." In other words, they are designed to be made up several at a time. That is one of the principal reasons for the low prices, and they are available at prices quoted, *only* in the four styles shown here, and with specifications as printed. Made on best grade Hamley trees . . . have good rigging . . . good stirrup leathers . . . good cinchas, stirrups and latigos. Seat jockeys, back jockeys and fenders are doubled and stitched. Built as good saddles should be built!

## ↑ The MONTROSE ROPER
### No. F696

Made on genuine Hamley Lieuallen tree. Weighs about 31 pounds. Seat measures; 13½", 14", 14½" and 15". STIRRUP LEATHERS—2½" wide—to lace.
STIRRUPS—Round or flat bottom. (See note on page where stirrups are listed.)
CINCHA—No. 66 or No. 180. Other cinchas furnished at slightly higher cost. (See note on cincha page in catalog.)
RIGGING—¾ single with flat ring.
PRICE—

## $65.00
As described

Furnished with ¾ double or full double rigging for $4.50 extra.

## ↑ The CHALLENGER
### No. F697

Made on genuine Hamley Standard tree. A low saddle for roping and other ranch work. Weighs about 31 pounds.

SEAT MEASURES: 13½", 14", 14½" and 15". Single style, 2½" stirrup leathers.

STIRRUPS—Round or flat bottom. (See note on page where stirrups are listed.)

CINCHA—No. 66 or No. 180. (See note on cincha page).

RIGGING—¾ single style with flat rings.

PRICE.............................. $65.00

# AT LOW PRICES

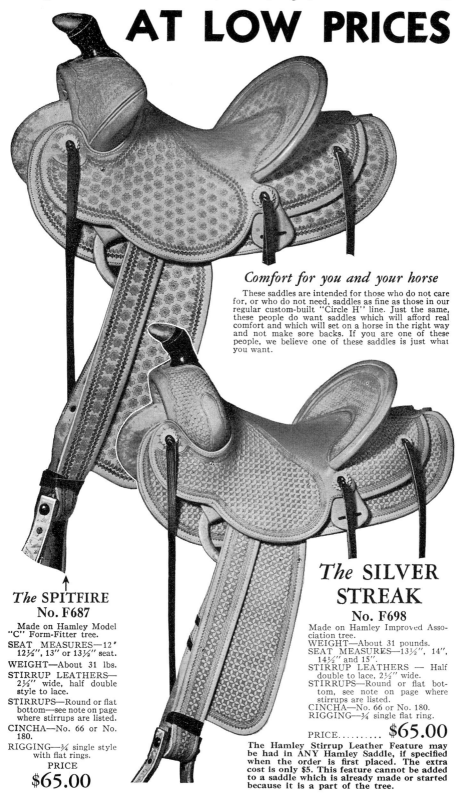

## Comfort for you and your horse

These saddles are intended for those who do not care for, or who do not need, saddles as fine as those in our regular custom-built "Circle H" line. Just the same, these people do want saddles which will afford real comfort and which will set on a horse in the right way and not make sore backs. If you are one of these people, we believe one of these saddles is just what you want.

## *The* SPITFIRE
### No. F687

Made on Hamley Model "C" Form-Fitter tree.

SEAT MEASURES—12″ 12½″, 13″ or 13½″ seat.

WEIGHT—About 31 lbs.

STIRRUP LEATHERS— 2½″ wide, half double style to lace.

STIRRUPS—Round or flat bottom—see note on page where stirrups are listed.

CINCHA—No. 66 or No. 180.

RIGGING—¾ single style with flat rings.

### PRICE
## $65.00

## *The* SILVER STREAK
### No. F698

Made on Hamley Improved Association tree.

WEIGHT—About 31 pounds.

SEAT MEASURES—13½″, 14″, 14½″ and 15″.

STIRRUP LEATHERS — Half double to lace, 2½″ wide.

STIRRUPS—Round or flat bottom, see note on page where stirrups are listed.

CINCHA—No. 66 or No. 180.

RIGGING—¾ single flat ring.

### PRICE......... $65.00

The Hamley Stirrup Leather Feature may be had in ANY Hamley Saddle, if specified when the order is first placed. The extra cost is only $5. This feature cannot be added to a saddle which is already made or started because it is a part of the tree.

# HAMLEY'S IMPROVED "EAST-WEST" SADDLE

The comfort and security of a western saddle . . . and the light weight and trim appearance of an English saddle

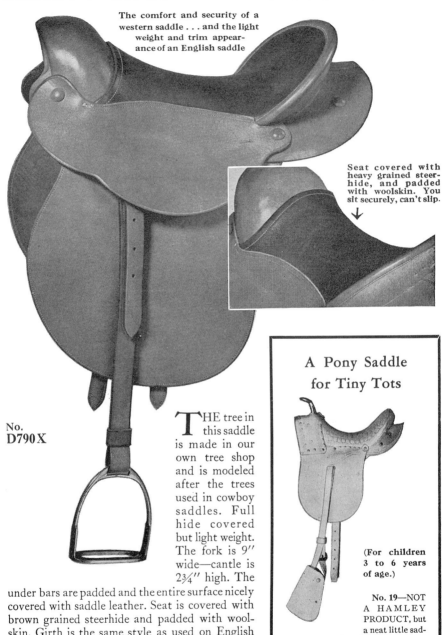

Seat covered with heavy grained steerhide, and padded with woolskin. You sit securely, can't slip.

No.
**D790X**

T HE tree in this saddle is made in our own tree shop and is modeled after the trees used in cowboy saddles. Full hide covered but light weight. The fork is 9" wide—cantle is 2¾" high. The under bars are padded and the entire surface nicely covered with saddle leather. Seat is covered with brown grained steerhide and padded with woolskin. Girth is the same style as used on English saddles and is equipped with two buckles.

The saddle is finely finished throughout—a real quality article and riding club members who have seen and used the saddle tell us it is one of the finest they have seen—especially suited to cross country riding. Each **$65.00**

Will be fitted with small sterling horn if so ordered.

### A Pony Saddle for Tiny Tots

(For children 3 to 6 years of age.)

No. 19—NOT A HAMLEY PRODUCT, but a neat little saddle in a quality that is just right for fast-growing youngsters. 11" seat, quilted calfskin. Felt lined bars; nickle plated horn; 2½" wood stirrups with taps. Webb cincha equipped with buckle. ⅞" adjustable stirrup leathers. Delivered **$12.95**

# Trick Riding Saddles *MADE TO ORDER*

**No. 193**

Nearly all professional trick riders and a majority of amateur **trick** riders have their own ideas about trick riding saddles. The saddle shown here, embodies practically all the features of a good trick saddle but you may select features from it and add others of your own when sending your order. We have made scores of these saddles, each one is a special job, and we know we shall understand your instructions and questions.

**No. 193**—Price, as shown, including under-the-belly cables (shown) and shoulder stand straps (not shown).....  **$112.50**
Same saddle, full check stamped...............**$117.50**
Same saddle—full hand flower stamped..............**$135.00**
If under-the-belly cables and shoulder stand straps are not wanted, deduct $14.00 from prices quoted.

*Your new Trick or Relay saddle may not look exactly as it is represented here. Improvements are made from time to time, and as they are made they are built into the saddles to make them better for their intended use.*

## *Chain Lightning*
### RELAY SADDLE     No. 9373

THE fact that Hamley saddles, from the most elaborate range saddle, on down the line to guest saddles, and including such special rigs as Relay and Trick Riding saddles are made on trees which are designed and made in our own shops gives us an advantage over all other makers of western riding equipment. Most users of this type of equipment recognize that this advantage passes on to customers in the same degree. It makes it possible for them to really get what they want.

The first real Relay saddles on the market were made by Hamley & Company—Hamley Relay saddles led the field then and they do today.

**No. 9373**—Price, complete as shown...... **$39.50**
Without rubber cincha **$34.50**
Rubber cincha with extra ring piece and connecting unit for using cincha on an ordinary stock saddle..**$9.00**
Cincha alone......... **6.00**

*Weighs only*

**13 lbs.**

*including Cincha*

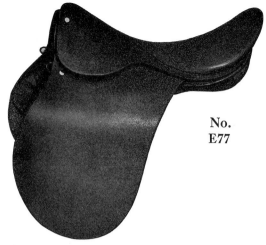

No.
E77

# English - Made Saddles

*Made in England especially for Hamley & Co.*

**No. E77**—Imported English Saddle, guaranteed non-breakable head. Deep seat, full grain leather, folded leather girth—two buckles. Safety stirrup leather hooks, 1¼″ stirrup leathers. Straight head, round cantle. Full calf lined under bars......... **$42.50**

**No. E77X**—Same as No. E77 but with cut back head........ **$42.50**

**No. E78**—Same as No. E77 but with square cantle, straight head.................... **$42.50**

**No. E78X**—Same as No. E77 but with square cantle, cut back head.................... **$42.50**

No.
E88

**No. E88**—Imported English Saddle. Non-breakable patent head, full lined skirts, deep seat, safety stirrup leather hooks, non-rust stirrups; folded leather girth, 1¼″ stirrup leathers, straight head, round cantle; full calf lined pads. A real saddle, and only................ **$49.50**

The reputable British firm from whom we import this fine line of English riding equipment (part of which is shown on the succeeding page) has given us continued co-operation and good service for a great many years and we have yet to find a line that compares with its quality and craftsmanship. In spite of their terrible difficulties over there, they have written us that "business and deliveries will carry on as usual."

### FIRST GRADE NUMNAHS
*{Saddle Pad for English Saddle}*

All of above English saddles have full calf covered pads. No cloth covered pads to soil—just good solid leather well padded.

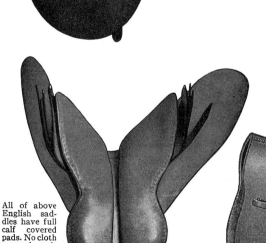

**No. 5**—Shaped felt numnah with leather straps— reinforced splice in center. Each.. **$4.00**

**No. 6**—One-piece, heavy, solid felt numnah. Each........ **$3.75**

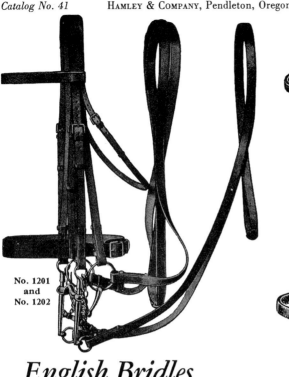

**Bridle
No. 1401
and
No. 1402**

**Bit
No. 3600**
(See
listing
below).

No. 1201
and
No. 1202

# English Bridles

### These Bridles Made in England Especially for Hamley & Co.

**No. 1201**—Ladies' genuine English made Weymouth Bridle. Hand sewed in the English style, double reins, one pair ½″, one pair ⅝″. Complete with caveson or nose band and never rust bits, postpaid.................................**$14.50**
If wanted with nickel-plated bits, complete postpaid.................................**$12.50**

**No. 1202**—Men's English made Weymouth Bridle. Same as No. 1201 but with ⅝″ and ¾″ reins. Complete with caveson or nose band and never rust bits, postpaid...........................**$16.00**
Or with nickel-plated bits, complete, postpaid.................................**$14.00**

**No. 1301**—English Pelham bridle, complete with ⅝″ and ¾″ reins, caveson, and never rust Pelham bit. Each, delivered.......................**$14.35**

**No. 1302**—Same as No. 1301 but with ¾″ and ⅞″ reins, complete, delivered.............**$13.35**

**No. 1401**—Snaffle Bridle, hand sewed, one pair English reins, ⅞″ cheeks and ¾″ reins. Each..**$7.45**
(Priced without bit)

**No. 1402**—Snaffle Bridle—same as No. 1401 but with 1″ cheeks and ⅞″ reins. Each..........**$7.95**
(Priced without bit)

(All above bridles and reins have stud fastenings—no buckles where straps fasten to bits.)

### Extra Reins

**No. 1501**—English Reins, stud hook ends, all hand sewed. Pair ⅝″, **$2.50**; ¾″, **$2.75**; ⅞″, **$3.00**.

---

## Bit Shown on Bridle No. 1401

**No. 3600**—The Never Rust "Hackamore Bit." No mouth piece. Nose band goes clear around instead of as shown and is neatly rounded in front. Made of "Star Steel Silver," Non-Rust. Price, complete with curb hooks and chain, less nose band...**$7.50**
Nose band, extra.........................**$2.60**

## English Riding Crops

Colors: Tan, Brown, Black. Covers: Smooth and braided leather, also braided thread covered.
When ordering state color wanted, whether braided or smooth leather cover or braided thread cover and advise approximate price.
Prices from **$1.25** for the braided thread covered crops to **$2.00** and **$2.25** for the smooth leather covered and **$3.50** and **$4.00** for the braided leather covered ones.
The finest crops we have ever seen. Prices are about half what crops of this quality usually sell for.

## English Style Halters

**Russet Color (Tan), or Black**

**No. 2500**—1⅛″, medium size, for 800 to 950 pound animal, cadmium plated fittings, round throat. Each.....................**$4.75**

**No. 2501**—1¼″, horse size, finely sewed, round throat, cadmium plated hardware. Each......**$5.50**

**No. 2600**—1¼″, horse size, finely sewed, round throat, brass hardware. Each.................**$5.75**

**No. 2600C**—⅞″, colt size, otherwise as No. 2600. Each.....**$3.85**

# How to Order a Saddle to Fit You

## SADDLE SEAT MEASUREMENTS

The length of the seat of a saddle is measured from the center of the fork at a point about one inch below the base of the horn, back to the center inside top edge of the cantle. The length of seat required for different riders depends partly upon his height and partly upon his weight. Some riders like a fairly tight fitting saddle and others like considerable room. The measurements as given in the table below are for an easy, comfortable fit.

When ordering your saddle it will be well to consult this table and also, when sending orders please tell us your height and weight.

Send along your questions if you are in doubt about any details. We want to help you get what you really would like to have.

| HEIGHT AND WEIGHT OF PERSON WHO IS TO RIDE SADDLE BEING ORDERED | | TREE STYLES AND APPROXIMATE SEAT SIZE TO ORDER | | | | | | | | | |
|---|---|---|---|---|---|---|---|---|---|---|---|
| Height | Weight Lbs. | Form Fitter Model B | Form Fitter Model C / Back Saver | Bronc / Low Bronc | Triangle / New Triangle | Standard / Lieuallen | Association / Improved Association | Hamley Roper / Bernard / Professional Roper | Improved Weatherley | Hamley Youngman | Denny Hunt / Wallowa / Wade |
| 5′ 2″ to 5′ 6″ | 110—120 | 11½ | 11½ | 12 | 12 | 13 | 13 | 13½ | 13½ | 13½ | 13 |
| 5′ 4″ to 5′ 6″ | 120—130 | 12 | 12 | 12½ | 12½ | 13½ | 13½ | 14 | 14 | 14 | 13½ |
| 5′ 6″ to 5′ 9″ | 120—130 | 12½ | 12½ | 13 | 13 | 14 | 14 | 14 | 14 | 14 | 14 |
| 5′ 5″ to 5′ 7″ | 130—145 | 12½ | 12½ | 13 | 13 | 14 | 14 | 14 | 14 | 14 | 14 |
| 5′ 6″ to 5′ 8″ | 140—155 | 13 | 13 | 13½ | 13½ | 14 | 14 | 14½ | 14½ | 14 | 14½ |
| 5′ 6″ to 5′ 8″ | 155—170 | 13 | 13½ | 13½ | 14 | 14½ | 14½ | 15 | 15 | 15 | 15 |
| 5′ 6″ to 5′ 8″ | 170—185 | 13½ | 14 | 14 | 14½ | 15 | 15 | 15 | 15 | 15 | 15 |
| 5′ 6″ to 5′ 8″ | 185—200 | 14 | 14½ | 14½ | 14½ | 15 | 15 | 15 | 15 | 15 | 15 |
| 5′ 8″ to 5′ 10″ | 130—145 | 12½ | 12½ | 12½ | 13 | 14 | 14 | 14½ | 14½ | 14 | 14 |
| 5′ 8″ to 5′ 10″ | 140—155 | 12½ | 13 | 13 | 13 | 14 | 14 | 14½ | 14½ | 14½ | 14 |
| 5′ 8″ to 5′ 10″ | 155—170 | 13 | 13½ | 13½ | 14 | 14½ | 14½ | 14½ | 14½ | 14½ | 14½ |
| 5′ 8″ to 5′ 10″ | 170—185 | 13½ | 13½ | 13½ | 14½ | 15 | 14½ | 15 | 15 | 15 | 15 |
| 5′ 8″ to 5′ 10″ | 185—200 | 14 | 14 | 14 | 14½ | 15 | 15 | 15 | 15 | 15 | 15 |
| 5′ 8″ to 5′ 10″ | 200—220 | 14½ | 14½ | 14½ | 14½ | 15 | 15 | 15½ | 15½ | 15 | 15 |
| 5′ 10″ to 6′ | 140—155 | 12½ | 12½ | 13 | 13 | 14 | 14 | 14 | 14 | 14 | 14 |
| 5′ 10″ to 6′ | 155—170 | 13 | 13½ | 13½ | 14 | 14½ | 14½ | 15 | 14½ | 14½ | 14½ |
| 5′ 10″ to 6′ | 170—185 | 13 | 13½ | 13½ | 14 | 15 | 14½ | 15 | 15 | 15 | 15 |
| 5′ 10″ to 6′ | 185—200 | 13½ | 14 | 14 | 14½ | 15 | 15 | 15½ | 15½ | 15 | 15 |
| 5′ 10″ to 6′ | 200—220 | 14 | 14½ | 14½ | 14½ | 15½ | 15 | 16 | 16 | 15½ | 15½ |
| 6′ to 6′ 2″ | 175—200 | 14 | 14½ | 14 | 14½ | 15 | 15 | 15½ | 15½ | 15 | 15 |
| 6′ 2″ to 6′ 4″ | 220—250 | 14½ | 14½ | 15 | 15 | 16 | 15½ | 16 | 16 | 15½ | 15½ |

**WHEN ORDERING LADIES' SADDLES.** Please be sure to tell us the height and the weight of the lady who is to ride the saddle, also tell us her approximate hip measurement. With this information we shall know what size tree to suggest in the particular style being ordered.

# About Extras for Your Saddle

When ordering your new saddle there may be special features you would like included and which are not pictured as being part of the saddle you have selected. Every Hamley Saddle is a special job and changes can be made.

**For some of the extras on saddles,** the following list will give considerable information:

**For saddles with trees longer than 15 inches,** add $1.00 for each inch over the 15 inches.

**For square skirts larger than 15x30 inches on saddles** listed at $70.00 and over, add $1.00 extra for each additional inch of width and 75 cents extra for each additional inch of length.

**For California Round Skirts,** extra dip on the skirt so that it will extend down under the rigging ring, add $2.00 to the price quoted for the regular round skirts on the saddle under consideration.

**For One-piece Fenders and Stirrup Leathers,** when not shown that way in picture of saddle quoted add $3.00 on flowered saddles, and $2.00 on check stamp or plain saddles. 50c more for D171 style.

**For Rope Roll Front and Cantle Bindings** on saddles shown with regular style bindings, add $12.00.

**For Rawhide Braided Horn on Saddles** showing wrapped or leather covered horn, add $1.00 to price of saddle.

**Dees for rear** of ¾ double rigging, without rear cinchas, and latigos, $1.50 extra.

**Quilted Seats:** To base of cantle, $3.50; to top of cantle, $4.50; Jockeys and entire seat to top of cantle, $6.50.

**Cheyenne Roll Cantle Binding, $3.50; Semi-Cheyenne, $2.50; Streamline, $1.50** (see page 23); **Wade, $5.50** (see page 20).

**Plain or Button Top Sterling Horn** furnished at no extra charge. These horns have special thick edge.

**Initials or Brand** stamped on back cantle of saddle without charge.

**For Swell Forks** wider than quoted in description of saddle, add $1.00 for each inch of swell over the width specified.

**Double Rawhide Cover on Tree, $5.00 extra.** Our trees all have bull hide covers and double cover is not really necessary.

**If double stirrup leathers** are wanted on saddles shown with half double leathers, add $1.50 to price quoted.

**For Hamley Flat Plate Rigging,** on saddles shown with other style single riggings, add $3.50 to price.

***Hamley Stirrup Leather Feature available only on new saddles, $5.00 extra.***

# Cincha Riggings on Saddles

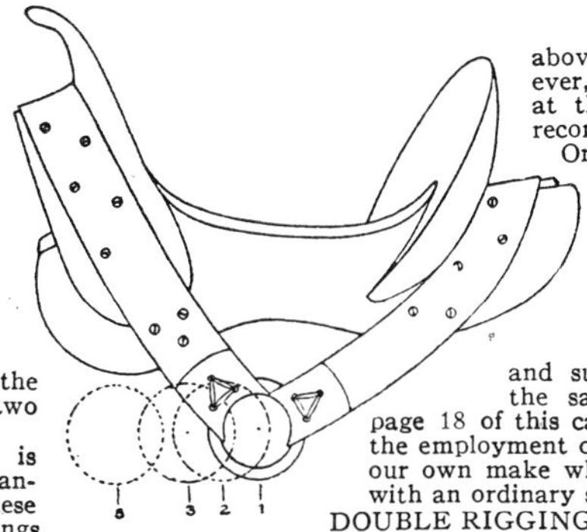

During the year we receive many, many letters from customers asking for specific information with regard to saddle riggings, and believe it will be a good plan if we give some definite information on rigging right here.

To begin with, saddle riggings are divided into two main classes, single riggings and double riggings. The single rigged saddle, of course, is intended for one cincha and the double rigging usually requires two cinchas.

THE SINGLE RIGGING is made in the following styles—Spanish, ¾, ⅝ and Center Fire. These different names for the riggings merely indicate the position at which the ring is hung, or point at which draft of the latigo comes. On the drawing shown herewith, the ring marked No. 1 is hung at about the Center Fire position. The dotted lines showing the positions at which the ring might be placed are explained as follows: No. 2 indicates a ⅝; No. 3 a ¾ and No. 5 a Spanish rigging. It will be noticed that this Spanish position is about the same as the position of the front ring on a full double rigged saddle.

For single rigged saddles we use the following rings: Ordinary round rings, Flat Hercules Bronze rings, or our own patent "E-Z" rings, and other special types which may be specified by customers. These different rings mentioned, with the exception of the "E-Z," can be used for any of the different riggings as shown by the sketch, and as explained above. The "E-Z" rigging, however, works most satisfactorily at the ¾ position, and is not recommended for other positions.

One other single rigging which we use quite extensively and which has become a favorite wherever known is the Hamley Flat Plate. It is a plate of special construction embedded in a large flat piece of leather and such a rigging is shown on the saddle No. F628, shown on page 18 of this catalog. The extra charge for the employment of this rigging on a saddle of our own make which is described and priced with an ordinary single rigging is $3.50.

DOUBLE RIGGINGS: There are two main types of double rigging, the regular double with the front ring at the same position as the Spanish single rigging, and the back ring hung slightly back of the point of the cantle of the saddle. The other main type of double rigging is the ¾ double. The back ring on this style rigging is placed in the same position as for the regular double rigging, but the front ring is placed in the ¾ position, the stirrup leather running through the ring and the ring being of a larger size than is used at the front on a regular double rigging.

The Hamley Flat Plate rigging can be supplied in double riggings if the rear attachment is a ring or dee. We do not recommend the use of the Flat Plate for both front and rear rigging. It is a good one to use at the front, however, and then at the back either a dee or a ring should be used.

## Hamley Patent Cincha Riggings

### Hamley E-Z Rigging

**Patented**

The "E-Z" rigging was developed as an improvement for saddles fitted with riggings set at the ¾ position. The patented feature of the rigging is a large flat "dee" shaped metal piece which because of its shape, allows extra freedom for the stirrup leather and, being flat, reduces the bulk between the rider's leg and the side of the horse. This adds to the comfort of the saddle as far as the rider is concerned and also minimizes the chance for sore sides on the horse.

The "E-Z" rigging is used only on saddles with ¾ single rigging and on saddles with ¾ double rigging. It is shown on saddles, pages 27 and 34, with single riggings.

"E-Z" rings, alone—pair, nickel finish........$2.25

XC Finish.............................$1.50

### Hamley Flat Plate Rigging

**Patented**

The Hamley Flat Plate rigging consists of a large piece of heavy saddle leather cut in the proper shape to fit at the back and front ends of a saddle tree in the same manner that other rigging straps fit. Into the central part of this large piece of leather is fit a patented metal plate of proper shape to accommodate the latigos which pass through a hole in the leather just above the top edge of the plate.

The main advantage of this rigging is the fact that it entirely eliminates all unnecessary bulk between the leg of the rider and the side of the horse by eliminating the ordinary rigging ring and leathers which fold around it. It is the most comfortable rigging yet developed—both for horse and rider. Can be had in ¾, ⅝, and center fire single riggings and in ¾ double.

See saddle No. F628, page 18. This rigging is $3.50 extra when ordered on saddles regularly fitted with "E-Z" or ring riggings.

## Improved Hercules Bronze Rigging Rings

The rings shown here are made of Hercules Bronze, a new and very tough metal which will not corrode and will not rust. Furnished on any of the saddles quoted with "E-Z" rigging at no extra charge.

If you are repairing your saddle and need rigging rings, we shall be glad to furnish them. When ordering please tell us what style rigging you are putting on the saddle so we can be sure you are getting the proper size rings. Prices on these rings are given on page 62.

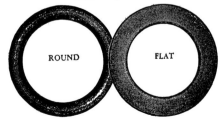

ROUND      FLAT

*Be sure to read about the new Hamley Stirrup Leather Feature, page 6*

# *Extras to Repair Your Saddle*

| Stirrup Leathers, per pair— | Price | Postage |
|---|---|---|
| Plain, with liners, 3″........... | $ 7.85 | $0.40 |
| Check Stamp, with liners, 3″..... | 8.50 | .40 |
| Half Double Style, flower stamp.. | 10.75 | |
| Full double stirrup leathers $1.50 extra. | | |

Fenders (Rosedaros), per pair—

| | Price | Postage |
|---|---|---|
| 17½x7½″, Plain.............. | 4.25 | .40 |
| 17½x7½″, Check Stamp....... | 5.25 | .40 |
| 17½x7½″, Flower Stamp...... | 7.90 | .40 |

New Skirts, pair—real Hamley quality:

| | Price | Postage |
|---|---|---|
| Plain round.................... | 12.50 | .60 |
| Check round................... | 14.00 | .60 |
| Flower round.................. | 17.00 | .60 |
| Plain, square, 15x29″, or 30″.... | 16.75 | .70 |
| Check, square, 15x29″ or 30″.... | 18.25 | .70 |
| Flower, square, 15x29″ or 30″.... | 24.75 | .70 |
| All skirts lined with best grade bark tanned wool skins. | | |

| New Strings, full set, less rope strap— | | |
|---|---|---|
| First grade, ⅝″ wide........... | 1.75 | .10 |
| New Rope Strap, buckle sewed on ¾″ | .50 | .02 |
| New Leather Buttons for Strings, dozen...................... | .15 | .02 |
| "E-Z" Rings, pair— X.C. finish, $1.50; Nickel finish... | 2.25 | .10 |
| New Heavy Latigos, each......... 1½″ wide, $1.25; 1¾″, $1.50; 2″. | 1.70 | .10 |
| Sterling Horns, each............. | 2.50 | .15 |
| Heavy Latigo Strings, ⅞″x7′, for wrapping horn................ | .75 | .05 |
| First Grade Wool Skins, full hides and heavy wool (price governed by size and quality wool) $3.50 to. | 5.00 | .25 |
| Hercules Bronze Rings, for cincha rigging, and cinchas, flat or | | |

round, per pair—

| | Price | Postage |
|---|---|---|
| 3¼″.. (When ordering rings for) ..$ 1.75 | | $0.10 |
| 3½″.. ∫saddle rigging be sure to∫ .. 1.85 | | .10 |
| 4¼″.. ∫tell us the style of rig-∫ .. 2.00 | | .15 |
| .. ∫ging they will be used in∫ | | |
| When ordering these rings be sure to state whether you want FLAT or ROUND rings. | | |
| Rawhide strip for capping horn before wrapping............... | .20 | .05 |
| Hamley's Patent "Flat" Plates, solid white nickel, pair......... | 2.50 | .10 |
| Hamley's Patent "Flat" Rigging, Complete with leather, etc., ready to put on saddle. (See note below)...................... | 10.50 | .35 |
| "E-Z" Rigs and leathers complete, ready to put on saddle. (See note below)................... | 7.75 | .35 |
| Hamley's Patent "Flat" Rigging, attached to your old saddle..... | 13.00 | |
| "E-Z" Rigging, complete, attached to your old saddle............. | 9.75 | |

### REPAIRS ON SADDLES

| | |
|---|---|
| Saddle cleaned, re-oiled and soaped......... | $ 2.50 |
| Horn capped—re-wrapped................. | 2.50 |
| Horn leather covered.................... | 4.00 |
| New horn put in saddle and either leather covered or wrapped................... | 8.00 |
| Steel repair horn with cap. Rawhide covered, and necessary instructions and materials for attaching............................ | 1.75 |
| Skirts relined with first grade woolskins, Round | 7.00 |
| Square.............................. | 8.00 |
| Fork re-covered...................$5.50 to | 9.00 |
| New cantle binding sewed on by hand....... | 2.50 |
| New tree put in old saddle.........$22.50 to | 30.00 |
| Saddle re-strung thruout, including rope strap. | 3.25 |

**Notice** When ordering "E-Z" rigging or "Flat" rigging complete, intending to attach it to your saddle yourself, be sure to give measurements of your saddle, as follows: Seat measure from fork back to cantle; leg room from center of swell back to cantle edge at tie button on side jockey; and from front edge of fork, measuring under seat, to back side of cantle at center.

---

# *Flat and Round Rigging Dees and Stirrup Leather Buckles*

No. 10 →

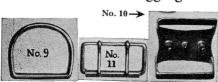

**No. 9**—Round Rigging Dees, 2¾″, for regular double rigging, either solid brass or nickel composition, each..............35c
2″ size, for back ring on ¾ double rig, each...............................20c

**No. 9X**—Improved Hercules Bronze Rigging Dee. This dee is real heavy around the circular part and is perfectly round where the rigging strap connects. 3″ across straight side, each.........$0.90
2¼″, each................................$0.60

**No. 10**—Conway buckle for stirrup leathers, solid brass, 3″, pair...............$1.30

**No. 10X**—Conway stirrup leather buckles, brass plated, pair:
2¼″..............................60c
2½″..............................70c
3 ″..............................85c

**No. 11**—Double-tongue stirrup leather buckle, Cadmium plated, 2½″, 25c each; 3″, 30c each.

**No. 20**—Improved Hercules Bronze Rigging Rings. The ring is nearly ⅜″ thick where the latigo goes around and tapers off to about ⅛″ at the extreme edge. A real ring much heavier than the old style Hercules Bronze rings.
3 ″ each..........................$1.15
3½″, each.......................... 1.25
4¼″, each.......................... 1.35

(Prices quoted above include delivery)

## AL RAY Stirrup Leather Buckle

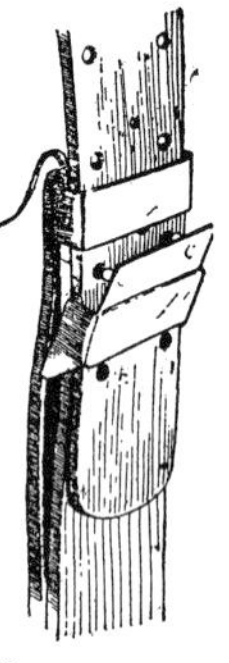

**No. 16**—A fine idea in stirrup leather buckles that permits quick, positive change of stirrup leather length. Notice the sketch—"rocker" plate of heavy metal pulls out and stirrup leather may be adjusted to desired length. Positive; won't slip; no bulge. If you want this improved buckle on your new Hamley saddle, just specify same in your order, and add $2.50 to price of saddle. Sizes for 2½″, 2¾″ and 3″ stirrup leathers. Buckles only, pair, delivered.................$2.00

## Hamley Improved Stirrup Leather Buckle

**No. 17**—A simplified, flat, solid bronze stirrup leather buckle that permits quick, positive change of stirrup leather lengths. Made in one solid piece. Has metal loops with curved hooks in back that fit into holes as pictured. Heavy leather loop or keeper below metal loop. Positive, quick action. No bulge; cannot come loose once it's in position. If you want this buckle on your new Hamley Saddle, just specify same and add $2.50 to regular price of saddle. Sizes 2½″ and 3″. Buckles only, pair, delivered............$2.00

## Good Equipment Deserves Proper Care!

Leather, without proper care, soon becomes dry and hard and short lived. Proper care consists of occasional soaping or oiling.

**No. 23**—Fiebing's Yellow Saddle Soap. A real softener, preservative. 8-oz. can delivered ..$0.25
12-oz. can, delivered........................ 0.35

**No. 26**—Propert's Saddle Soap. Made in England and used all over the world for fine saddles, boots, etc.
5-oz. can, delivered......................$0.35
12½-oz. can, delivered...................... 0.50

**No. 39**—Pure Steam Refined Neatsfoot Oil. A preservative, not for waterproofing.
1 pint can, delivered......................$0.45
1 gallon in gallon can...................... 1.75
(Postage extra on gallon can, about 60c)

**No. 62**—Asco English Style Saddle Soap; occasional application gives your saddle extra life, velvety finish. 6-oz. can, postpaid..........$0.35
12-oz. can, postpaid...................... 0.50

### DRI-SHU

**No. 25**—Waterproofing for shoes, boots and all leather goods. Three shades: Dark, Light, and Colorless. Prevents water penetration effectively and takes a nice polish.
Price, 5½-oz. can (postage 5c)...................$0.25

### LEXOL

**No. 244**—Lexol renourishes and strengthens leather of all colors and finishes, prolonging its life. Excellent for decorated saddles, bridles, etc.—will not injure metal parts. Takes polish by rubbing; will not soil clothing. makes leather soft and pliable. Protects boots against corral acids, etc. 3-oz. can, delivered..............$0.25
Pint can, delivered.............................. 1.00
Quart can, delivered.............................. 1.75
Gallon can, delivered.............................. 4.00

## Snowshoe . . . for waterproofing boots and chaps

**No. 28**—Just a few years ago a man in the Pacific Northwest developed "Snowshoe" Leather Dressing, and it has proved itself the best waterproofing for chaps and boots that we have ever seen. Chap leather is not naturally waterproof. It must be treated with a dressing of this kind. Boots are the same way. Proper care makes good equipment last longer. Directions for application printed on can.
Price, 7-ozs. delivered.................................................... **$0.50**

### WREN'S WORLD RENOWNED "DUBBIN"
#### Leather Preservative

**No. 73**—A famous leather preservative and finisher which is made in England and used throughout the world on fine leather goods. It is especially suitable for all kinds of saddlery, including bridles, etc., as well as boots and shoes. Per can, postpaid.......**$0.35**

#### GLYCERINE BAR SADDLE SOAP

**No. S1**—America's finest glycerine saddle soap. ¾ pound bar is about 6¾" long. Easy to handle; easy to apply. Bar, postpaid................**$0.50**

## TRAILER GOGGLES

**No. 169**—Made of good double fill 8 oz. khaki duck, with easily replaced celluloid lenses. Adjusting tie strings so will fit any average horse.
Each, delivered .....$3.75
Lens replaced........ 1.60

#### CANVAS SHIPPING BAG FOR SADDLE

**No. 74**—Heavy canvas bag, properly designed to carry saddle. Has full leather bottom, brass handles, padlock and key. Each (Postage, 50c)........$8.50

## Saddle Pockets

**No. 104**

8 x 9 inches
Pair
Plain......$ 8.25
Creased...... 8.75
Check stamp. 9.25
Flower stamp,
as shown.. 13.75
Postage, 50c

If made on back jockeys of saddles:
Plain......$ 6.50
Creased
border.... 7.25
Check stamp 7.75
Flower stamp 10.50

### STABLE BLANKETS AND SHEETS

### THE BEST

**No. HB1**—Striped good quality burlap unlined stable sheet. Bound neck and front. Double surcingle. Each, postpaid..............72" $3.75
76" 3.95

**No. HB2**—Good quality burlap blanket, full kersey lined; plain burlap color, double surcingle. Each, postpaid.......................72" $4.15
76" 4.35

**No. HB3**—Medium weight brown canvas blanket. Full kersey lined. Made to stand the weather. Very desirable for trailer use.
Each, postpaid...................................72" $5.00
76" 5.25

(Size 68" or 80" on special order; two weeks delivery).

# Saddle Cinchas

### Any cincha on this page furnished with buckle ends when so ordered

**CINCHAS WITH SADDLES**—Cinchas priced as high as $2.50 may be had with saddles quoted at $85.00 and over. On cheaper saddles, cinchas up to $1.50 in price may be had. If better cincha than allowed is wanted, add the price of the cincha to the price of the saddle ordered, and deduct the allowance of $1.50 or $2.50.

**No. 22M**—(At right.) Hand made, pure soft mohair. Extra heavy 3½″ cadmium rings.

  4¼ inches.......$1.80
*5  inches....... 1.90
*5¼ inches....... 2.15
6  inches....... 2.50

**No. 22**—Diamond Center Hair Cincha, best quality, hand made, 5″ wide......................$2.25
6″ wide......................................................................... 2.50
**No. 31—Famous Tommy Grimes Roping Cincha.** Similar in appearance to No. 22M, but wider. This cincha was designed and the first one made by Tommy Grimes. Width, 7″, extra heavy hand made strands of soft mohair. Rings, 4″ heavy gauge, solid brass. Length, end to end, 30″. Each....................$4.50
(See below for End Covers to fit.)

**No. 23M — (At left.)** Hand made, pure soft mohair. Extra heavy 3½″ cadmium rings.

  4½ inches......$1.65
*5  inches....... 1.75
*5½ inches....... 2.10
6  inches....... 2.30

Postage and packing on all cinchas 15c each.
**No. 23**—Best quality, Three Bar, Hand Made Hair Cincha, 5″ wide..........................$1.90
6″ wide......................................................................... 2.10

**No. 180 — (At left.)** Hard Cotton Cord. Extra Heavy 3½″ cadmium Rings.

5 ″ wide....$0.70
5½″ wide.... 0.80
6 ″ wide.... 0.90

Postage and packing on all cinchas 15c each.

**No. 66**—(At right.) Hard Cotton Fish Cord. Extra heavy 3½″ cadmium rings.

**5 inches..$0.75
6 inches.. 0.95**

**Laced-on Cincha Connecting Straps for Breast Collars, on any Cincha** $0.50
Connecting strap for use with rear cinch, laced on, 30c

## CINCHA END COVERS

**N⊃. 8**

    **Pair, put on**
Plain............**$0.75**
Check stamp..... 1.00
Flower stamp.... 1.75
  Postage, 10c pair

**Special size for No. 31 Cincha:**
Plain............**$1.75**
Check stamp..... 2.25
Flower stamp.... 3.00
  Postage, 10c pair

**No 7**
**No. 7 —** Folded cincha end cover, Pair........**$0.75**
**No. 10** —Woolskin Cincha End Cover. (Same style as No. 7.) Pair........**$0.65**

**No. 21**—Cincha buckle as pictured, delivered.....**$0.45**

**New Bar Center Ring**

**No. 902**—A sturdy Cadmium plated bar center ring that is light weight, strong, and economical.

3″ inside diameter....**$0.25**
3½″ inside diameter.. 0.35

*No. 22M and No. 23M, 5′ and 5½′ cinchas equipped with No. 902 Bar Center ring; 25c extra one end; 50c extra both ends.

**BAR CENTER RING,** with tongue. Solid Cast Brass. Furnished on No. 22M Cincha in 5½″ and 6″ widths only. Add to price of Cincha, Bar Center Ring one end............**$1.25**
Both ends.......... 2.50

---

*Angora Cord for Making Cinchas*

**No. 14**—Good heavy Angora cord in length 20 strand cincha. Per piece, delivered..**$1.65**

# Wide Bottom Stirrups

**No. 15X**—4″ stirrup that is very popular in some sections. Heavy galvanized iron binding. With leather lining. Pair.........**$3.50**
(Postage 35c)
Without leather lining. Pair...............**$2.50**
(Postage, 35c)

## ALUMINUM STIRRUPS

**No. 16** (At left)—A 1¼″ flat bottom type stirrup of solid cast aluminum; polished to shine like silver. Has the strength of wrought iron with less than half the weight, Pair, delivered **$2.50**

**No. 16L**—Ladies' size, for 2½″ stirrup leather. Pair, delivered......**$2.50**

**No. 17** (At right)—This is a 1¼″ bottom round type stirrup, built for uniform strength throughout. Solid cast aluminum, and highly polished. Order a pair of aluminum stirrups, and if they don't more than please you upon arrival, just return for full refund. Pair, delivered..............**$2.25**

---

**LADIES' AND BOYS' STIRRUPS**
Available in styles No. 37 and No. 30. Price same as quoted for men's.

---

# TAPS ... *to Match Your Saddle*

### PRICES PER PAIR

| Length | Plain | Creased | Check Stamp | Flowered |
|---|---|---|---|---|
| 18-in. | $12.50 | $13.25 | $14.00 | $17.75 |
| 22-in. | 13.50 | 14.00 | 15.00 | 19.50 |
| 24-in. | 14.75 | 15.50 | 16.00 | 21.00 |
| 26-in. | 15.75 | 16.50 | 17.00 | 22.75 |

**No. 032**

This tap is made on a special new pattern and over a form which provides plenty of room for the toes. The tap also hangs straight. Material is heavy and firm.

The taps pictured here can be furnished with saddles and stamped to match the saddle. Can also furnish to match your old saddle. **We deliver taps at prices quoted.**

## Stirrups with Saddles

In figuring costs on saddles it is necessary to include stirrups of a certain price, and you will notice that Nos. 37 and 30 are usually mentioned. If you want a special leather-covered, tipped or aluminum stirrup instead of the style specified in the description of the saddle you select, just deduct $1.50 from the price of the special stirrup you wish and add difference to price of saddle. (The $1.50 is the allowance for the regular stirrups mentioned in saddle description, which are not to be taken if special stirrups are wanted.)

**No. 30,** Ox Bow (At left)—Round bottom stirrup, wood, bound with extra heavy galvanized iron. Prices are without leathers. Add 50 cents pair if leathers are wanted.

|  | Pair |
|---|---|
| 1″ bottoms.......... | **$1.35** |
| 1½″ bottoms....... | 1.40 |
| 2″ bottoms......... | 1.50 |

Postage, 20 cents, pair.

LEATHER COVERED
**No. 30L**—This stirrup is exactly like No. 30, except that it is full leather covered—laced like No. 37L.

| 1¼″ bottoms, pair... | **$3.95** |
|---|---|
| 2″ bottoms, pair..... | 4.25 |

Postage, 20c pair.

**No. 37L** (At right)—Wood stirrup, regular No. 37, covered with leather. Prices:

|  | Pair |
|---|---|
| 1″ bottoms.............. | **$3.75** |
| 1½″ bottoms............ | 3.95 |
| 2″ bottoms............. | 4.25 |
| 2½″ bottoms............ | 4.75 |
| 3″ bottoms............. | 5.25 |

Postage, 20 cents, pair.

**No. 37**—IRON BOUND. Same style as No. 37L, but without leather; bound with 24-gauge galvanized iron.

|  | Pair |
|---|---|
| 1″ bottoms.............. | **$1.25** |
| 1½″ bottoms............ | 1.40 |
| 2″ bottoms............. | 1.50 |
| 2½″ bottoms............ | 1.85 |
| 3″ bottoms............. | 2.15 |
| 3½″ bottoms............ | 2.40 |

Leathers on bottoms and rollers, 50c pair extra. Postage 20c pair. Also in ladies' size, for 2½″ stirrup leathers. 1½″ bottoms, $1.40, 2″, $1.50.

**No. 37T** (At right)—Flat bottom wood stirrup, same shape as No. 37. Covered with heavy galvanized iron and covered with leather at tips, around bottoms, and around rollers.

|  | Pair |
|---|---|
| 1½″ bottoms.............. | **$2.95** |
| 2″ bottoms............... | 3.25 |
| 2½″ bottoms............. | 3.60 |
| 3″ bottoms............... | 3.95 |

Postage, 25 cents pair.

**No. 15**—This is a real stirrup for the rider who likes a narrow tread. Tops are widened for strength and tread is ⅝″ wide. Heavy metal binding and 3″ rollers, leather on bottoms and rollers. Pair.....**$1.75**
Without leathers, pair......**$1.35**
Postage, 15c.

← No. 15

## OVERSHOE STIRRUPS

(Not pictured)
**No. 030**—Over-size stirrups made especially for use when you wear overshoes. Same style as No. 30 stirrup. 2″ bottoms only, pair **$1.85**
Postage, 20 cents pair.

## Decker Pack Outfit

### Made on Genuine O. P. R. Tree

**No. 162**—This outfit is used by the hundreds by the government forestry service in the rugged mountains of the West. Experienced packers who have used it will have nothing else.

The canvas part of the outfit is doubled No. 000 extra heavy. It is bound all around with heavy leather which is stitched with waxed thread. The rigging rings on the outfit are fastened by hand-riveted copper rivets. The tree consists of a pair of bars with round iron forks front and rear. All leather parts are first grade and the outfit throughout is made for real service. When in use the space between the two layers of canvas is filled with straw, small tree boughs or some other substance to make a pad against the animal.

Price, complete with tree................$21.50
Price, without tree...................... 17.50

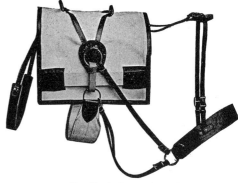

Woolskin covered bars on this tree
$1.50 extra.

## Pack Saddle

| Repairs | Price | Postage |
|---|---|---|
| Tree only............. | $3.75 | $0.35 |
| Breast Collar........ | 1.00 | .10 |
| Breeching and Straps.. | 2.85 | .15 |

**No. 16**—A first-grade Pack Tree with saddle tree bars, built to fit the horse; fitted with full double rigging, 1½" rigging straps, web breeching and breast collar, strong web cinchs, sling cincha with iron hook, 1½" latigos. Complete as described and shown.....$12.50
**No. 17**—Same as above, complete without breeching and breast collar.............$ 9.75
**No. 18**—Same as No. 16 with breeching and breast collar, but with single cincha rigging instead of double..............$11.50
**No. 19**—As pictured, but without breeching and breast collar and with single rigging instead of double..................$ 9.50
Postage and insured safe delivery on pack saddles, 75c each.

## Pack Cinchas

**No. 5**—Heavy webbing cincha with jap rings, harness leather reinforcements. Each........$0.75
Postage 10c

**No. 6**—Long heavy webbing cincha with hook one end for sling cincha. Each..............$1.10
Postage 10c

## Tarps

Best, full weight, white duck. Full one-piece, no center seams. Snap and ring fastenings down sides and both ends hemmed.

| Sizes | 14-oz. duck | 16-oz. duck |
|---|---|---|
| **No. 250**—6 ft. x 16 ft...... | $ 9.25 | $10.60 |
| **No. 251**—6 ft. x 17 ft...... | 9.95 | 11.50 |
| **No. 252**—6 ft. x 18 ft...... | 10.70 | 12.35 |

Any of these tarps will be made with zipper fastener across one end and up side for $1.50 extra.
Prices quoted include delivery

## Quality Pack Bags

No. 59

**No. 59**—Made of 000 heavy duck. Full leather ends and binding; leather strip 9" wide reinforces front 5" up and bottom 4" under (not shown in picture). 4" strips reinforce material on carrying stick. Top flap extends past edge of bag at both ends. Proper size to take a 10-gallon oil case. The finest bag on the market. Postage, 50c. Per pair............$15.50
**No. 49**—A high-grade pack bag made from the same heavy material as No. 59, but without some of the features which make the No. 59 so expensive. Ends are full leather, all points of strain reinforced with leather, heavy straps all around, a better bag all through than most people are accustomed to. Postage, 50c. Per pair....................$13.50

## Hobbles

**No. 3**—Forestry Service Hobble. Heavy 1½ inch leather with heavy swivel chains. Has folded leather lining. Pair, first grade, postpaid............$1.85
Dozen................................$20.00

**No. 7**—Handy Hobble. Made especially to carry on the saddle or in a bed roll. Good grade black harness leather, lined with latigo leather. Each, for one horse, postpaid........................$1.60
With Sheepskin Lining.................... 2.00

# HAND WOVEN NAVAJOS

## Direct from the Navajo Indian Reservation

This picture is of a 1A grade rug, approximately 34" x 68" in size. Folds to a 34" x 34" double saddle blanket
This grade generally used for floor rugs.

## *Fine for Floor Rugs . . . Wonderful for Saddle Blankets*

THESE Navajos are made entirely by hand by the Navajo Indians. They raise their own sheep, shear the wool, scour it, dye, spin and weave it into fine rugs. As you know, Navajos have their own ideas about design. Seldom do they make two rugs alike. The predominating colors are black and red for designs and the background or body of most of them is white and gray. We receive shipments regularly direct from the reservation so our stocks are always complete. Sizes square or single about 30"x30". Double blankets from 28" to 34"x56" to 68" (length approximately twice the width). For different grades available and prices per pound just read the column below.

No. 1A—Very choice Navajo rugs. Selected patterns and weaves suitable for floor rugs or fine saddle blankets, double size only. This grade is scarce. Per pound.................................$2.25
(These 1A blankets weigh about 6 pounds each.)
No. 1 grade, selected for good weave and quality, per pound................................$1.90
No. 2 grade, real good but not quite up to No. 1 grade, per pound...........................$1.60
No. 3 grade, good blankets, but not equal to No. 1 and No. 2 grades, per pound................$1.35

Single weight from 2 to 3½ pounds. Doubles from 4 to 7 pounds. (We pay the postage.)

# BEAUTIFUL *Corona* BLANKET

No. 877—BEAUTIFUL CORONA BLANKET. A blanket like this will certainly dress up your outfit. The nice part of it is that you couldn't get a nicer one for the money. Made of first grade carpet, leather bound, with best quality woolskin lining underneath. Fringe is pure wool yarn, and may be had in a combination of any two of the following colors: *White, Black, Brown, Red,* or *Wine.* When ordering, be sure to send an exact paper pattern of the skirts on your saddle indicating where the rigging ring (or rings) hangs over the edge of the skirt. Delivery two weeks,

Each, postpaid......... **$35.00**

# TWO FINE WOVEN ANGORA PADS "A1" QUALITY

**No. 50**—(At right) Outside of a good Navajo, this is the finest saddle pad we have ever seen. A thick woven Angora, soft, yet hard as nails for wear. It is a nice looking pad you'll be proud to own, and one your horse will enjoy working under.
Size 30"x30" for square saddle. Each, delivered...**$4.95**

**No. 37**—Just like No. 50, above, except size 28½"x 28½" for round skirted saddle. Each, delivered....**$3.75**

**No. 85**—(At left) This is the same fine quality as No. 50 pad, except that it is doubled, rounded, and the edges bound as pictured. Made in such a way that it is twice as serviceable as others— there are four different sides you can place next the horse's back. Size 27"x27", folded once. Each, delivered.....................**$8.50**

**No. 86**—Special large size, shaped like No. 85, folds to 30" x 30". Each......................**$9.25**

---

## *Quilted Hair Pads — Duck-Covered*

**No. 400**—(At right) Approximately 90 per cent Pure Curled Hair felted blanket, about 1" thick, firmly interlaced through burlap. Top (or back) covered with heavy army duck to take the wear. A reliable and sanitary cushion under the saddle. Similar in style to No. 12, for round skirt saddles. Size 29"x29". Each delivered........**$3.25**

**No. 402**—(Left, above) Same pad as No. 400, but for square skirt saddles. Size 30"x30"; same style as No. 7. Each, delivered.................................................................**$3.25**

Pads No. 400 and 402 can be cleaned in the same manner as No's. 7 and 12 at the top of page 77. Leather chafes may be had on either of these two new pads for $1.00 extra. Please specify whether for single or double rigged saddle.

---

# Top Blanket Values

**A wool camp blanket; or cut it in half and get two fine 3-fold saddle blankets for the price of one.**

**No. 700**—This is a guaranteed 100% wool blanket in an army O.D. Khaki color and passes all U.S. government tests. The material is pre-shrunk from an 86" width down to 62" in width, and it is 82" long. The blanket weighs from 3½ to 3¾ lbs., and is one for which the government has paid up to $6.00 and $7.00 each when buying them by the thousands. While they are available the price will be, delivered..............**$4.95**

**No. 800**–This is a Maltese gray, guaranteed all wool, pre-shrunk blanket, size 62"x82". It is ideal for home or camp use, weighs 3½ lbs. and is a real article. Price, each, delivered..........**$3.85**

**EXTRA FINE—100% WOOL—7-lb. BLANKET**

**No. 900**—A large full double blanket, size 62"x72", guaranteed 100% wool. Weighs 7 pounds. Dark gray color. A wonderful blanket for the price. Each, delivered....................**$7.95**

## Pure Curled Hair Saddle Pad and Alaskan Hair Pad

Note that these curled hair pads are larger than those listed by most dealers.

No. 12—26" x 30". This pad is made of pure curled hair and is nearly one inch thick, but is very light, weighing only two pounds. Gall sores are quickly healed with the pad, by placing next to the sore a piece of clean white cloth and leaving it there while the horse is in use. The air circulating freely under all parts of the saddle prevents scalding. Price, each **$4.00** Postage, 20 cents.

No. 7—Pure Curled Hair, same as No. 12, but for square saddles. Size 30" x 30".............. **$4.75** Postage, 25 cents.

No. 830—A curled and quilted hair pad, same style as No. 12 pad but not such high quality. A real pad, however, for real service and easy on the horse. For round skirt saddles, each, postpaid.............. **$2.75**
No. 831—Same pad as No. 830, but for square skirt saddles, 30" x 30", each, postpaid............ **$2.75**
These pads are great for wear and are easily and quickly cleaned by placing in running water and wriggling to loosen the dirt. Leather chafes put on any of the above pads, $1.00 extra. Specify whether for single or double rigged saddle.

## Woven Goat Hair Pad

No. 81—(For tender backs.) Size 30"x30". Porous woven saddle pad, made of hair. The manner of the weaving of this blanket makes it very porous, allowing free circulation of air under the saddle, which prevents scalding. Just the blanket for tender-backed horses **$2.50** Postage, 35 cents

No. 71—Size 27"x36" porous woven saddle pad, very similar to No. 81, but made of Angora Goat Hair, and white in color. Same free circulation of air and the finest blanket of this kind on the market.............. **$3.50** Postage, 35 cents.

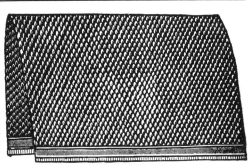

## THE "BIG SIX"

Here is a big high-grade double thick blanket for the horse with a tender back. A wool mix blanket, thick and stiff, so will not wrinkle under saddle. Guaranteed to be the biggest and best blankets you have seen at these prices—send them back if they're not.

No. 77—BLUE. A mighty good one. Size 28"x84", each...................... **$5.65**
Size 28"x56", each................... 3.85
Size 28"x28", each................... 1.90

No. 79—CHECKERBOARD STRIPES. A thick, wooly blanket with several different colors in 3 checkerboard stripes on solid dark color background stripes; weighs about 4 lbs. Size 28"x84". Each................... **$3.95**
(Prices above include delivery).

## Quilted Hair and Deer Hair Pads for Service

Here are some fine, inexpensive quilted pads for use either under your riding saddle or with pack saddles. Heavy duck canvas.

No. 42—"Swabak" round shape, size 25"x26". 10-oz. army duck covering and filled with 100% pure deer hair. Cool on the horse, light weight.
Each, delivered................... **$1.80**

No. 43—"Swabak", square shape, size 25"x27". 10-oz. army duck covering. Filled with 100% pure deer hair. "Swabak" pads are shaped to fit the animal's back.
Each, delivered................... **$2.00**

# Silk Giant Rope

Recognized by professionals and others all over the country as the best throwing and strongest lariat rope on the market. The smoothest rope made. Stocked in 6 different sizes. Illustrations below show actual sizes.

The No. 1 (⅜-in. scant) is a dandy little rope for trick roping and for catching calves—it's just a dandy calf rope. The No. 2 (⅜-in. exact) is the regular ⅜-in. size which we have sold for years. Its best use is for light work from the saddle. The No. 3 size (13/32-in.) is used by hundreds of men for all-around purposes, especially with small stock. The No. 4 (7/16-in. exact) is the size supplied in most makes of lariat rope when the customer asks for 7/16-in. It is the strongest and smoothest rope of this size on the market. The No. 5 (7/16-in. full) is the standard size for heavy work and is used almost universally in steer roping contests. The No. 6 (½-in. exact) is slightly heavier than the contest (No. 5) size and is recommended only for the heaviest of lariat work.

All sizes furnished in any length desired. *Order by number.*

*Prices*    (*Postage Paid*)

Per foot—No. 1, ⅜″ scant......... **4  c**
No. 2, ⅜″ exact.......... **4½c**
No. 3, 13/32″ (7/16″ scant) **5½c**
No. 4, 7/16″ exact....... **6  c**
No. 5, 7/16″ full........ **6½c**
No. 6, ½″.............. **6½c**

*Below are pictured
the 6 different sizes
in Silk Giant Rope*

**ACTUAL SIZE**

# LINEN RATTLER
## *Lariat Rope*

Has a waxed waterproof finish.

This is a 3-strand hard twist linen rope which, while a comparatively recent invention, has already become favorably known throughout the West for its lasting qualities. Some users claim Linen Rattler will outwear four or five other good ropes. Made in two sizes, 3/8″ full for average light saddle work, and 7/16″ full for work with heavy stock. Another feature of this rope is that there are no slivers—it's as smooth as a piece of leather. Prices quoted here include delivery:

3/8″ full, per foot....**$0.11½**
7/16″ full, per foot... **0.14**
(*Postage Paid*)

# Genuine Mexican Maguey Rope . . . for Trick Ropers
## (Not recommended nor guaranteed for lariat purposes)
**A DEPOSIT OF $1.00 IS REQUIRED ON ALL MAGUEYS ORDERED FOR C.O.D. SHIPMENT.**

For fancy catch work there is nothing so fast and snappy and so accurate to throw as a good, clean, smoothly made Mexican Maguey.

Maguey rope is a product of Old Mexico, made from a native grass of that country. The rope is unlike Manila or cotton rope in that it will not become soft and raggy from use. For this reason it is used by all fancy ropers, in contests and in exhibitions, for doing fancy roping stunts. Being of a firm nature, the rope will hold a loop better than ordinary lariat rope, and throws very accurately.

Maguey rope does not make a good spinning rope. If you want rope for that purpose, order No. 12 Samson Spot Cord, regular finish. If you want the highest class lariat rope, order Silk Giant. Maguey is not recommended nor guar-

Postage paid on Magueys when full remittance accompanies order.
No. 6M — Beginner's Maguey about 35 feet, each.........**$1.25**
No. 7M—Best grade Amateur Maguey, about 35 feet, each..**$1.65**
No. 8M — Professional grade, about 70 feet, ⅜″ diameter, hard and smooth, each..........**$3.50**
No. 9M—Finest selection Professional—our "Mefford" grade. Each rope weighs about 4-lbs. 70 feet, ⅜″ diameter, each..**$4.00**

anteed for lariat ropes, but is the finest trick rope in the world for throwing fast loops and making fast catches.

**PIGGIN' ROPE, Comes about 20 ft. to the lb.**, per lb., postpaid ..... **$0.40**

# *Waterproofing for Lariat Rope!*

During the past few years we have supplied hundreds of our customers with a special preparation for waterproofing twisted Manila lariat ropes. The preparation has proved very practical. We buy it in large containers, and supply it to our customers in quantities of one pound upward. Price is 50 cents per pound, and one pound is sufficient to treat about 35 feet of lariat.

Instructions for application:

The job should be done in a very warm room. Heat the rope—care of course should be taken not to burn it. Place the can containing the waterproofing compound in a dish or pan containing boiling water and when the compound becomes melted saturate a very hot woolen cloth with the compound. Holding this hot cloth in the hand, pass the heated rope through the folds of the saturated cloth.

After the rope has been well treated with the compound wipe off any excess compound with a clean cloth.

## *Hair Ropes... Good Ones*

We are prepared to give you good quality and good service on orders for hair ropes. Lengths are 15 feet to 22 feet.

No. 9A—15 ft. first quality, clipped.........$4.00
No. 9B—15 ft., second quality..............3.50
No. 9C—20 to 22 ft. first quality, clipped.....5.00
No. 9D—20 to 22 ft., second quality.........4.25
(Postage paid when remittance accompanies order).

## *Samson Spot Cord*

### FOR ROPE SPINNERS

Spot Cord is used by all rope spinners because it is smoother than any other similar rope made. The No. 12 size is best for ropes 20 feet and longer, and No. 10 is used for some short ropes. The No. 12 waterproof is used for lariat purposes by some folks in damp weather. The usual length for a spinning rope is about 20 feet.

**PRICES**

No. 12—Regular finish, per foot..............6  c
No. 12—Waterproof finish, per foot..........7  c
No. 10—Regular finish, per foot..............4½c
No. 10—Waterproof finish, per foot..........5½c
NOTE: No. 12 rope measures ⅜" in diameter. No. 10 rope measures 5/16" in diameter. (We pay postage on all sizes when remittance accompanies order).

## Hamley's
## SWIVEL HONDA

*For rope spinners and trick ropers.*

This swivel works best on Maguey ropes.

Most trick ropers and some rope spinners are now equipping their ropes with Hamley's Rawhide Swivel Hondas. Hand made. Price, postpaid, each....**$1.50**

## HOGUE'S HANDY HONDA

Light weight, just a fraction more than one ounce. Attached by simply slipping over the end of the honda loop and closing down three prongs which project on each side—it takes just a little pounding. No need to plait the rope back of the loop, as is necessary with other style hondas. Each, postpaid.........**$0.20**
Attached to twisted ropes, Silk Giant, etc....**$0.50**
Attached to braided ropes, Spot Cord, etc....**$0.75**
(Prices, "attached to ropes," include honda).

---

**Charges for Fitting Hondas on Ropes**
(*Including Hondas*)

No. 407 or 409 Brass Honda.......$0.65
Hogue's Handy Honda.............50
Loop tied and covered with leather.. .50
Brass or aluminum hondas or wire-wrapped loop on Spot Cord..............$0.75

---

### *Brass Hondas*

No. 407—Each.....$0.15
No. 409—Each.....$0.15
No. 409X — Aluminum Honda. Same shape as No. 409. For spinning ropes; each...............$0.15

No. 407        No. 409

---

← This one by
Bernard S. Mason

This one by →
Chester Byers

**Two Different Books Entitled**

## "ROPING"

### Learn the Art of Rope Spinning Easily

Chapters on Ropes and Roping, Rope Spinning, The Flat Spins, The Vertical Spins, Trick Knots, Lariat Throwing, Roping Exhibitions and contests. Price...... **$1.00**

Chester Byers, a Champion Trick Roper is recognized as tops in handling a rope. His book contains passages by Will Rogers; you'll enjoy it. Price.... **$1.50**

(Postpaid, in the United States. In foreign countries add 25c)

# Silver Trimmed Bridles and Heads

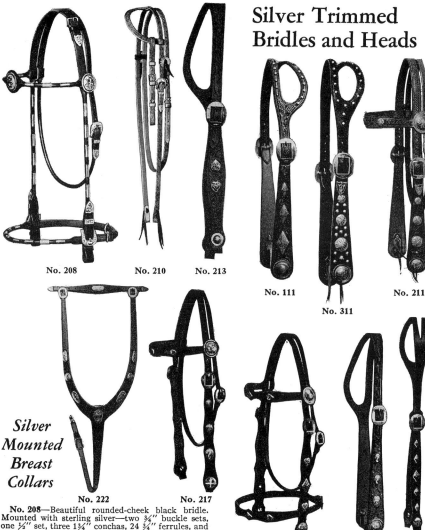

No. 208　　No. 210　　No. 213

No. 111　　No. 211

No. 311

## Silver Mounted Breast Collars

No. 222　　No. 217

No. 216　　No. 218　　215

No. 208—Beautiful rounded-cheek black bridle. Mounted with sterling silver—two ¾" buckle sets, one ½" set, three 1¾" conchas, 24 ¾" ferrules, and one extra tip. Expertly finished to give distinctive appearance. Complete, as shown, delivered...**$55.00**
(Not available in brown color)

No. 210—Sturdy ½" embossed head mounted with one ½" sterling silver buckle set. (Shown with ear piece on wrong side to display stamping and curb.) Complete as shown, postpaid.........**$7.50**

No. 213—Tan head, with dyed brown background, and sterling silver ornaments. Full lined, and a Hamley quality product throughout.
Each, delivered............................**$17.50**

No. 111—Very fine tan bridle head, nicely hand stamped, mounted throughout with sterling silver ornaments; silver tips on billet ends; all parts full lined. Each, delivered.....................**$35.00**
(Also made in black if so ordered)

No. 311—Very fine, full lined, black bridle head, mounted throughout with sterling silver buckles, ornaments, etc., silver tips on billet ends. Each, delivered...............................**$38.50**
(Made in tan color if so ordered)

No. 211—Tan color, full lined, hand stamped, elaborately silver mounted bridle head, tan saddle leather, all ornaments sterling silver. Each, postpaid...................................**$45.00**
(Also made in black if so ordered)

No. 222—Tan saddle leather breast collar, full lined and mounted with seven large hand-engraved sterling silver ornaments. Sterling silver buckles at top, silver tips on ends of neck piece, with silver name plate in center. Entire article hand flower stamped. Each, delivered...................**$38.50**
(Will be furnished in black if so ordered)

No. 217—Black (or tan) bridle, full lined cheeks and brow band, 1¾" sterling silver conchas, ¾" silver buckles. Silver screw ornaments at bottoms of cheeks. Each, delivered......................**$32.50**

No. 216—Fine silver mounted black (or tan) bridle head, full lined cheeks, brow band, and nose band, all buckles and ornaments sterling silver, except buckles on throat latch and nose band which are white nickel. 1½" screw back ornaments at bottoms of cheeks. Each, delivered..........**$35.00**

No. 218—Tan color, full doubled and stitched, hand stamped, sterling silver mounted head, ⅞" billet, 2" sterling conchas, sterling silver ornaments. Each, delivered..............................**$27.50**
(Made in black color at $1.00 extra)

No. 215—Black (or tan) head, sterling silver buckles and silver screw ornaments at bit ends, ten silver ornaments on cheeks. Each, delivered.......**$18.75**

When you order, please specify color of bridle wanted.

# Good *Bridles and Earheads*

**No. 442**—Solid saddle leather bridle—tan color, nickel buckles, nickel rosettes, and double head rivets. Cheeks and browband 1″ wide—throat latch ⅝″.
Each, delivered.............**\$3.75**
With nose band to match....**\$4.70**
(No. 442, black color, 25c extra)

**No. 565**—Solid saddle leather bridle head—hand flower stamped cheeks and crown. Hand sewed laps, nickel concha buckles. ¾″ billets.
Each, delivered...................**\$6.25**
(No. 565, black color, 50c extra)

**No. 443**—Solid tan saddle leather bridle head with shaped browband and noseband hand stamped to match hand stamping on cheeks. ⅞″ crown billet, ⅝″ throat latch. Nickel buckles, sewed laps. Each, complete as shown........................**\$7.25**
(No. 443, black color, 50c extra)

**No. 440—TAN. No. 441—BLACK.**
A double crown ½″ bridle arranged at top so adjustments can be made easily. Thick solid leather heavily edged to give a rounded appearance. Ring in noseband for tie down. All laps sewed. Nickel buckles and leather loops. Complete as shown with curb strap to match. Each, delivered........................**\$5.75**

No. 442    No. 565    No. 443    No. 440—Tan
No. 441—Black

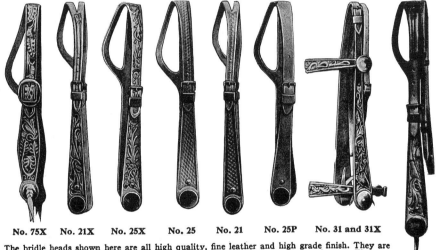

No. 75X    No. 21X    No. 25X    No. 25    No. 21    No. 25P    No. 31 and 31X

No. 286X

The bridle heads shown here are all high quality, fine leather and high grade finish. They are suitable companions for use with the very finest saddles and other quality equipment. They are all regularly made in tan color but will be dyed and finished in black when so ordered—extra charge 50c, except no extra charge on No. 25P and 21P.

**No. 75X**—1¼″ crown, nickel ornaments, hand sewed and hand stamped. Each.............**\$6.25**
Nose band—1″ wide at buckle—swelled in center and stamped to match No. 75x head. Each....**\$2.00**

**No. 75**—Same as No. 75x but stamped like No. 25. Each................................**\$4.40**
Nose band—swelled center—for No. 75 head. Each....................................**\$1.35**

**No. 21X**—1″ buckle ends, adjusting buckle on each cheek—all hand sewed and hand stamped—nickel ornaments. Each....................**\$4.35**

**No. 21P**—Same as No. 21x but all plain rubbed finish....................................**\$2.85**

**No. 25X**—1¼″ buckle ends—adjustable on near side. Nickel buckle and ornaments. Hand sewed and hand stamped to match Oak Leaf saddle. Each **\$4.85**

**No. 25**—Same as No. 25x, but hand check stamped................................**\$4.25**

**No. 21**—Same as No. 21x, but hand check stamped.................................**\$3.35**

**No. 25P**—Same as No. 25x, but plain rubbed finish....................................**\$3.25**

**No. 31**—Same quality, style and finish as No. 31x but stamped like No. 25....................**\$4.50**
Nose band to match—shaped as on No. 31x.. 1.35

**No. 31X**—This is a high quality all hand flower stamped head, made of selected saddle leather as are the other bridles on this page. Nickel trimmings and hand sewing. Each without nose band....**\$6.25**
Hand stamped nose band as pictured........ 2.00

**No. 286X**—Here is one of the finest and most practical bridle heads ever designed. Has the advantages of a regular split ear head and in addition, has the safety of a bridle like No. 31x. The cheeks are each fitted with buckle for adjustment and the throat latch slides through leather loops attached to the crown. All hand flower stamped.........**\$5.75**

**No. 286**—Same as No. 286x, all plain rubbed finish. Each................................**\$4.50**

**ALL ITEMS LISTED ON THIS PAGE DELIVERED AT PRICES QUOTED**

# Bridles and Ear Heads

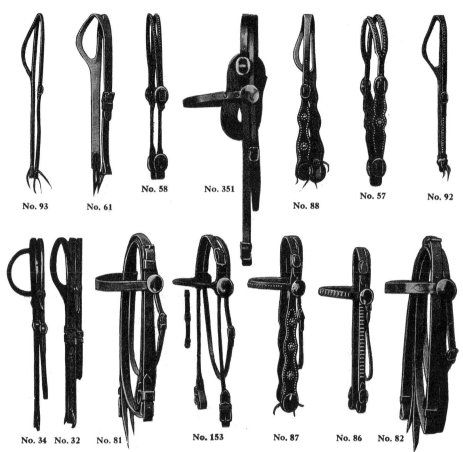

No. 93     No. 61     No. 58     No. 351     No. 88     No. 57     No. 92

No. 34   No. 32   No. 81     No. 153     No. 87     No. 86   No. 82

**No. 93**—Black ear head, loop slides on crown for adjustment, ½" wide, each.................**$1.05**
Nose Band to match **40c** extra.

**No. 93T**—Same as No. 93, tan color, each...**$1.20**

**No. 61**—Plain head, real quality. Black, 1" wide. Nickel buckle sewed on, each..............**$1.80**

**No. 58**—Round sewed cheeks with ¾" nickel concha buckles. Sewed laps, nickel ornaments, black, each...............................**$3.00**

**No. 351**—An inexpensive ¾" black bridle with throatlatch and browband. Riveted laps, nickel ornaments, with ⅝" reins, each............**$3.25**

**No. 352**—Same as No. 351, but without reins, each......................................**$2.10**

**No. 88**—Fancy black bridle head with all nickel ornaments, ⅞" wide at buckle on crown, each..**$3.70**

**No. 57**—Black head, split crown, nickel buckles and ornaments. Sewed laps, no rivets, with straight crown as shown $3.10; or, with shaped crown like No. 61.................................**$3.70**

**No. 92**—A fine little black head of neat appearance. ¾" wide at buckle. Nickel plated buckle and solid nickel spots and conchas, each........**$2.60**

**No. 32**—A real bridle head. Combination **split** ear and throat latch bridle. Cheeks 1" wide and **each**

fitted with nickel adjusting buckle. Throat latch slides through leather loops attached to crown. Leather rosettes. Embossed flower decoration—color, tan. Each..........................**$4.75**
Entirely plain............................... 3.75

**No. 34**—Here's another combination head, same style as No. 32, but light weight. Only ½" wide. Plain rubbed finish. Tan saddle leather, each..**$2.50**

**No. 81**—An old reliable service bridle in tan or black. Selected materials—all sewed, no rivets. 1⅛" wide, nickel buckles and rosettes. Without reins $3.75; with long ⅞" reins..............**$5.40**

**No. 81X**—Same as No. 81 but 1" wide, each **$3.60**
With long ¾" reins.........................**$5.10**

**No. 153**—Extra quality ¾" round head with curb strap, black color....................**$5.00**
(If wanted tan color, add $1.00)

**No. 153X**—Same as No. 153 but heavier, ⅞" at buckles, with curb strap...................**$5.45**

**No. 87**—Fancy black head, all nickel trimmings, sewed, ⅞" wide at buckles, each..............**$4.40**

**No. 86**—Black, ⅞" head—solid nickel mountings, each....................................**$4.35**

**No. 82**—Full double crown, sewed laps, nickel ornaments, complete with throat latch and brow band, without reins, black color............**$3.85**
With reins, long and ⅞" wide, each........ 5.50
⅝" Throat Latches, not pictured. Each, postpaid **60c**

**ALL ITEMS LISTED ON THIS PAGE DELIVERED AT PRICES QUOTED**

# QUALITY BREAST COLLARS
*Made of selected materials and finished to match up with your HAMLEY Saddle*

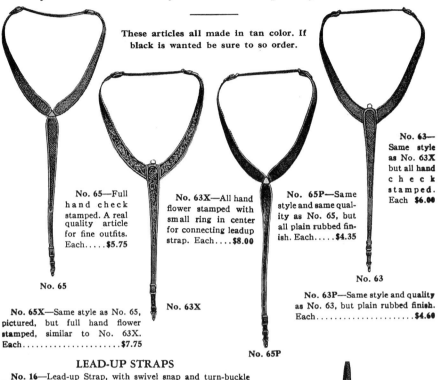

These articles all made in tan color. If black is wanted be sure to so order.

**No. 65**—Full hand check stamped. A real quality article for fine outfits. Each.....**$5.75**

No. 65

**No. 65X**—Same style as No. 65, pictured, but full hand flower stamped, similar to No. 63X. Each.....................**$7.75**

**No. 63X**—All hand flower stamped with small ring in center for connecting leadup strap. Each....**$8.00**

No. 63X

**No. 65P**—Same style and same quality as No. 65, but all plain rubbed finish. Each.....**$4.35**

No. 65P

**No. 63**—Same style as No. 63X but all hand check stamped. Each **$6.00**

No. 63

**No. 63P**—Same style and quality as No. 63, but plain rubbed finish. Each.....................**$4.60**

### LEAD-UP STRAPS

**No. 16**—Lead-up Strap, with swivel snap and turn-buckle for above breast collars. Plain rubbed finish, 5/8" wide. Each...............................................$0.85
Stamped, 5/8" wide, each.............................$1.10

**No. 17**—Straight Nose Band to go with lead-up strap. Plain rubbed finish, 7/8" wide, each........................$0.85
Stamped, 7/8" wide, each.............................$1.10

## Billeted Leather Rear Cincha for ¾ Double Rigged Saddles

**No. 15**—Rear cincha, all leather, for ¾ double rigged saddles. The rear end has doubled tug which in picture is slipped through the leather loop back of buckle. The off side has tug attached and equipped with turn buckle. Each.......**$3.50**

**No. 54**—Flank cincha for Association saddles. Each..**$2.25**
(If wanted wool covered. Each **$3.00**)

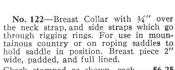

No. 122

**No. 122**—Breast Collar with ¾" over the neck strap, and side straps which go through rigging rings. For use in mountainous country or on roping saddles to hold saddle in position. Breast piece 2" wide, padded, and full lined.
Check stamped as shown, each....**$6.25**
Plain, each........................ **5.75**
Plain, wool skin lined............... **4.25**
Plain, unlined, no padding.......... **3.75**
Flower stamped, padded, lined....... **8.50**

All items on this page delivered at prices quoted, unless otherwise specified.

No. 72

## BUCK ROLLS
### No. 72

Best grade of rolls, will fit any saddle, easily attached. Welted tops, fancy stitched and stuffed with hair.
**Style 1**—Made with rings and strap for tightening.
**Style 2**—Instead of rings on top ends, this style has long ends for fastening under fork in front of seat. Price, either style......**$3.75**
Postage, 25 cents.

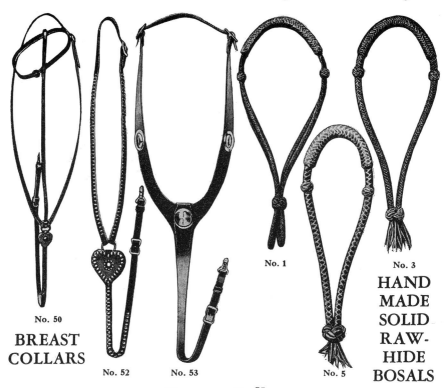

No. 50

**BREAST
COLLARS**

No. 52    No. 53

No. 1

No. 3

**HAND
MADE
SOLID
RAW-
HIDE
BOSALS**

No. 5

## Breast Collars

No. 50—Tan or black ½" breast collar, complete with lead-up strap and nose band. (Lead up strap made with swivel snap instead of loop as shown.)
Each.....................................**$3.00**
Breast collar alone........................ 1.75
Lead-up alone............................ 0.75
Nose band alone.......................... 0.60
   No. 52—¾" x ⅞", breast collar, with nickel trimmings, black or tan....................**$3.25**

No. 52P—Without nickel trimmings.......**$1.85**
   No. 53—"Fit-Rite" Breast Collar, with three silver plated conchas, black or tan. Each.........**$5.75**
With engraved silver plated conchas.........**$7.65**
   No. 53X—Same as No. 53, except that buckles and conchas are sterling silver. Loop and snap to fasten at cinchas are X.C. plated..........**$16.50**

## Bosals, or Nose Bands

Heavy solid rawhide bosals strictly hand made from first class materials.

No. 1—Double, 8-plait. Each...............**$2.60**
No. 5—Single, 6-plait. Each................. 2.00

No. 3—Single, 12-plait. Each..............**$2.60**
No. 3—Single, 8-plait. Each................. 2.25

Any of above bosals fitted with leather head and Theodore of braided cotton rope, $1.50 extra.

All items on this page delivered at prices quoted.

## Curb Straps

No. 2—Round, sewed **90c**

No. 4—Flat, 2 buckle **50c**

No. 6—Flat, 1 buckle **35c**

## Hackamore

   No. 64—12-plait, hand-made, rawhide nose piece, single with solid knot, ¾" latigo leather head, braided cotton Samson cord Theodore. Ea. **$4.35**

   No. 65—Same as No. 64, but with 6-plait, nose piece, latigo head riveted, and to buckle on side, with the same Theodore. Each.............**$3.65**

Theodore Rope only— knots tied. Each..**$0.75**

Nos. 64 and 65

## Curb Chains

   No. H18—Light weight, nickel plated steel curb chain (pictured at right). Each, with hooks, delivered..............**$0.50**
   No. H19—Like No. H18 but Star Steel Silver. Each, postpaid..............**$1.25**
   No. 3616—Star steel silver curb chain heavy weight, with hooks. Each....**$1.25**

No. H18

# *Whips, Reins, Latigos, Saddle Strings and Quirts*

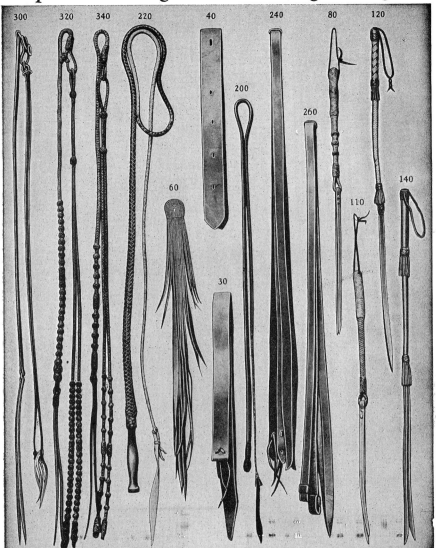

## SNAKE WHIPS

**No. 200**—"Pocket," small, shot loaded, 6-ft. (postage 35c extra). Each.....................**$3.75**

**No. 200A**—Same as above with larger butt, twisted popper, 5-ft. Each. (Postage 20c extra)....**$2.15**

## DROVER WHIPS

**No. 220**—12-plait rawhide, 12-ft., shot loaded; leather covered, swivel, steel handle, nickel knuckle joint. Buckskin tip and popper....**$4.75**
(Postage 40c extra)

**No. 220A**—12-plait, lace leather, 10-ft., otherwise same as No. 220. Each.....................**$4.50**
(Postage 40c extra)

**No. 225** — 4-plait, 14-ft., lace leather, swivel handle. Each..**$3.75**

**No. 226** — 4-plait, 12-ft., lace leather, swivel handle. Each..**$3.25**

## BRIDLE REINS

**No. 240**—Soft, select latigo, extra long, 1½". Pair.......**$2.40**
**No. 240A**—1¼". Pair.....**$2.20**
**No. 240B**—1⅛". Pair.....**$2.10**
**No. 240D**—1". Pair.......**$1.85**
**No. 240E**—¾". Pair.......**$1.50**
**No. 260**—Solid leather, black or tan, extra long, 1". Pair.....**$1.80**
**No. 260A**—⅞". Pair.....**$1.65**
**No. 260B**—¾". Pair.....**$1.50**
**No. 260C**—⅝". Pair.....**$1.35**

These reins are cut from the best part of the leather; no flank used. For buckles at bit end instead of loops, add 50c per pair.

**No. 300**—Narrow reins to tie in bit, long round romal. Pair..**$2.50**
**No. 320**—Solid rawhide, hand made, 12-plait. Pair........**$11.00**
**No. 320A**—8-plait. Pair...**$7.75**
**No. 340**—4-plait. Pair....**$5.25**

## LATIGOS, SADDLE STRINGS, QUIRTS

**No. 30**—Select latigo, extra long, 2¼" wide, **$1.80**; 2", **$1.70**; 1¾", **$1.50**; 1½", **$1.25**.

**No. 40**—Short tug for off side of saddle, doubled, stitched, 2¼", **$1.85**; 2", **$1.65**; single, 1¾", **$1.25**; 2", **$1.40**; 2¼", **$1.60**.

**No. 60**—1st grade saddle strings, set.....................**$1.75**
**No. 60X**—Second grade strings, set.....................**$1.40**
**No. 80** — Hand-made rawhide quirt, shot loaded, 16-plait...**$3.75**
12-plait...................**$3.00**
**No. 110** — Hand-made rawhide quirt, 8-plait, shot loaded....**$2.25**
**No. 120**—12-plait, calf quirt **$2.40**
**No. 140**—Heavy leather quirt, shot loaded. Each...........**$1.50**

All articles on this page delivered at prices quoted, unless otherwise noted.

# CROCKETT ALUMINUM BITS
## STOUT AS STEEL—WILL NOT RUST
## HAND-FORGED—FEATHERWEIGHT

### *Guaranteed Against Breakage in Use*

**No. 1043**—Although this bit has 8⅝″ cheeks, it is not a clumsy looker. It is gracefully designed, nicely engraved, and it really looks good in a horse's mouth. In spite of its length, it weighs only 8 ounces. Has 5⅛″ medium port mouth; each cheek is mounted with button ornament. Mirror finish.

Each, as shown, postpaid .......................... **$7.50**

Plain.................................................**$6.00**

**No. 1041**—Hackamore bits of featherweight, hand-forged aluminum are becoming increasingly popular every day. When other bits fail, this type succeeds. This one has 5⅛″ mouth, weighs 16 ounces, has 9¼″ cheeks and woolskin wrapped noseband.

Each, as shown, postpaid.......................... **$9.50**

Plain................................................**$7.25**

**No. 1043**

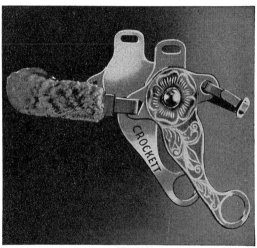

**No. 1039**—Here's a Crockett hackamore bit with three leverage adjustments —mild, medium, or severe. This feature gives positive control without injury to the horse's mouth. Mouthpiece is removable. Has 10″ cheeks, woolskin padded noseband and weighs only 20 ounces. If it doesn't suit you send it back.

Each, as shown, postpaid.............. **$10.00**

Plain..........................**$7.95**

**No. 1042**—A top notch roping type bit with special curb loops and a low port mouth (5⅛″). It weighs only 7 ounces, is as strong as steel, shines like silver, has 7⅝″ cheeks, and will do its job well. Each cheek is mounted with a raised ornament. Each, as shown, postpaid.......... **$5.70**

Plain..........................**$4.50**

**No. 1041**

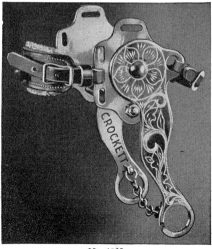

**No. 1039**

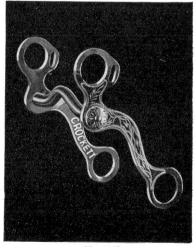

**No. 1042**

# CROCKETT
## *"Hand-Forged"* BITS

The bits shown here are also of shiny Hand-Forged Featherweight Aluminum and we guarantee to replace, without cost, any one of them returned to us as a result of *breakage in use*. They will not rust.

**No. 1023**—Believe us, the bits on this page are all beauties; we know you'll like this one. Light as a feather, strong as steel. 5⅛" mouth, 8⅜" cheeks with loose rings and weighs only 7½ ounces.
Delivered, as shown...................... **$6.75**
Plain............................................**$6.00**

**No. 1022**—Here's a dandy new roping bit with plenty of what it takes—weighs only 7½ ounces, strong as steel, and does its work like a veteran. 5⅛" mouth, 7⅞" cheeks, solid bottom bar.
Engraved as shown, postpaid.............. **$5.70**
Plain............................................**$4.50**

**No. 1024**—About the neatest job of bit making yet; it doesn't seem possible that anything so light and easy on your horse could be as strong as this little bit, yet it's guaranteed. 5⅛" mouth, 7" cheeks, weighs only 5½ ounces. Engraved as shown, postpaid. **$6.00**
Plain............................................**$5.25**

**No. 1020**—Safety pattern bit—plenty of leverage and still it won't hurt your horse's mouth, because bridle swivels are on outside of cheeks. 5⅛" low port mouth, 8" cheeks, and weighs 9 ounces. Carries regular guarantee. Each, postpaid......... **$6.00**
Plain............................................**$4.90**

**No. 905**—A great many hackamore bits like this one have been sold throughout the country during the past several years, and its users recommend it highly. It was just a short time ago that it was first shown made from *Hand-Forged Aluminum*. The design has been improved, and the cheeks shine like silver; they are 9¾" long. Curb chain is adjustable on either side by leather straps. Plain leather nose band.
Engraved, as shown, postpaid. **$12.50**

Same bit, but entirely plain. **$7.95**

(This beautiful No. 905 Bit may also be had with a removable mouthpiece 5⅛" long in either the engraved or plain style for $1.00 extra.)

No. 1023

No. 1020

No. 1022

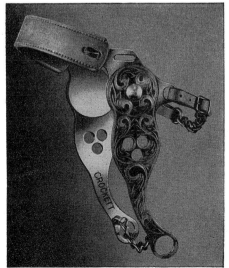

No. 905

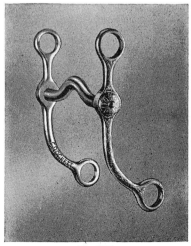

No. 1024

No. 037

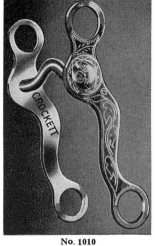

No. 1010

No. 1036

## *"Featherweight Aluminum"*
### Will Not Rust or Frost Your Horse's Mouth

No. 1016

**No. 037**—You'll never grow tired of this beauty. Hand-forged of featherweight aluminum, it weighs about 12 ounces complete with chains. Has 5⅛" mouth, 7½" cheeks with 2" 'hat-shaped' raised conchas. Price, engraved as shown, postpaid............................ **$11.25**

Plain..........................................................$9.00

**No. 1010**—Another beautiful number we take pride in showing. Although it is a conservative bit, it has all the distinction that one could ask for. 8½" cheeks with raised ornaments, 5⅛" low port mouth, and weighs 8 ounces.

As shown, postpaid............................... **$6.75**

Plain..........................................................$5.25

**No. 1036**—This bit should become one of the most popular numbers ever shown in a Hamley catalog; at least, that's the way we feel after examining it. Weighs about 12 ounces complete with chains; has 5⅛" mouth, and 7¾" cheeks with 2" raised ornaments.

Each, engraved as shown, complete, postpaid.......................... **$12.75**

Plain ........................................................$10.50

**No. 1016**—A good, common sense, polo type humane bit that will hold the bad ones. Notice the loops near bottom of cheeks in which to attach thong to hold curb strap in place; also special curb loops. Has 6⅞" cheeks with raised ornaments, 5⅛" low port mouth, and weighs 7 ounces.

Each, as shown, postpaid.......................... **$6.45**

Plain.......................................................$5.25

No. 1017       No. 1003

**No. 1017**—A lightweight, sturdy little bit with 5½" cheeks, and 5⅛" low port mouth. Its extra smooth finish and nicely engraved cheeks make it outstanding. Button ornament on each cheek. Weighs 4 ounces. Mirror finish, Each, as shown, postpaid........ **$4.00**

Plain..................$3.00

**No. 1003**—Mirror finish and nicely engraved. Weighs only 6 ounces; has 5⅛" mouth, with 7¾" shaped cheeks, concha style, with small four leaf clover mounted on each side.

Each, as shown, postpaid........ **$5.70**

Plain..................$4.50

# "*Shines Like Silver*"

**No. 1051**—An ideal roping bit that can't be surpassed when it comes to bringing results. It has a curved bar mouth 5⅛" across, and weighs only 7 ounces. Cheeks are 8" long. Engraved
as shown, postpaid....................... **$5.70**
Plain.......................................... **$4.50**

**No. 1058**—Here's a nice bit with a little "sex appeal", not only in its general design, but in the way it does its job—so smoothly, so prettily, so easily. Has 5⅛" low port mouth, 7⅞" cheeks, and weighs only 7 ounces.
Engraved as shown, postpaid.............. **$6.00**
Plain.......................................... **$4.90**

**No. 1059**—Another splendid bit with 5⅛" low port mouth. Taking nearly everything into consideration, this bit really is well designed; its lines are well placed. It would grace any silver mounted bridle. Has 7" cheeks and weighs only 8 ounces.
Engraved as shown, postpaid.............. **$7.20**
Plain.......................................... **$6.00**

No. 1051

**No. 1061**—It's difficult to describe so many swell bits as are shown in this catalog without repetition, but they're all good and we want you to know it. This one has 5⅛" low port mouth, 7½" cheeks, and weighs only 6 ounces.
Engraved as shown, postpaid........................... **$4.85**
Plain.................................................... **$3.75**

**No. 1053**—Light as a feather, strong as steel. This little bit, with 5⅛" low port mouth, will accomplish its purpose and then some. 6⅞" cheeks; weighs only four ounces. Engraved as shown,
postpaid..... **$4.75**
Plain.............. **$3.75**

**No. 1067** — Weymouth type bit, but different in that its cheeks curve slightly toward the loose-ring end. 5⅛" low port mouth and 8¾" cheeks. Weighs eight ounces. As shown only,
postpaid...... **$6.00**

No. 1059

No. 1058

No. 1061

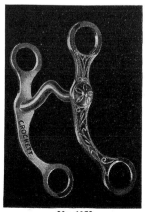
No. 1053

No. 1067

# HUGH STRICKLAND, CROCKETT
# MARTIN 'ZEPHYR', SCHMELZ BITS

### *Featherweight, Strong as Steel*
### *Guaranteed Against Breakage in Use*

No. B444

**No. B444—Martin "Zephyr" Show Bit.** Just about the neatest bit we've seen in the fine "show" class yet also light in weight (about 19½ ounces complete with Star Silver Steel rein chains). It has 8¾" cheeks with one 2½" Sterling Silver concha and one smaller ornament on each. Special curb loops, open port mouth, and comes cut engraved only. Each, postpaid.......... **$25.00**

**No. B3—Hugh Strickland Walking Horse Bit.** Hugh Strickland, better known as "Strick" in the rodeo world has spent his entire life around horses. He understands them and knows their needs. Though this bit weighs only 13 ounces, the mouthpiece is heavy. Has 9" cheeks and 5" mouth. As shown only,
postpaid......................................... **$7.50**

**No. 99H—Schmelz "99" Bloodless Bit.** So named because it will adjust to properly suit and handle 99 out of every 100 horses. Since it has a *removable mouthpiece*, it can be a three adjustment hackamore for the green colt; a very mild bit, a medium firm bit, or a *right now stopper* for the runaway, and all without blood or pain. Cut from hard tempered Duraluminum. 8¾" cheeks, 5⅛" mouth, weight 15 ounces. Engraved as shown.
postpaid....................................... **$10.00**
мirror finish............................................ 7.75

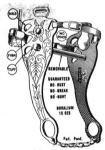

No. B3

**No. B102—**(At left). Another beautiful **Martin "Zephyr".** This particular bit is a favorite everywhere it is in use. Has 7¾" cheeks, weighs about 10 ounces, and has half breed mouth as shown. Comes complete with Silver Steel rein chains. Cut engraved,
as shown....................... **$15.00**
Engraved.............................. 11.00
Plain.................................... 7.00

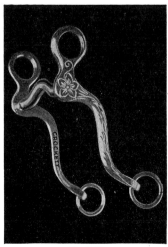

No. 99H

**No. 1056—Crockett Special.** An outstanding and cleverly designed bit with exceptionally smart lines. Loose rings and 5⅛" low port mouth. Similar to No. 1059, page 81, but without the bottom bar. 7" cheeks; weighs 6 ounces. Engraved as shown, postpaid **$6.25**
Plain............................ 5.25

**No. B401—Martin "Zephyr" Roping Bit.** Tested and proved by outstanding cowboys and horsemen all over the country. Weighs about 8½ ounces. Has 7¾" cheeks. Delivered to you at prices quoted.
Cut engraved, as shown.................. **$10.50**
Engraved..................................... 7.50
Plain......................................... 5.25

**No. B400—Martin "Zephyr" Special Bit.** A standard bit with plenty of class. Open port mouth; weighs about 7½ ounces; has 7¾" cheeks. Raised concha on each cheek similar to No. B401. Delivered to you at prices quoted. Cut engraved as shown...... **$8.75**
Engraved..................................... 6.75
Plain......................................... 4.75

No. 1056

No. B401

No. B400

# MEXICAN
# HAND-FORGED

## *Solid Silver Overlaid*
## *Hand-Engraved Bits*

Made to our specifications by a man who has devoted his entire life to the making of fine bits and spurs. All are made of hand-forged steel, Sterling silver overlaid, and hand-engraved in beautiful design. They may be had with special length cheeks or different spread between cheeks on special order, delivered in about two weeks. No extra charge. May also be had with different style of mouth piece on special order.

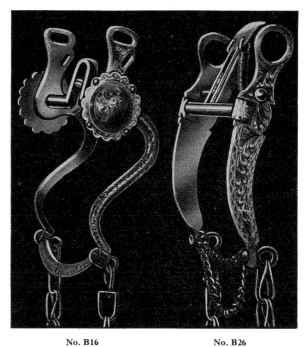

No. B16                    No. B26

**No. B16**—Open port mouth with barrel roller; 7¾" cheeks with 2¼" raised engraved silver conchas. 5" between cheeks. Can be had with spade or half-breed mouth on special order. Sterling silver overlaid and engraved, including bottom bar. Complete with hand made rein chains. Port mouth, as pictured will be sent unless other type of mouth is specified. Weight about 28 ounces.

Each, delivered...... **$32.50**

**No. B26**—Here is a really fine loose check bit that will give you lots of good service in addition to keeping its fine appearance. Has 7" cheek overlaid with Sterling silver and finely engraved. 3⅜" spade mouth. 5¼" between the cheeks. Double chains at bottom. Swivel post and hand made rein chains. Weight about 22 ounces.

Each, delivered...... **$18.75**

**No. B381**—A Mexican silver overlaid bit, hand engraved. Finely finished steel base—a real strong service bit of exceptional beauty and light weight. Conchas are completely protected by the swelled cheeks. Spade or half-breed. Half-breed sent unless otherwise specified. 7" cheek.

With bottom bar, delivered..... **$23.50**

Less bottom bar, delivered.. **$21.00**

**No. B422** (at right)—One of the most popular fancy bits ever made. Weight about 28 ounces complete. The cheeks and bottom bar are overlaid with Sterling silver and hand engraved. Notice the big concha at end of the mouth piece. Pictured with spoon spade mouth, but may also be had with half-breed or Montana mouth. Please be sure to specify type of mouth desired in ordering.

Price as shown...... **$19.75**

No. B422

# Silver Steel ... *Overlaid with Sterling Silver*

## POLISHED TO MIRROR BRIGHTNESS...WILL NOT RUST

It is impossible to picture and describe the real beauty of these bits. They shine like mirrors. The sterling silver overlays are hand engraved by the best craftsmen in the business. This engraving is almost as delicately done as is the engraving on fine platinum rings. Order the style you like best. If it does not more than please you upon arrival, just return for full refund. We know you will be delighted!

This one
mounted with
silver and gold

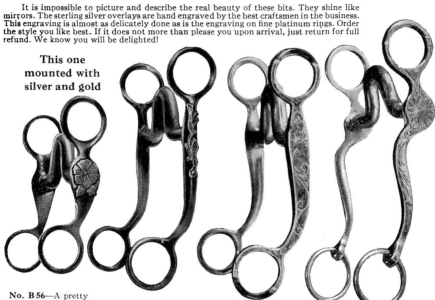

**No. B 56**—A pretty little bit that will give loads of satisfaction. 5½″ cheeks, 5⅛″ mouth. Decoration on each cheek of Sterling silver with flower in gold. Never Rust Silver Steel. Weight about 12 ozs. Each, delivered. **$10.75**

**No. B46**—A good conservative bit of Never Rust Silver Steel, mounted on each side with engraved Sterling silver. 6⅞″ cheeks, 5¼″ spread, weight about 14 ounces. Each, postpaid. **$11.75**

**No. B211**—Never Rust Silver Steel with hand-engraved Sterling silver overlaid mouth; weight about 15 ozs. Shines like a mirror. Each, postpaid. **$16.75**

**No. B51**—6½″ cheeks overlaid with Sterling silver beautifully engraved. Hand-forged from Never Rust Silver Steel. Loose rings; 5⅛″ mouth. Weight about 14 ozs. Each, postpaid. **$15.75**

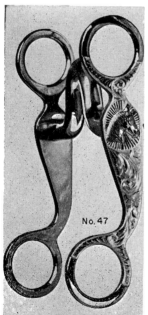

No. 47

### Horse-Head in Gold Relief

**No. B47**—One of the most beautiful bits in its class. Shines like a diamond and is made of Silver Steel that will never rust. Cheeks are mounted as shown with finely engraved Sterling silver. The horse's head stands out in *gold* relief. This bit weighs only 14 ounces; has 6½″ cheeks. Each, delivered... **$20.00**

**No. B48**—The picture of this bit cannot do it justice. The diamond mounting is about ⅛″ high, and of course is of Sterling silver as is the rest of the mounting. When you see this bit you will agree that it is a wonderful job of bit-making and engraving. Silver Steel, never-rust, so it will keep its original sparkle for years to come. 5½″ cheeks. weighs 12 ounces. Each, delivered... **$16.75**

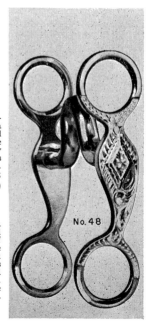

No. 48

# Crockett *"Never Rust"* Silver Steel

## *Guaranteed Against Breakage in Use*

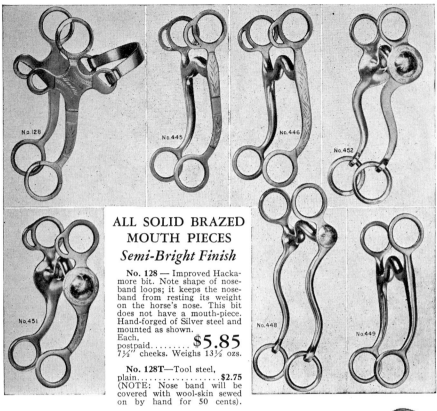

No. 128    No. 445    No. 446    No. 452    No. 451    No. 448    No. 449

### ALL SOLID BRAZED MOUTH PIECES

#### *Semi-Bright Finish*

**No. 128** — Improved Hackamore bit. Note shape of noseband loops; it keeps the noseband from resting its weight on the horse's nose. This bit does not have a mouth-piece. Hand-forged of Silver steel and mounted as shown. Each, postpaid........ **$5.85**
7½" cheeks. Weighs 13½ ozs.

**No. 128T**—Tool steel, plain................**$2.75**
(NOTE: Nose band will be covered with wool-skin sewed on by hand for 50 cents).

**No. 445**—Hand-forged of never-rust Silver Steel. Notice solid mouth-piece rounded at cheeks—cannot pinch a horse's mouth. Special loops for curb strap at top of cheeks. Each, delivered...................... **$5.85**
7¼" cheeks. Weighs 14 ounces.

**No. 446**—Mounted as shown. Hand-forged, all one piece, and guaranteed. Note special loops for curb strap at top of cheeks.
Each, delivered............................................... **$5.85**
7¼" cheeks. Weighs 12½ ounces.

**No. 452**—A loose-ring bit of exceptionally fine appearance. Silver Steel, will not rust. Big, hand-engraved concha mounted on cheeks as shown. **$7.85**
Each, delivered.....................
6½" cheeks. Weighs 16½ ounces.

**No. 451**—Silver Steel, hand-forged, and mounted as shown. Will keep its appearance all during its long life. Note loops for curb strap at top of cheeks. Each, delivered...................... **$7.85**
6¾" cheeks. Weighs 16½ ounces.

**No. 448**—Notice how mouth-piece is welded at cheeks. Hand-forged, all one piece; Silver Steel. Mounted and engraved as shown.
Each, delivered................................................. **$6.00**
7½" cheeks. Weighs 15½ ounces.

**No. 449**—A plain, light-weight, high quality bit. Easy on the horse; notice how mouth-piece is rounded at cheeks. Hand-forged; Silver Steel; **$5.00**
guaranteed. Each, delivered....................
7" cheeks. Weighs 12 ounces.

### STERLING SILVER OVERLAID

**No. B619**—Again it's a Crockett, with the **improved curb loops.** 5½" open port mouth. Made of polished Silver Steel, and overlaid with finely engraved Sterling Silver (including front of bottom bar). Equipped **$15.50**
with Silver Steel rein chains. Each, delivered.................

TOOL STEEL BIT, with same mountings, delivered.................**$13.75**
6⅛" cheeks. Weighs 18 ounces with chains.

No. B619

# TOOL STEEL

**No. B34**—A Crockett bit that has loads of class and is sturdily built for years of service. Made of tool steel and neatly engraved. The rosettes are 2¼" in diameter. Comes complete with rein chains attached. Half-breed mouth piece. As shown and described
Postpaid............... **$8.50**

# SILVER STEEL

**No. B861**—A good solid hand-forged all one piece silver steel bit of the famous Crockett make. Has 6" cheeks, and weighs 14 ounces. 1½" welded rings in cheeks as pictured. This bit is mighty easy on the horse—yet the leverage is such that it will hold the roughest of them. Bridle cheeks attach in the two large rings in center of cheeks. Price,
delivered............... **$4.75**

# MORE CROCKETT BITS
## *Silver Steel*
### *WILL NOT RUST*

**No. 110S**—Highest grade hand-forged bit, nicely finished and mounted as shown. Weighs only 13½ ozs. Has 6¼" cheeks. A Crockett. Each, delivered......**$5.25**

**No. 280S**—Just the bit for tender mouthed horses. Weighs only 13 ounces, and has 7" cheeks. Hand-forged and mounted as shown. A Crockett. Each, delivered.........**$4.90**

No. 110S        No. 280S

No. 21S     No. 140S     No. 57S

**No. 21S**—A short cheek, light weight, hand-forged Crockett guaranteed bit; engraved and mounted as shown. Cheeks 5½" long; weighs 9 ounces. Each, delivered **$3.85**

**No. 140S**—Especially fine for horses with tender mouths. Crockett hand-forged quality. ⅝" mouth piece and cheek circles to the front. 6¼" cheeks; weighs 16 ounces. A dandy. Each, delivered........... **$5.85**

**No. 57S**—A light-weight favorite, with just the right hang and proper port. Finest materials, hand-forged, and Crockett guaranteed. Weighs only 12 ounces; has 5⅞" cheeks. Each, delivered...... **$3.95**

**No. 116S**—Always a popular favorite, this good looking bit, mounted as shown, is hand-forged from the finest and strongest Silver Steel that can be put in a bit. Made for heavy use. Weighs 13 ounces; has 6½" cheeks. Guaranteed not to break in use. Each, postpaid....... **$4.65**

This one
TOOL
STEEL

**No. B37**—A Crockett racking bit, made of select tool steel, with special curb strap rings so that curb strap cannot pinch corners of horse's mouth. Carries both the Crockett and the Hamley guarantee. Mounted as shown, postpaid....... **$4.25**
Plain, blued, postpaid..**$3.90**

# MOUTHPIECES STAR STEEL SILVER
# CHEEKS DURALUMINUM

### *Mirror Finish . . . No Rust*

These bits carry the same GUARANTEE as full Star Steel Silver Products—if they are broken in use, a new bit will be sent upon the return of the broken one.

The MOUTHPIECE WILL NOT PIT or become rough and will not irritate the horse's tongue. Neither will they create excessive saliva resulting in undesirable "slobbering".

The cheeks of the bit are FORGED—not cast, which means they are STRONG. At the same time, the bits are very LIGHT WEIGHT.

**No. B220**—Conservative design makes this a plenty nice little bit, since all of these specially constructed items have such a shiny finish. This one has 5″ low spade mouth with barrel roller. Cheeks are 7¾″ long. Bit weighs only 12½ ounces.
Each, postpaid.................................. **$3.85**

No. B220

**No. B225**—Cheeks somewhat similar to those on No. B220, 7¾″ long. Mouthpiece is half breed style with cricket and has 5″ spread. Bit weighs about 11½ ounces.
Each, postpaid.................................. **$3.85**

**No. B233**—This bit has 7½″ cheeks with bottom bar and comes completely equipped with Star Steel Silver rein chains. Raised concha on cheeks. Smooth shiny finish. 5″ half breed mouthpiece with barrel roller. Weighs about 19 ounces complete with chains. **$9.10**
Each, postpaid..................................

# FRONTIER METAL BITS

### *Featherweight*
### *Inexpensive . . . Guaranteed*

**No. B67**—This new, special lightweight metal is taking the country by storm, and it's not hard to understand when it's good enough to carry the regular Hamley guarantee and sell at such low prices. Here's a bit with 7½″ cheeks and 5″ mouth; it weighs only **$1.95** 6½ ounces. Nicely finished. Each, postpaid...........

No. B225

**No. B63**—A very popular shaped bit which has proved itself many times. You'll like its shiny durable finish, and the way it treats your horse. Has 6″ cheeks, and 5⅛″ mouth. Weighs only **$1.95** 4½ ounces. Each, postpaid.........................

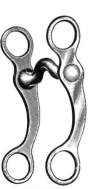

No. B67

No. B63

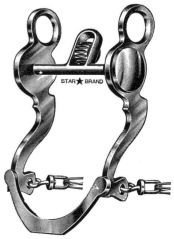

No. B233

# SERVICE
# BITS

**No. 55S**—It's a Crockett, hand-forged from Silver Steel; weighs 10½ ozs. 6¼" cheeks, 5⅛" mouth.
Each, postpaid........ **$4.15**

**No. B64**—Same metal as used in bits No. B67, and B63 on page 87. Hamley guaranteed. Has *shaped* cheeks 7½" long, and 5" mouth. Weighs only 6½ ounces.
Each, postpaid..... **$2.50**

**No. B66**—Exactly the same bit as above without bottom bar. Weighs only 5½ ounces.
Each, postpaid.... **$2.50**

### No. 1037

## *Mexican Ring Bit*

**No. 1037**—A good sturdy ring bit made of cast steel, polished and chased. Welded rein chains. 5" mouth, 4" ring.
Each, delivered......... **$2.25**
Nickel plated and chased..... **$3.60**

**No. 1987**—Light weight, extra strong bevel edge bit. Nickel plated. Each........... **$1.85**

## SILVER STEEL... *can't rust*

**No. 2634**—Kentucky Style Racking Bit—A real forged bit, made of finest silver steel, 5" mouth, 6¼" cheeks.
Each, delivered.............. **$2.95**

**No. 634**—Kentucky Style Racking Bit—Hand-forged steel, nickel plated. First quality, 5" mouth, 7" cheeks.
Each, delivered.............. **$2.35**

**No. 62**—Light weight cast steel bit. Nickel finish. Each...... **$0.95**
**No. 62X**—Same as No. 62, cadmium finish. Each... **$0.65**

**No. 61**—A plenty nice little bit that can't be beat for the money; it's made to do its job well, and it has a polished chrome finish. 5⅝" cheeks; weighs 12 ounces.
Each, postpaid..... **$1.95**

**No. 1455**—Full nickel plated bit with nickel chains and ornamented bottom bar. Each, delivered..**$3.55**

**No. 98**—Solidly made bit with medium length cheeks. Fine blued finish. Each, delivered........**$0.85**

**No. 167**—Popular one piece bit. Light weight but strong. Blued finish, delivered....**$1.50** Nickel finish, delivered... **2.10**

## These bits made to give SERVICE at LOW COST

**No. 230**—A good grade plain bit with bottom bar and chains. Each, delivered........**$1.90**

### TENDER MOUTH BIT
Mouth-piece curves slightly to front.

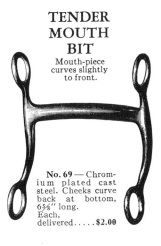

**No. 69** — Chromium plated cast steel. Cheeks curve back at bottom, 6⅝″ long. Each, delivered.....**$2.00**

## PONY BIT

4½ inches between cheeks.

# ENGLISH STYLE BITS

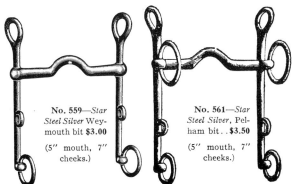

**No. 988**—Blued finish, cast steel bit with open port. Also has small copper roller which is not shown in picture. Each **$0.75**

**No. 559**—*Star Steel Silver* Weymouth bit **$3.00**

(5″ mouth, 7″ cheeks.)

**No. 561**—*Star Steel Silver*, Pelham bit..**$3.50**

(5″ mouth, 7″ cheeks.)

# Rein Chains

**No. 563½**
Star Steel Silver, "Never Rust," hand forged. 7/16" jointed mouth, 5" long. One or more of these should be on every ranch, 2" rings. Each, delivered..............................................$1.50

**No. 526½**
Same style bit as No. 563½ but hand forged steel, nickel plated. Each, delivered.......................................$1.25

## Barrel Head Bit

**No. 16½**
Best quality forged steel. Each, delivered.................$2.00
**No. 216½**
Never rust, silver steel. Each, delivered.................$3.00

**No. 13 Welded Rein Chain. Pair....$0.40**

**No. 15L**

No. 14—Hercules Welded Rein Chain. Pair...............$0.90
No. 15—Star Steel Silver "Never Rust." Pair...............$1.25
No. 16—Nickel plated. Pair, delivered...................$1.10
No. 17—Hand-made chains with swivels as used on silver mounted bits.......................$1.75
No. 15L—Star Steel Silver (will not rust); light weight; hand-made style links, with swivel. Pair..$1.65

### DANDY HORSE BRUSHES

No. BR1—High grade pure white fibre finishing brush. Trimmed 2". Size 2¾" x 8¼". Each, postpaid........$1.10

No. BR4—A "Dandy" style brush with heavy wood handle and gray fibre bristles known as "Union" type. Each, postpaid.............$0.35
No. BR5—Exactly the same as No. BR4 but with brown, stiffer bristles. Each, postpaid....................................$0.35

### LEATHER BACK HORSE BRUSH
No. LB18—Very fine quality brush. Oval face, all stiff black bristle. Russet split leather back with wide, curved hand strap. Size 9"x4¾". Each, postpaid.........................................$2.25

### ALUMINUM MANE COMB
No. C229—Made of pure, polished aluminum. Very light weight, and very durable. Each, postpaid.........................$0.60

### CURRY CARD
No. C4—Exceptionally fine mane and tail card. Size 3½"x6". Copper wire set in rubber. Wooden back and handle. Each, postpaid.........................................$0.50

### SCOTCH CURLING COMB
No. SC34—Generally used for curling hair on 4H Club stock. Best quality, 6" comb; wooden handle. Each, postpaid.......$1.35

---

## Curry Combs—Spring Steel, Crinkled Sheet Steel, Rubber

No. 15—Circular pattern Curry Comb of spring steel. Double life because it is reversible—use both sides. Black wood handle. Each, postpaid.....$0.25

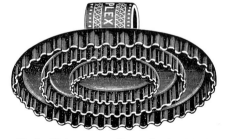

No. 1—Fitch pattern Curry Comb. Crinkled sheet steel, leather handle. Duplex model. Each, postpaid....................................$0.35
No. 1X—Same as above, but made of best quality rubber. Each, postpaid....................$0.60

No. 1029

No. 1030

No. 1031

No. 1032

No. 1033

No. 1034

No. 1035

# CROCKETT SPURS

*Hand-Forged
Featherweight Aluminum
Stout as Steel*

Crockett Bits and Spurs need no introduction. Their quality and dependability has been proved many times over during the many years they have been on the market. Likewise the guarantee against breakage in use offered by Crockett and Hamley together gives positive assurance of this fine quality; this guarantee could not be made possible had the manufacturer not endeavored, from the very beginning, to maintain a standard of quality that could not be questioned. On this page Hamley & Company takes pleasure in presenting seven of the newest and prettiest spurs ever manufactured. Constructed of the new *hand-forged, featherweight aluminum,* they represent all the good things that go to make up the finest spurs money can buy; simply, they "take the cake."

(Any spur shown on this page available in ladies' or boys size at same price).

No. 1029—Here's a little spur with plenty of class, and don't forget this new Hand-Forged Aluminum will really stand the gaff. Has ¾" heel band, 1⅝" shank, 1¼" rowel. Pair weighs about 6 ounces and will be delivered as shown for..........................$7.75
If wanted plain............................$6.75

No. 1030—A neat number for bronc riders, yet classy enough for any purpose. Pair weighs about 8 ounces. 1¾" shank, 1" heel band and 1½" rowel with split points. Pair, engraved as shown, postpaid....................$8.75
Plain................................$7.75

No. 1031—If you want a good looking spur with a chap guard, you need look no further. Pair weighs about 8 ounces. Spur has 2⅝" shank, 1" heel band and 1½" rowel. Pair, delivered as pictured.........................$8.75
Plain................................$7.75

No. 1032—Now we have one with a 16-point rowel (2"), and like all the others, it's a knockout. Pair weighs about 9 ounces. 2½" shank, 1" heel band. Pair, as shown, postpaid.........................$8.75
Plain................................$7.75

No. 1033—Patterned after a popular bronc spur. Notice the sloped buttons for more leverage in tightening the spur to your boot. Fancy engraving. Pair weighs about 9 ounces. 1⅞" shank, 1" heel band, 1½" rowel. Pair, as pictured, postpaid..................$8.75
Plain................................$7.75

No. 1034—A plenty nice small spur with a 20-point rowel. Pair weighs about 8 ounces. 2¼" shank, ¾" heel band, 2¼" rowel. Pair, delivered as shown..................$8.25
Plain................................$7.25

No. 1035—This number might look delicate, but it's plenty tough. You'll know when you try it. Pair weighs about 5½ ounces. 2⅛" shank, ½" heel band, 1½" rowel. Pair, engraved as shown, postpaid.................$5.95
Plain................................$4.95

# HAMLEY Silver SPURS

*Shining Silver Steel*

**No. 114**—(Above). Appearance and lasting qualities have a lot to do with buying a good silver mounted spur. Here's one of Silver Steel, never-rust construction that can take it! Popular standard style. Has 1⅛″ heel band, and 2″ shank. Order a pair, and if you don't like them, just return for full refund. Pair, delivered....... **$22.50**

Length of shank, width of band and style of rowel will be changed at no extra cost.

**No. 814**—(At left). One of the most beautiful spurs you can imagine. Made of Silver Steel; shines like a mirror, and will not rust. Overlaid with Sterling silver and hand engraved like a piece of fine jewelry. Short, 1¼″ shank; 1″ heel band. Sterling silver heel strap button as pictured.

Pair, delivered..... **$21.00**

**FOR THE LADIES**

**No. 815**—(At right). A pair of these spurs will be one of her most prized possessions. They are regular pieces of jewelry as well as extremely serviceable. Hand-forged never-rust Silver Steel and brightly polished. Overlaid with Sterling silver, and exquisitely engraved. Neat and dressy. Heel band is ¾″; shank 1½″. Pair, postpaid.... **$17.50**

**No. 816**—(At left). Many prefer this style spur because it can be fastened so securely. Notice the angle of the strap buttons. Hand-forged of highly polished Silver Steel. Will not rust. Overlaid with Sterling silver and beautifully engraved as pictured. Order a pair. If, upon arrival, you don't agree that this is the finest spur you have ever seen at the price, just return for full refund. Pair, postpaid...... **$26.50**

*Gold and silver mounting*

# FANCY SPUR LEATHERS

**No. 177S**—Spur straps complete with ¾″ silver buckles, loops, and tips, and 1¾″ scalloped edge Sterling silver conchas; all silver pieces very finely finished and nicely hand-engraved. Straps themselves made of kip leather in tan, brown, or black; brown or black dyed background, finely hand-stamped, and doubled and stitched . . . a classy job to match up with classy spurs. Set, complete for two spurs, delivered.......... **$19.25**

# 2 More Silver Hand Engraved Beauties

**No. 80M —A MAN'S SPUR.** The most beautifully engraved pure silver overlaid spur you have ever seen. It is truly a piece of jewelry, so fine is the engraving and mounting. This is a shining silver steel spur —never rust nor tarnish, plus the silver overlay work on one side. Heel band tapers from 1⅛" next to shank to ¾" at tip of heel band. 2" shank, and comes regularly with 2¼" 10-point rowels.

Per pair, delivered.. **$22.50**

**No. 21M — LADIES' SPUR.** What finer gift can you imagine for the lady who rides. This spur is of a popular design, and made of shining silver steel—will never rust nor become tarnished. Overlaid on this is the finest engraved pure white silver. We are sure you will agree that the engraving is as beautiful and carefully worked out as that found on the backs of good watches or on rings. ⅝" heel band; 1¾" shank; 9-point 1½" rowel, mounted one side only.

Per pair, delivered.... **$16.00**

## POPULAR CROCKETT SPURS

### Airplane Metal

**Guaranteed Against Breakage In Use**

**No. 908**—An individual style among new spurs. Pair weighs only 14 ounces. ¾" heel band (wider at oval), 2½" shank, 2¼" 20-point rowel. Pair, as shown, postpaid....... **$6.65**
Plain....................................$5.65

No. 908

**No. 910**—An ideal bronc spur with shanks that hang low; has special tie down loops for under-heel strap. Pair weighs 14 ounces. 1" heel band with smooth beveled edge, 1¾" shank, 1¼" rowel. Pair, as shown, delivered...... **$6.65**
Plain....................................$5.65

No. 910

**No. 457**—Glistening Airplane Metal spur for men. Pair weighs 6 ounces. ⅝" heel band, 1" shank, 1¾" rowel. Pair, postpaid... **$4.85**

**No. W457**—Same spur as No. 457, but in size for ladies and boys. Pair, delivered.............$4.85

No. 457

**No. 900**—A serviceable bronc spur. Shines like a mirror. Pair weighs 8 ounces. 1½" shank, 1" heel band, 1¼" rowel. Pair, postpaid...................... **$5.75**

No. 900

**No. 444**—A really neat spur for men. Pair weighs about 7 ounces. 2" shank, ½" heel band, 1¼" rowel. Pair, delivered..... **$3.25**

**No. 441**—Same spur as No. 444, but in size for ladies and boys. Pair, postpaid..............$2.85

No. 444

### MARTIN "ZEPHYR" BRONC SPUR

**No. B88**—A beautiful duraluminum spur. Light weight. Carries full Hamley guarantee. Short shank with 1½" rowel. Engraved as shown, per pair................. **$11.00**
Plain....................................$5.50

**No. B77**—Exactly the same spur but *ladies' size.* Prices same as men's.

## *This one Airplane Metal*

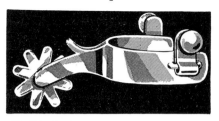

**No. 906**—Crockett Airplane Metal spur. Has 1″ heel band, 1¾″ shank. Pair weighs about 8 ounces. Guaranteed against breakage *in use*. Pair, delivered...................... **$5.50**

**No. 216**—Tapered heel band—1¼″ at shank, and ¾″ at end. Rowels, swinging buttons and shank tips finely mounted and engraved as pictured. 2¼″ shank; 12-point 2¼″ rowels. Hand-forged of Silver Steel. Pair, delivered.. **$6.95**

**No. 0249**—Light weight Crockett spur. Tool steel, mounted and polished. ⅝″ heel band; Crockett swinging buttons.
**Style 1**—Mounted as shown.............................. **$3.00**
**Style 3**—Plain..........................$2.75

**No. 350**—Bronc Spur by Crockett. Hand-forged of Never Rust Silver Steel polished to shine like a mirror. Notice strap button on bottom part of heel band; when you strap this spur on your boot it will stay. 1½″ shank, and heel band 1″ wide. Pair, nicely mounted as shown, postpaid........................ **$7.95**

---

# *Hamley Special* BRONC SPUR
## *... one that stays put*

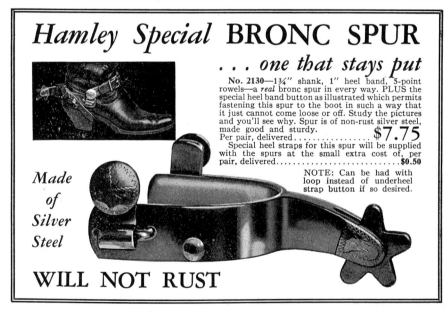

**No. 2130**—1¾″ shank, 1″ heel band, 5-point rowels—a *real* bronc spur in every way. PLUS the special heel band button as illustrated which permits fastening this spur to the boot in such a way that it just cannot come loose or off. Study the pictures and you'll see why. Spur is of non-rust silver steel, made good and sturdy.
Per pair, delivered.................. **$7.75**
Special heel straps for this spur will be supplied with the spurs at the small extra cost of, per pair, delivered...........................**$0.50**

NOTE: Can be had with loop instead of underheel strap button if so desired.

*Made of Silver Steel*

WILL NOT RUST

---

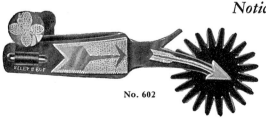

No. 602

## *Notice... Made of Silver Steel*
(No. 602 shown at left below)
Shanks 2¾″ long

**No. 602**—MONTANA JOE—Heel band tapered from 1¼″ at shank to ¾″ at strap button. 2½″, 20 point rowels.

**Style 1**—Mounted one side as shown. Pair...... **$8.75**

## "Paddy Ryan Special"

**No. 219**—This Crockett carries both the Hamley and the Crockett guarantes. It is made of selected tool steel, hand-forged. 1″ band and 2¼″ rowel. Mounted as pictured.
Pair, delivered...................... **$4.50**

**No. 183**—A bronc spur of that famous Crockett quality. Designed by Paddy Ryan, well-known rider. 1″ heel band, 1¾″ shank, 1½″ rowel. Silver steel.
Style 1—Mounted
  one side................... **$6.50**
Style 3—Plain............................$5.50
If wanted made of tool steel, plain, polished... 4.50

## Ladies', Boys' Spurs

**W201**—Ladies' and children's size. Stainless never rust steel. ¾″ band.
Pair, delivered....... **$6.75**
Plain polished tool steel....$4.50

**W183**—Proper size for ladies and children. Stainless never rust steel. ¾″ band.
Pair, delivered....... **$6.75**
Plain polished tool steel.....$4.50

## *A Better* BRONC SPUR

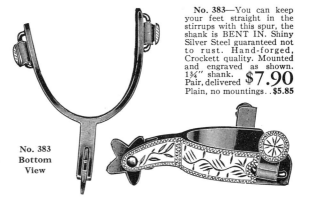

No. 383
Bottom
View

**No. 383**—You can keep your feet straight in the stirrups with this spur, the shank is BENT IN. Shiny Silver Steel guaranteed not to rust. Hand-forged, Crockett quality. Mounted and engraved as shown. 1¾″ shank.
Pair, delivered **$7.90**
Plain, no mountings.. **$5.85**

No. 306

**No. 306**—This classy little spur is another Crockett made in the solid button style. Made by hand of good materials, and carries both the Crockett and Hamley guarantees. ⅞″ heel band, 2″ rowel. Pair, delivered............. **$4.95**

### *Never-Rust*
No. 1145

**No. 1145**—Another spur as a new low price. Super silver steel, never rust. 1⅛″ heel band, 2¼″ rowel.
Pair, delivered...................... **$4.65**

No. 127

*(The picture here shows mounting on shank and buttons, but this spur made without these mountings).*

**No. 127**—A special plain, blued, unfinished, hand-forged spur. The highest grade material and made for service. Furnished only as described.
Pair, delivered to you............... **$2.65**

No. 453

**No. 453**—Top notch bronc spur. 1″ heel band; 1¾″ shank. Notice the slope of the buttons, and the special loop for heel strap. Fastens in such a way that it simply cannot come loose. Hand-forged, all one piece; beautifully mounted as pictured. Silver steel; will not rust. Made and guaranteed by Crockett. Pair, delivered.......... **$7.95**

### No. 0243

**No. 0243**—Light weight, all hand forged, nicely finished steel spur. A product of the famous Crockett factory. Mounted as shown. A bargain at the price, per pair, delivered.........................**$2.65**

## All One Piece!

### No. 2022

**No. 2022**—7/16″ heel band, 2⅞″ shank. Hand forged, solid shank. 1½″ rowel. Bright silver steel. Pair, delivered...............................**$2.25**
Made of "Silver Steel," will never rust.

## For Ladies and Boys

**No. 1254X**—A few dimes and nickels and you can make that youngster a happy kid with this dandy little spur. Steel, filed and chased. Mexican "jingle" style—the weights on the shank clank against the rowels. Pair, delivered.........**$0.85**

# ENGLISH STYLE SPURS

## For Men, Ladies and Boys

**No. 1912**—Star Steel Silver Spur. 1″ neck. Pair................**$2.00**
**No. 105L**—Ladies' and boys' weight, 1″ neck. Pair....................................**$1.70**
Straps for above spurs, either style—Brown or Black, 4 straps to set.......................**$0.75**

**No. 912**—Polo Style. Silver Steel Spur, medium weight, man's size, will not rust. Complete with rowel. Pair.....................**$1.75**
**No. 205L**—Ladies' size, otherwise same as No. 912. Pair..**$1.35**

Straps for the men's or ladies' spurs—black or brown, 4 straps to set.......................**$0.75**

### HERCULES BRONZE

**No. 513**—Shiny bronze finish. 2¼″ shank, ¾″ heel band ornamented with solid white nickel buttons. 1¾″, 10-point rowel. Pair, postpaid.....**$3.00**

### FOR LADIES and BOYS

**No. 387½**—Same style and finish as No. 513, but in size for ladies and boys. A beautiful little spur, and sturdy. 1¼″ rowels, and shorter shank. Pair, postpaid...........................**$2.55**

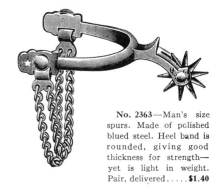

### SILVER STEEL—Never Rust

**No. 391½**—Star Steel Silver spurs of exceptional strength and beauty. Horseshoe and horse's head raised on heel band. About 2¼″ shank; 1¾″, 10-point rowel. Pair, postpaid......................**$3.30**

**No. 520**—Same style and finish as No. 391½, but in size for *ladies and boys*. 1½″ shank, 1¼″ rowel—14-point. Pair, postpaid....................**$2.85**

**No. 2363**—Man's size spurs. Made of polished blued steel. Heel band is rounded, giving good thickness for strength—yet is light in weight. Pair, delivered.....**$1.40**

**No. 9**—Here's a dandy solid brass spur with short shank and very small rowel. Proper size for ladies' and boys' boots and shoes. Pair, with straps delivered..................**$1.25**

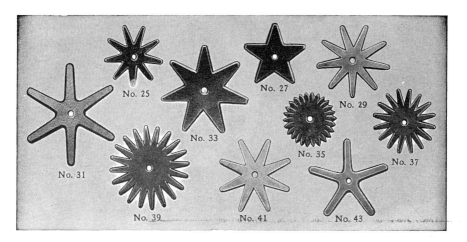

## *Spur Rowels—All Kinds and Sizes*

**No. 25**—Regular size 1½". Pair............$0.50
Size 1¾" and 2"........................... .75
2¼"........................................ 1.25
**No. 27**—Regular size 1½" and 1¼". Pair.....$0.50
Size 1¾" and 2"........................... .60
**No. 29**—Pair: 1½", 50c; 1¾", 75c; 2", $1.00;
2¼", $1.25.
**No. 31**—Pair: 1¾", 75c; 2", $1.00; 2¼" and 2½"
$1.25; 3", $1.50.
**No. 33**—Regular size 1½" and 1¾". Pair....$0.60
Size 2", pair............................... .85
Size 2¼" and 2½"........................ 1.25
**No. 35**—Regular size 1¼" and 1⅝". Pair.....$0.50

**No. 37**—16 points, size 1¾"................$1.00
Size 2".................................... 1.25
Size 2¼" and 2½"........................ 1.50
**No. 39**—20 points, 2". Pair.................$1.25
Size 2¼"................................... 1.50
Size 2½"................................... 1.50
**No. 41**—1¾" and 2". Pair.................$0.75
Size 2¼".................................. 1.00
**No. 43**—Pair: 2", $1.00; 2¼", $1.25; 2½", $1.25
**No. 29S**—"Star Steel Silver"—Never rust.
Pair.........$0.75    Pair, 2¼"......$0.75
**No. 39S**—"Star Steel Silver"—Never rust.
Pair, 2".........$0.75    Pair, 2¼"......$0.75

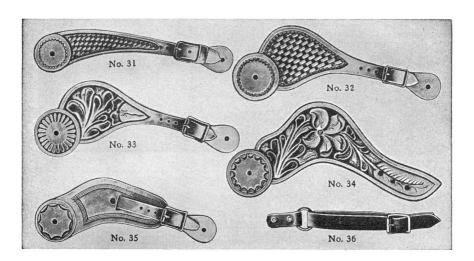

## *"A" Quality Spur Leathers*

**No. 31**—Full hand check stamped as pictured,
leather loop back of buckle. Pair............$1.00
Full flower stamped, otherwise as shown.....$1.25
Plain, no stamping, leather loop back of buckle..$0.85

**No. 32**—Full hand check stamping, as pictured,
¾" buckle. Pair............................$1.25
Plain, no stamping, ¾" buckle. Pair.........$1.00
Full flower stamping, ¾" buckle. Pair.......$1.50

**No. 33**—Full flower stamped as pictured. Pr. **$1.50**

**No. 34**—Full hand-flowered, stamped as pictured.
Pair......................................**$2.00**
Full check stamped, like on No. 32. Pair.....**$1.25**
Plain, no stamping. Pair....................**$1.00**

**No. 35**—Creased border stamping, as pictured,
¾" buckle. Pair...........................**$0.90**
All plain, no stamping, ¾" buckle. Pair.....**$0.75**

**No. 36**—Double strap made of heavy ¾" latigo
leather. One end slides through ring and back to
buckle; easy to tighten spurs. Pair..........**$0.75**

# HOLSTERS

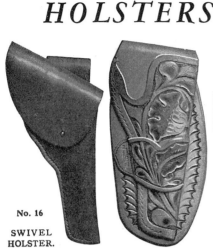

### Hamley De Luxe Shoulder Holster

**No. 600**

The finest material and workmanship you've seen in a holster. Fits the famous .22 Colt automatic pistol or any other caliber or make *and accommodates an extra clip.* Made from a choice piece of saddle leather, lined with coltskin. Price, postpaid........ **$5.75**
Be sure to give caliber, make and length of barrel with order.

**No. 16**

**SWIVEL HOLSTER.**

Made with swivel belt loop so that when wearer sits down the holster swings with the leg. First grade materials. Plain, laced edge as pictured......**$4.00**
Without laced
edge..........**$3.25**

**No. 30**

**No. 34**

| | No. 30 | No. 34 |
|---|---|---|
| Plain Leather, first grade... | $2.50 | $3.50 |
| Crease Border, first grade.. | 2.75 | 3.85 |
| Check Stamped, first grade. | 3.60 | 4.65 |
| Full Flowered, first grade.. | 4.75 | 5.75 |

Postage and insurance on any of above styles, 15c each.

Prices on Nos. 16 and 30 include barrel lengths to 5½". If ordering holster for gun with barrel longer than 5½", add 15c for each extra half inch.
**BE SURE to give model of gun, caliber and length of barrel with your order so that we can send holster of the proper size.**

## CARBINE SCABBARD

**No. 20**—Made of high grade saddle leather. Shown below.
Plain leather, with straps..**$5.50**    Crease border, with straps..**$5.85**
Full check stamped (pictured), with straps..................**$6.50**
Full flower stamped, with straps............................**$9.00**
Postage on scabbards 25c.

For regular rifle scabbard (long barrel), add 50c to above prices. In ordering be sure to give make, model, caliber, and length of barrel.

### HAMLEY SPRING HOLSTER

**No. 32**—A holster for cylinder guns that permits user to take gun from holster quickly by pulling *out* instead of *up.* Neatly made, with spring sewed inside the leather; convenient shoulder strap carries gun comfortably.
Each, delivered... **$6.25**

Be sure to give make, model, caliber, and length of barrel in ordering.

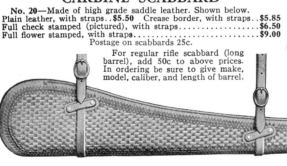

**No. 20**

**No. 32**

## CARTRIDGE BELTS

Made of Tan Saddle Leather. Nickel Buckles. Loops sewed on with waxed thread.

| | | |
|---|---|---|
| **No. 2**—1¾" wide. Each....................**$3.25** | **No. 4**—2½" wide. Each (pictured)..........**$3.75** |
| **No. 3**—2" wide. Each...................... 3.50 | Be sure to give waist measure and caliber of gun. |

⌐ WANT A REAL GOOD BELT? Those listed below have loops which are not stitched on the under side so cannot rip open or become loose; belts are fully lined on under side. Nickel buckles.

| | |
|---|---|
| **No. 7**—2" wide. Each....................**$3.50** | **No. 8X**—2½" wide, folded.................**$6.00** |
| **No. 7X**—2" wide, folded................... 5.50 | **No. 9**—3" wide. Each.................... 4.00 |
| **No. 8**—2½" wide. Each.................... 3.75 | **No. 9X**—3" wide, folded.................... 6.50 |

Be sure to give waist measure and caliber of gun.

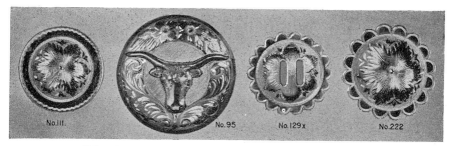

No.III.    No.95    No.129x    No.222

## CONCHAS

**No. 129X**—Scalloped Tie Concha. Prices, each: 1½", **$1.90**; 1¾", **$2.10**; 2", **$2.30**.

**No. 111**—Straight Edge Concha, with bar in back. Prices, per pair: 1¼" **$3.20**; 1½", **$4.00**; 1¾", **$4.60**; 2", **$5.20**; 2¼", **$5.70**.

(This concha may be had with screw back—if that is what you want, add 25c each to the above prices. Made special, will take about 10 days to deliver).

**No. 222**—Sterling silver, hand-made, hand engraved, scalloped edge concha. Has strong brazed loop on back. For use on bridles, etc. 2" diameter. Each, **$2.50**; 2¼" diameter. Each **$2.75**

## STERLING SILVER HORN CAP

**No. 95**—Hand-made, sterling silver, hand engraved, horn cap with steer head ornament mounted on top. Each.........................**$3.75**
(This ornament has heavy wood screw brazed in center on back side and can be attached to the top of most any sufficiently large topped horn which has smooth leather cover.)

### SILVER SADDLE PLATE

**No. 15**—Hand-made silver plate for saddle. 4" long, 2¼" wide. Engraved border, plain center, **$2.75**. Engraved border with initials engraved in center, **$3.00**. With border and full name in center, **$3.50**. With name, town and state nicely engraved, **$4.25**.

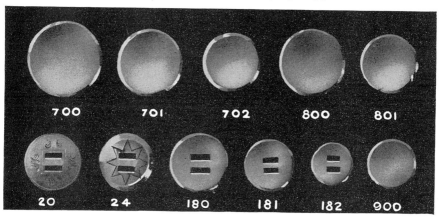

700    701    702    800    801

20    24    180    181    182    900

## ROSSETTES AND TIE ORNAMENTS

Beveled edge, solid nickel top, lead filled rosettes:

**No. 700**—2½" with 1⅛" loop on back. Pair, delivered...............................**$0.50**

**No. 701**—2" with ⅞" loop on back. Pair, delivered...............................**$0.45**

**No. 702**—1¾" with ¾" loop on back. Pair, delivered...............................**$0.40**

**No. 800**—Nickel plated rosette, 2", with 1" cast loop on back. Pair, delivered.............**$0.35**

**No. 801**—Nickel plated rosette, 1¾" with ⅞" loop on back. Pair, delivered............**$0.30**

**No. 20**—Sterling silver tie ornament, very heavy, for saddles, chaps, etc., ½" slots:

**Hand Engraved**
1½" diameter. Ea..**$1.75**  1¾" diameter. Ea..**$2.15**

**Plain Finish**
1½" diameter. Ea..**$1.35**  1¾" diameter. Ea..**$1.50**

**No. 24**—Star silver (solid nickel) tie ornament, very heavy, with sterling silver plate, ½" slots: 1¼". Each.........**$0.25**  1¾". Each.........**$0.35** 1½". Each......... .30

Heavy solid white nickel tie ornament, highly polished:
**No. 180**—1¾" with ½" slots. Per dozen....**$0.85**
**No. 181**—1½" with ⅜" slots. Per dozen.... .75
**No. 182**—1¼" with ⅜" slots. Per dozen.... .60
**No. 900**—Nickel plated bridle rosette, 1½" diameter with ¾" loop on back. Pair, postpaid.....**$0.25**

**No. 7**—Button ornaments for ornamenting bridles, breast collars, chaps, etc.

| **Star Silver** (solid white nickel) | | **Sterling Silver** | |
|---|---|---|---|
| ¼" per hundred..........**$0.45** | ¼" each................**$0.09** |
| ⁵⁄₁₆" per hundred.......... .54 | ⅜" each................ .20 |
| ⅜" per hundred.......... .63 | ½" each................ .30 |
| ½" per hundred.......... .86 | ⅝" each................ .40 |
| ⅝" per hundred.......... .95 | ¾" each................ .50 |

### SHEET SILVER FOR ORNAMENTING BITS, SPURS, ETC.

We have in stock at all times pure sheet silver in strips 3" wide and proper thickness for inlay and overlay work on bits and spurs. A piece 3" wide and 4" long costs from $1.00 to $1.50, depending upon the silver market.

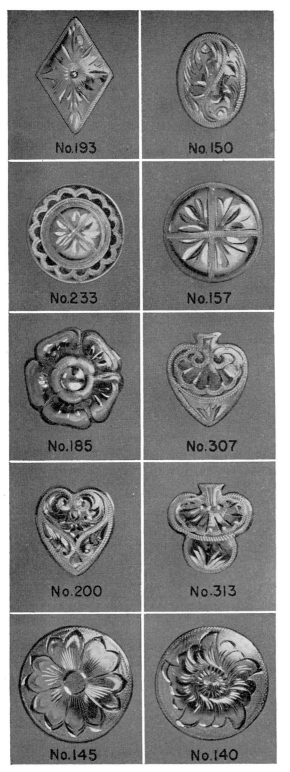

# HAND-MADE
# Sterling Silver
# Mountings
### for Bridles, Breast
### Collars, Saddles, etc.

Every article on this page is made of sterling silver, and hand engraved—like a fine piece of jewelry. It costs very little more to ornament your equipment with first grade silver. All ornaments shown have attachments on back for fastening to leather.

(These ornaments regularly furnished with copper wire fasteners on back, can be had with screw back on special order, delivery 10 days, extra cost on each ornament 25c.)

(Sizes are measured across ornament the longest way.)

No. 193–Raised Diamond Ornament Prices, each: ⅝″, 25c; ¾″, 30c; ⅞″, 35c; 1″, 40c; 1⅛″, 50c.

No. 150—Oval Raised Ornament. Prices, each: ⅝″, 40c; ¾″, 50c; ⅞″, 65c; 1″, 80c; 1-3/16″, $1.00; 1⅜″, $1.25.

No. 233—Raised Concha Ornament. Prices, each: ½″, 35c; ⅝″, 40c; ¾″, 50c; ⅞″, 65c; 1″, 70c; 1¼″, $1.15; 1½″, $1.50.

No. 157—Round, raised ornament. Prices, each: ⅜″, 25c; 7/16″, 35c; ½″, 40c; ⅝″, 50c; ¾″, 60c; ⅞″, 70c; 1″, 85c; 1⅛″, $1.00.

No. 185—Raised Flower Ornament. Prices, each: ½″, 40c; ⅝″, 55c; ¾″, 65c; ⅞″, 95c; 1″, $1.15.

No. 307—Raised Spade Ornament. Prices, each: ⅝″, 40c; ¾″, 50c; ⅞″, 60c.

No. 200—Raised Heart Ornament. Prices, each: ½″, 30c; ⅝″, 40c; ¾″, 50c; 15/16″, 65c; 1⅛″, 80c.

No. 313—Raised Club Ornament. Prices, each: ⅝″, 40c; ¾″, 50c; ⅞″, 60c.

No. 145—Round, Raised Ornament. Prices, each: ⅝″, 50c; ¾″, 65c; 1″, 95c; 1¼″, $1.40; 1½″, $1.70.

No. 140—Round, Raised Ornament. Prices, each: ⅝″, 50c; ¾″, 65c; 1″, 95c; 1¼″, $1.40; 1½″, $1.70.

(Prices quoted include delivery.)

## NEW TIE HOLDERS

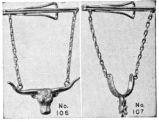

No. 106—Sterling Silver Steer Head Tie Holder—hand engraved. Delivered . . . . . . . . . . . . . . . . . . . .**$2.50**
No. 107—Sterling Silver Spur Tie Holder—hand engraved. Delivered . . . . . . . . . . . . . . . . . . . .**$2.50**
No. 107X—Spur Tie Holder, similar in appearance to No. 107, but made of coin silver. Delivered . . . . . . . . . .**$1.00**

# NEW 1941
# STERLING SILVER
# BUCKLE SETS

The buckle sets shown on this page are all new numbers and are solid Sterling silver. The beautiful engraving is done by expert craftsmen who have spent most of their lives training themselves to do the best type of engraving. You will agree that only an artist could turn out such magnificent pieces as these and the ones on a few succeeding pages. Dress your belt up with one of these Sterling silver sets, and *it needn't be a western belt, either.*

**No. H25**—Ovalled, and yet slightly flatter than the average Sterling set. A distinctive number with a smooth rope edge. For ¾" strap. Per set...........**$8.50**
Buckle only, **$6.25**; Loop, **$1.10**; Tip, **$1.65**.

**No. H26**—Here's one we know you'd like. It's a conventional shape, but it is better proportioned than the ordinary buckle of this general shape.
For ¾" strap. Per set......**$7.25**
Buckle only, **$5.65**; Loop, **$1.00**; Tip, **$1.10**.

**No. H27**—Exactly the same as set No. H26, but it has been dressed up with a smooth rope edge. For ¾" strap. Per set..**$7.75**
Buckle only, **$6.00**; Loop, **$1.00**; Tip, **$1.25**.

**No. H28**—Just the same buckle as No. H25, but without the smooth rope edge. For ¾" strap.
Per set....................**$6.75**
Buckle only, **$4.75**; Loop, **$1.00**; Tip, **$1.50**.

**No. H29**—Same general shape as No. H28, above, but neatly proportioned for ⅝" strap.
Per set....................**$4.75**
Buckle only, **$3.40**; Loop, **$0.80**; Tip, **$1.05**

**No. H30**—Neat, but not gaudy. Unique engraving on plain background. For ¾" strap. Per set **$5.50**
Buckle only, **$4.00**; Loop, **$0.90**; Tip, **$1.10**.

**ALL HAMLEY SILVER BUCKLES SMOOTHED ON BACK SO THEY WILL NOT CHAFE YOUR BELT.
ALL SETS DELIVERED TO YOU AT PRICES QUOTED**

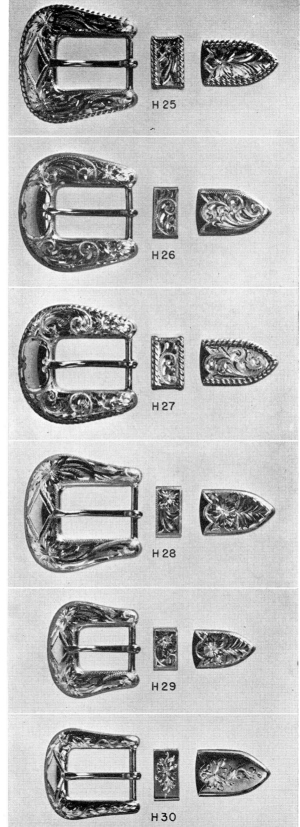

H 25

H 26

H 27

H 28

H 29

H 30

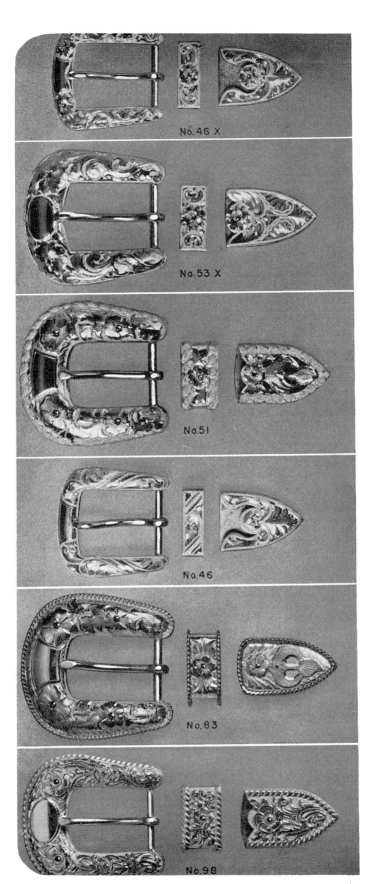

No. 46 X

No. 53 X

No. 51

No. 46

No. 83

No. 98

## Sterling Silve

# BELT
# BUCKLE
# SETS

The buckles and buc
sets pictured and descrit
here are of fine Sterling silv
hand made and engrav
Made for straps 1" wide.

**No. 46X**—A neat set, 
extra large, 4 rubies, overl
with gold. Per set.....**$13**
Buckle only, **$9.25;** Lo
**$2.25;** Tip, **$3.00.**
Also made for 1¼" stra
set..................**$16**
Buckle only, **$11.00;** Lo
**$2.50;** Tip, **$4.25.**

**No. 53X**—A larger set t
No. 46X; 4 rubies, overl
with gold. Per set....**$16**
Buckle only, **$12.50;** Lo
**$2.00;** Tip, **$3.25.**

**No. 44**—A set similar
No. 53X, but without g
overlay and rubies.
set..................**$9**
Buckle only, **$6.00;** Lo
**$1.50;** Tip, **$2.50.**

**No. 51**—An exception
nice one; 6 rubies, over
with gold, and finely
graved, rope edge. Per
set..................**$24**
Buckle only, **$18.00;** Lo
**$3.00;** Tip, **$4.25.**

**No. 50**—Like No. 51,
cept minus the gold over
and rubies—has rope e
engraving. Per set....**$11**
Buckle only, **$7.75;** Lo
**$1.75;** Tip, **$3.00.**

**No. 46**—Fine raised ce
buckle, hand engraved, 
loop and tip, set.......**$6**
Buckle only, **$4.00;** Lo
**$1.25;** Tip, **$1.75.**

**No. 83**—One of the m
beautiful sets we have 
seen. Large size. Flowers
leaves are gold overlays
engraved, with 6 rubies
flower centers. Gold rope 
on buckle, loop and 
Per set..............**$2**
Buckle only, **$20.50;** L
**$4.00;** Tip, **$5.50.**

**No. 98**—Somewhat s
lar in appearance to No.
except this one is a 
smaller. Heavily overlai
gold. Six rubies in flo
centers. Smooth, engra
rope edge. Per set....**$2**
Buckle only, **$16.00;** L
**$3.25;** Tip, **$4.50.**

Any of these buckle sets
be mounted on belts
prices ranging from $
to $10.00 each.

102

## Sterling Silver

# BELT BUCKLE SETS

**No. 23**—If you want a neat silver buckle but don't want to pay much for it, take a look at this one. Nicely engraved. For 1″ belt. Set, only......$7.75
Buckle only $6.00; Loop, $1.00; Tip, $1.25

**No. 23X**—FOR LADIES. The same thing exactly as No. 23, except made in smaller proportions for ladies' wear. Set, delivered........................$7.25
Buckle only, $5.65; Loop, $1.00; Tip, $1.10.

**No. 22**—Horseshoe buckle set for good. Made of sterling silver, with squares on horseshoe and flowers on loop and tip inlaid in gold. Six rubies in horseshoe. Gold flowers on tip and loop. For 1″ belt. ............................$10.75
Buckle only, $6.75; Loop, $2.25; Tip, $2.50.

**No. 20**—Fine hand engraved set of sterling silver, with gold overlay. Rope edge, gold flowers on buckle, loop and tip, with ruby centers. Gold engraved leaves inlaid on buckle. For 1″ belt. Set, delivered safely..................$18.50
Buckle only, $12.50; Loop, $3.00; Tip, $4.00.

**No. 20X**—FOR LADIES. The same thing exactly as No. 20, except made in smaller proportions. Set, delivered safely........................$17.50
Buckle only, $12.00; Loop, $2.75; Tip, $3.75.

**No. 21**—A mighty neat buckle set you'll be proud to own. Finely engraved; rope edge. For 1″ belt. Per set, delivered ...............................$8.50
Buckle only, $6.25; Loop, $1.10; Tip, $1.65.

**No. 82** — An exceptionally beautiful buckle set. Sterling silver, nicely engraved, smooth rope edge. Heavily overlaid with gold. Six rubies in flower centers. For belt. Set, delivered safely.......$22.50
Buckle only, $19.00; Loop, $2.00; Tip, $2.75.

**No. 81**—An outstanding good luck horseshoe buckle set. Sterling silver, beautifully engraved like a fine piece of jewelry. The head on loop is gold, as are horseshoe on buckle and flower on loop. For 1″ belt. Set, safe delivery guaranteed..$11.75
Buckle only, $8.75; Loop, $1.50; Tip, $2.25.

**No. 99**—(Bottom right). FOR THE LADIES. Another good luck set of sterling silver, beautifully overlaid with gold. Buckle has 2 rubies in gold flower centers. Horseshoe on loop is gold, and so is the head on tip. For 1″ belt. Set, delivered safely..........................$14.75
Buckle only, $11.00; Loop, $2.00; Tip, $2.50.

103

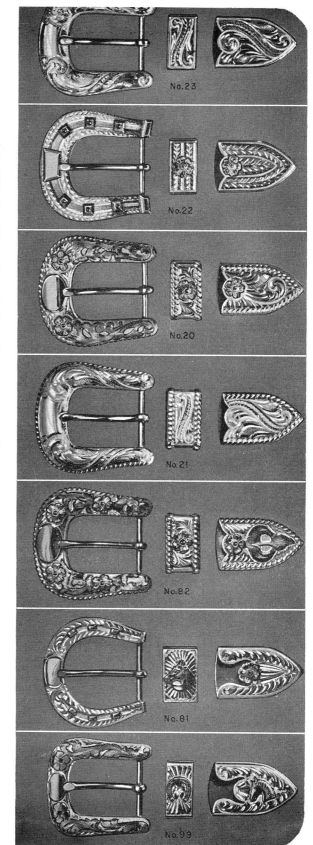

No. 23
No. 22
No. 20
No. 21
No. 82
No. 81
No. 99

# LOW PRICED *Sterling Silver* BELT SETS
# and *Gold and Silver* WRIST WATCH SETS

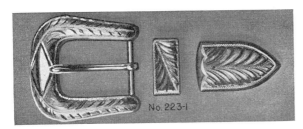

**No. 223-1**—Nicely engraved sterling silver set similar in shape to No. 23, Page 103, but not quite so elaborately finished. For 1″ strap. Set.......................$6.25

**No. 223-¾**—Just like No. 223-1 but for ¾″ strap. A good ladies buckle. Set...............$4.50

**No. 223-½**—Same as above for ½″ tapered end. Fine for the ladies. (See belt No. X324-1T on Page 111. Set.......................$4.00

**No. 223-⅜**—Same as above for ⅜″ tapered end. Used mainly on wrist watch straps. Set....$3.50

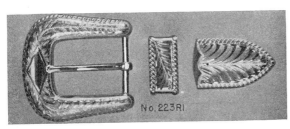

**No. 233R1**—Same set as No. 223-1, but it has a polished rope edge. Sterling silver, of course. For 1″ strap. Set..........$7.50

**No. 223R¾**—The ladies will like this one especially; it's neat, and not gaudy. Like No. 223R1 but for ¾″ strap. Set..........$6.50

**All buckles furnished with guards on the back to prevent chafing of the billet.**
**All buckle sets postpaid.**

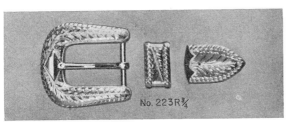

**No. 113**—(First strap at left). A wrist watch strap of HAZEL BROWN PIGSKIN fitted with No. 121 solid gold buckle set with silvered back. Complete, as shown, delivered.................$8.50

Mounted with No. 124 set, opposite page...............$9.50

Mounted with No. 125 set, opposite page.............$11.00

If strap is not wanted, deduct $1.00 from above price. When ordering strap specify width of strap where it joins watch and length of old strap when buckled.

**No. 133**—Fine hand-stamped wrist watch strap, calfskin, doubled and stitched, fitted with No. 121 solid gold buckle set with silvered back. Background dyed dark brown, or black. Complete, as shown, delivered.................$10.00

Fitted with No. H45 set, page 107.......................$ 6.00

Fitted with No. 124 set, opposite page.....................$11.00

Fitted with No. 125 set, opposite page.....................$12.50

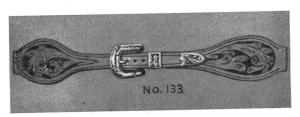

For plain, straight strap, tapered to buckle, brown, black, or tan leather, deduct $1.50 from above prices. When ordering specify length of lug on watch, and distance from one lug around wrist to other lug.

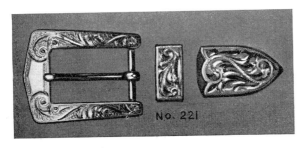

**No. 221**—Finely engraved sterling silver flat buckle with loop and tip to match. Smooth back, will not scrape belt. One of the neatest little sets we've seen yet. For ¾″ strap. Set.........$3.50

# NEW STERLING SILVER BUCKLE SETS

**No. H510-3/4** — Shiny Sterling Silver overlaid with solid gold flowers; no rubies. Neatly engraved rope edge. For ¾″ strap. Per set......................**$21.50** Buckle only, **$18.50**; Loop, **$1.75**; Tip, **$2.50**.

**No. H90**—Neatly proportioned and engraved Sterling set. Rope edge. For 1″ strap. Per set....................**$12.50** Buckle only, **$9.25**; Loop, **$1.60**; Tip, **$2.40**.

**No. H91**—Elaborate set with beautiful rope edge and solid gold overlay. Four rubies in flower centers. For ¾″ strap. Per set........................**$22.50** Buckle only, **$19.00**; Loop, **$2.00**; Tip, **$2.75**.

**No. H91X**—Same as No. H91. Gold overlay on buckle, loop and tip, but *no rubies.* Per set..........................**$19.75**

**No. H92**—Neat Sterling set proportioned similar to No. H91. Cleverly engraved. For ¾″ strap. Per set.....**$8.50** Buckle only, **$6.25**; Loop, **$1.10**; Tip, **$1.65**.

**No. H93**—Another classy little set uniquely engraved. There's nothing plain about it. For ¾″ strap. Per set....**$5.25** Buckle only, **$3.00**; Loop, **$1.00**; Tip, **$1.50**.

**No. H94**—Nicely designed flat set for ⅝″ wrist watch strap. Per set.....**$3.50**

**No. H97**—Same set as No. H94 but with solid gold overlay and 4 rubies. Beautifully finished. For ⅝″ strap. Per set........................**$10.00**

**No. 124**—Fascinating little rounded Sterling set with solid gold overlaid flowers and vine. For ⅜″ wrist watch strap. Per set..........................**$8.50**

**No. 125**—Exactly the same as No. 124 but is mounted with four rubies. For ⅜″ strap. Per set.................**$10.00**

105

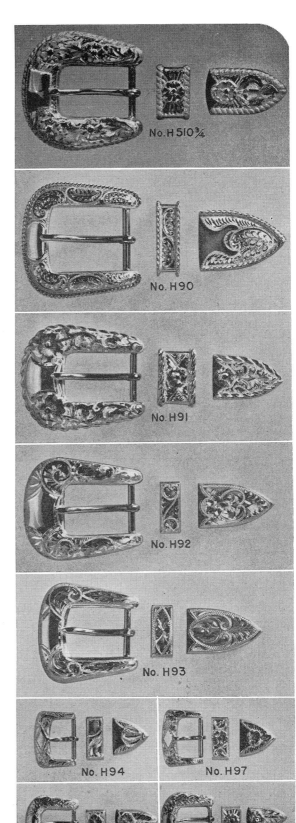

No. H 510¾

No. H90

No. H91

No. H92

No. H93

No. H94

No. H97

No. 124

No. 125

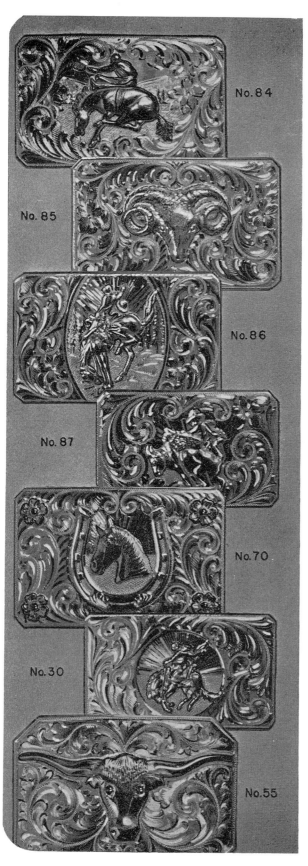

# Sterling Silve

All buckles shown on th
pages are hand made of sterl
silver and engraved by exp
craftsmen. Each one is an o
standing piece of jewelry. F
buckles come equipped w
sturdy loops and hooks on ba

*Do you want a Belt to go v
one of these Buckles?*

Machine flowered belt fitted to
buckle..........................$
Fine hand flowered belt...........$!

**No. 84**—HORSE AND RIDER
GOLD RELIEF. A flat buckle that yc
like. 2¾" long, 1¾" wide. Sterling sil
beautifully engraved. Each, postpaid **$12**

**No. 85**—All sterling silver flat buc
Ram's head in sharp relief—it stands
about ⅛". A real beauty. 2¾" long, 1
wide. Each, delivered.............$8

**No. 86**—Another all sterling silver
buckle that has real distinction. Horse a
rider stands out about ⅛". 2¾" lo
1¾" wide. For 1½" belt.
Each, delivered...................$8

**No. 87**—FOR THE LADIES, or
those who like a belt about 1¼" wide.
sterling silver. Steer and rider in sh
relief—stands out about ⅛". 2½" lo
1½" wide. For 1¼" belt.
Each, delivered...................$6

**No. 70**—GOLD AND RUBY MOUN
INGS. One of the prettiest flat buck
we have ever shown. Pure white sterl
silver, with horse shoe, horse head a
flowers in sharp relief. Flowers and ho
head in gold and so are the nails in t
horse shoe. Flowers have ruby cent
2⅞" long; 1⅞" wide. For 1⅝" b
Each, delivered...................$14

**No. 30**—A heavy, hand made sterl
silver belt buckle equipped with loop a
hook on back to accommodate a 1½" be
Buckle is superbly hand engraved and F
silver bucking horse and rider medalli
mounted in relief in center. Size of buc
2½" long, 1½" wide. Each........$6

**No. 55**—The popular flat plate ho
buckle. Solid sterling silver, engraved, w
steer-head in gold, ruby eyes. 2" wide a
3" in length. Each..............$15

**No. 55X**—Same buckle as No. 55 b
size 1½" x 2". Each..............$9

# Belt Buckles

**No. 24**--An exceptionally beautiful flat
ckle. The gold steerhead stands out from
e silver background in sharp (raised)
ief. Flowers in four corners are of gold
d have ruby centers. Gold steer has ruby
es. Same size as No. 25, 2¾" long.
4" wide. Each.................. **$15.00**

**No. 25**—Another dandy. No gold—all
ver, but steer head also stands out in
arp (raised) relief, and has ruby eyes.
4" long and 1¾" wide.
ch, delivered.................... **$7.75**

**No. 26**—(Not pictured—looks just like
). 25, but smaller) 2½" long and 1⅜"
de. However, it too has steerhead in
arp relief (raised), and in gold. Ruby
es. A neat buckle . . . and the price
only......................... **$9.25**

**No. 27**—Here is an unusual "picture
ckle." Made of white sterling silver, with
ld horse and rider, corral and foliage—
gold is in relief; that is, it stands out.
ne rest of the scene is nicely engraved
the silver. Each............... **$15.00**

## Other Sterling Silver
## Buckles and Buckle Sets

**No. 45**—Set for narrow ¼" hat band.
and made and engraved. Includes buckle,
op and tip. Sterling silver, (postpaid) **$3.00**

**No. H45**—Same as No. 45 but a little
rger for ⅜" strap. Set.......... **$3.50**

**No. 45X**—Solid gold............. **$6.00**
Any above set complete with hat band,
ack or tan, 50c extra.

**No. 121**—(Not shown). Solid gold set
aped like No. 45X for wrist watch strap;
", silver backed to prevent chafing.
et, postpaid...................... **$7.50**

**No. 47**—A beautiful and sturdy buckle
et for spur leathers, ⅝". Per pair.. **$9.00**
Single set, for one strap......... **$4.50**
If wanted complete with fancy, flower-
amped doubled calf skin spur leathers
ll ready to use)................ **$15.75**

**No. 477** — Hand made sterling silver
uckle set for ¾" spur straps.
ouble set, for two spur straps. Price **$9.50**
ingle set, for one strap. Price...... **4.75**

**No. 14**—Hand-made silver buckle suit-
ble for bridles, spur straps, etc., hand
ngraved. Each, for ⅝" strap, **$1.75**;
4" strap, **$2.00**; ⅞", **$2.25**; 1", **$2.50**;
⅛", **$3.00**; 1¼", **$3.60**; 1½", **$4.15**.

**No. 11**—Hand-made sterling silver, hand
ngraved buckle suitable for bridles, breast
ollars, spur straps, etc. Each, ⅝", **$2.00**;
4", **$2.20**; ⅞", **$2.50**; 1", **$2.75**; 1⅛",
**3.05**; 1¼", **$3.50**; 1½", **$4.45**; 1¾", **$5.45**.

**No. 60**—Nicely engraved buckle. Made
or 3 belt sizes. Each: 1", **$4.15**; 1¼",
**5.35**; 1½", **$6.40**.

**No. 80**—A neat little set for ⅝" strap,
uitable for wrist watch strap, hat bands,
tc. Set, delivered................. **$4.25**

### New Nickel Silver
### Hat Band Buckle Set

**No. 175**—(Not pictured, but similar in
appearance to No. 45 set). Hand-made,
icely engraved. ¼" set includes buckle,
oop and tip. Each, postpaid....... **$1.50**
Complete with rounded Leather Hat
Band........................... **$2.00**

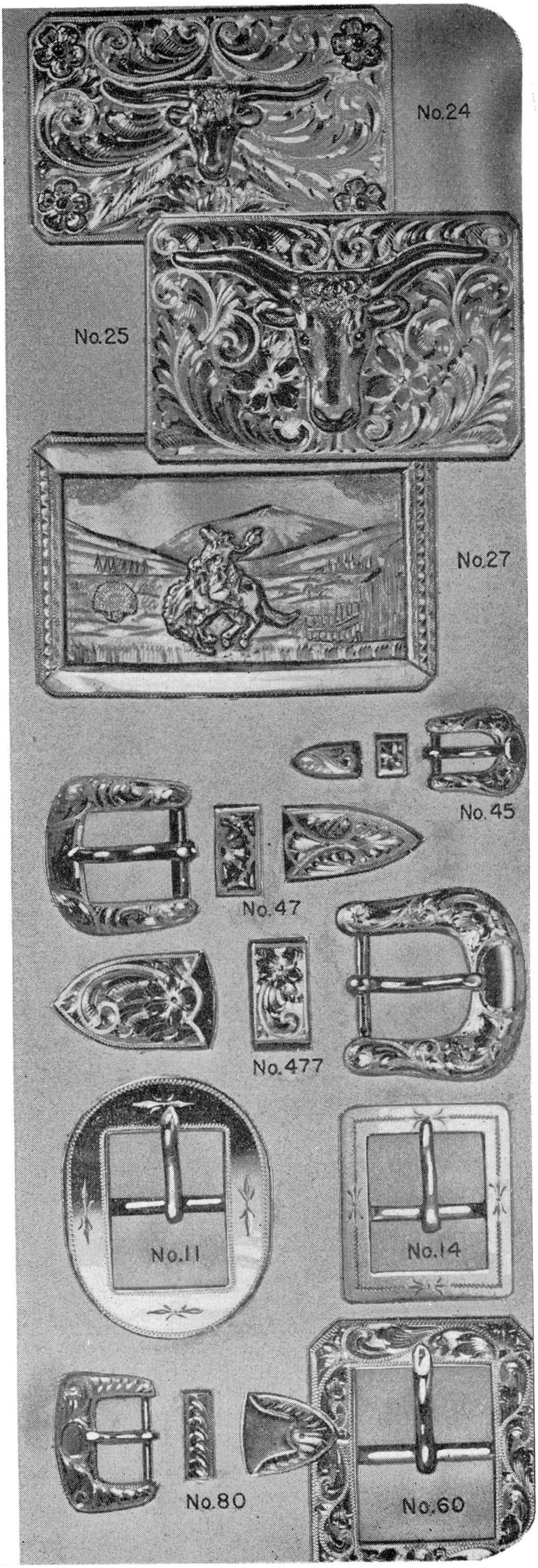

## Nickel Silver Buckle Sets
### Nicely Engraved—Shiny Finish

No. 171
No. 172
No. 173

**No. 171**—Has much the same appearance as Sterling silver and holds its beauty. Size 1". Set, postpaid............................**$2.25**

Hand checked 1½" belt with tapered ends, fitted to this set, complete with No. 171 buckle set.........................**$4.75**

Hand flowered 1½" belt with ends tapered and fitted to No. 171 buckle set, complete. **$7.50**

**No. 172**—FOR LADY'S BELT. Just like No. 171, but smaller size for ¾" strap. Set, postpaid............................**$2.00**

Hand checked 1¼" belt with ends tapered and fitted to this set. Price, complete...**$4.25**

Hand flowered 1¼" belt with ends tapered and fitted to this No. 172 set, complete..**$6.75**

**No. 173**—FOR SPUR STRAPS. This set is just like No. 171 but in still smaller size to accommodate ⅝" strap. Set, postpaid...**$1.75**

Double set for two spur straps, postpaid 3.25

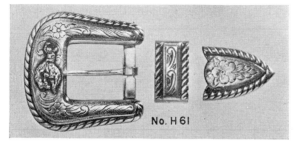

No. H 61

## Nickel Silver Sets
### *Dull Finish*

**No. H61**—A beautiful set of nickel silver with oxidized finish. Bronc and rider raised on front of buckle. Smooth rope edge. For 1" strap. An unusual value. Set, postpaid....................**$1.75**

**No. H62**—Exactly the same set as No. H61, but for ¾" strap. Just the thing for women's belts. Set, postpaid....................**$1.50**
(See Page 109 for embossed belts.)

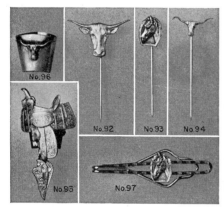

## Tie Pins and Scarf Holders

**No. 92**—Gold plated steerhead scarf pin. Measures 1⅜" from horn tip to tip. Each...........**$0.50**

**No. 93**—Oxidized silver horse head and horseshoe scarf pin. ½" across. Each.................**$0.50**

**No. 94**—Gold plated steerhead scarf pin. ⅞" across from tip to tip. Each.................**$0.50**

**No. 95**—Oxidized silver saddle scarf holder. Each...................................**$0.50**

**No. 96**—Oxidized silver scarf holder with small steer head on front. Each..................**$0.50**

**No. 97**—Tie clip with oxidized silver horse head and shoe ornament. Each..................**$0.50**

# BRONZE HORSES

Hand cast metal horses, perfect in detail and beautifully finished in Two-Toned bronze.

**No. G316**—Western Saddle Horse with complete outfit. About 2⅛" high over saddle.
Each........................................................................................... **$1.50**
Postage and packing 20c

**No. G204**—Three-gaited horse with bridle. About 2⅞" high over back.
Each........................................................................................... **$2.00**
Postage and packing 30c

**No. G119**—Western Saddle Horse with complete outfit.
About 4" high over saddle. Each......................................................... **$5.00**
Postage and packing 40c

# BUCKLES, BELTS, KEY and POCKET KITS

**No. 88**—DERIGOLD FLAT HOOK BUCKLE.
Reproduction of Cody Monument in bold relief. 3″
long and 1⅞″ wide. Equipped with loop and hook on
back to accommodate 1½″ belt. Each, postpaid. $2.00

**No. 89**—DERIGOLD FLAT HOOK BUCKLE.
The good luck buckle. Horseshoes and horse's head in
bold relief. 3″ long, 1⅞″ wide. Equipped with loop
and hook on back for 1½″ belt. Each, postpaid $2.00

**No. 825**—A very nicely embossed belt 1½″ wide tapered to fit any 1″ buckle. It is shown here fitted with
No. 223R-1 buckle set. This belt is of best quality cowhide and will catch anyone's eye. **$9.25**
You'll always enjoy it. As shown, with sterling silver buckle set, postpaid.....................
Belt tapered as shown but with solid nickel. or bronze buckle................................**$2.00**

**No. 610**—Grapevine embossed saddle leather belt 1½″ wide tapered to 1″ for solid nickel   **$3.50**
buckle set with raised horse and rider on buckle. Complete.................................
Buckle set only.................................................................**$1.75**

**No. 591**—Carefully embossed saddle leather belt 1¼″ wide tapered to 1″ for attractive   **$1.85**
nickel plated buckle set. Complete, postpaid, for only.....................................

**No. 590**—Saddle leather belt embossed with attractive design. 1″ wide straight through and mounted
with the same good looking nickel plated buckle set shown on No. 591.
Complete, postpaid, for only.............................................**$1.65**

## HAMLEY KEY KIT

You have never seen anything to compare in rugged
sturdiness with this Hamley "Key Kit". (Left).
Keys can't catch or come off. Made of best quality
heavy calfskin in Brown or Black; also English pigskin
in Natural Russet or Black.

**No. 35**—With 3 key hooks. Each..................$1.00
**No. 65**—With 6 key hooks. Each.................. 1.50
(Please specify kind and color of leather wanted.)

## HAMLEY POCKET KIT

**No. 10**—Put one of these cases in the hands of a friend
and watch his eyes snap as he rolls the leather between
his fingers.
Made of selected heavy calfskin, and designed for
carrying letters, note paper, a "fiver" or two, and other
loose papers. Colors, Black or Chocolate Brown. Size
4½″ x 9″. Each, postpaid........................$1.50

# Silver and Gold Mounted *Hand Stamped* Belts

**No. 363**—Best grade saddle leather, and beautifully stamped as pictured. 1½″ wide. Each, without buckle set and without tapered ends but full width entire length and fitted with solid nickel buckle and leather loops. .**$6.00**
   Complete belt as pictured with buckle set No.53X, hand engraved sterling silver with gold flower overlay. Two rubies in buckle, one in loop and one in tip. Each. . . . . . . . . . . . . . . . . . . . . . . . . . . . . . . . . . . . . .**$22.75**

**No. 366.** Another first grade saddle leather belt, hand stamped in acorn design. 1½″ wide. Each, without buckle set and without tapered ends but full width entire length and fitted with solid nickel buckle and leather loops. . . . . . . . . . . . . . . . . . . . . . . . . . . . . . . . . . . . . . . . . . . . . . . . . . . . . . . . . . . . . . . . . . . . . . . . . . . . . . . . . . **$6.00**
   Complete belt as pictured with buckle set No. 44, hand engraved sterling silver. Each. . . . . . . . . . . .**$15.00**

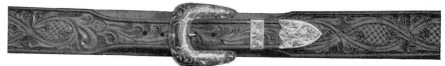

**No. 365**—Hand stamped scroll and criss-cross design. 1½-in. wide, and tapered at ends for 1-in. buckle. Each, without buckle set and without tapered ends but full width entire length and fitted with solid nickel buckle and leather loops. . . . . . . . . . . . . . . . . . . . . . . . . . . . . . . . . . . . . . . . . . . . . . . . . . . . . . . . . . . . . . . . . . . .**$6.00**
   Complete belt as pictured with buckle set No. 23. Beautifully engraved sterling silver. Each. . . . . . . .**$13.75**

**No. 361**—A neat 1-in. belt, nicely flower hand-stamped as pictured. Each, without buckle set but with solid nickel buckle and leather loops. . . . . . . . . . . . . . . . . . . . . . . . . . . . . . . . . . . . . . . . . . . . . . . . . . . . . . . . . . . . . . .**$5.25**
   Complete belt as pictured with buckle set No. 46X. Neat, hand-engraved sterling silver with gold flower overlay. 2 rubies in buckle, one in loop and one in tip. Each. . . . . . . . . . . . . . . . . . . . . . . . . . . . . . . . . . . . .**$19.00**

**No. 382**—A fine quality belt, beautifully stamped with floral design. Notice the dark finish on edges. 1½″ wide. Each, without buckle set and without tapered ends, fitted with solid nickel buckle and leather loops.$ **6.50**
   Complete belt as pictured, with Sterling silver buckle set No. 50. This buckle set has heavy rope edge, all silver; a big beauty. Each. . . . . . . . . . . . . . . . . . . . . . . . . . . . . . . . . . . . . . . . . . . . . . . . . . . . . . . . . . . . . . . . .**$18.25**

**No. 381**—Here is an outstanding belt. Hand stamped pattern in natural saddle leather color, but background is BLACK. 1½″ wide. Each, without tapered ends and without silver buckle, but equipped with solid nickel buckle and leather loops. . . . . . . . . . . . . . . . . . . . . . . . . . . . . . . . . . . . . . . . . . . . . . . . . . . . . . . .$ **7.00**
   Complete as pictured, with buckle set No. 20. Sterling silver, heavily overlaid with gold. Four rubies; rope edge. Each. . . . . . . . . . . . . . . . . . . . . . . . . . . . . . . . . . . . . . . . . . . . . . . . . . . . . . . . . . . . . . . . . . . . . . .**$25.50**

**No. 384**—Another outstanding hand stamped design in a solid saddle leather belt. 1½″ wide. Each, with solid nickel buckle—and without tapered ends and silver buckle. . . . . . . . . . . . . . . . . . . . . . . . . . . . . . . .$ **5.50**
   Complete as pictured, with buckle set No. 21—a neat Sterling silver set with rope edge and nicely engraved. Each. . . . . . . . . . . . . . . . . . . . . . . . . . . . . . . . . . . . . . . . . . . . . . . . . . . . . . . . . . . . . . . . . . . . . . . . . . . .**$14.00**

**No. 367**—Best grade genuine English pigskin with soft cowhide lining. A beauty. 1½-in. wide. Each, without silver buckle set but full 1½-in. width entire length and with solid nickel buckle and leather loop......**$4.50**
Complete belt as pictured with buckle set No. 50. Dandy sterling silver buckle, hand engraved in an ultra-fine manner; rope edge. Each ........................................................................**$16.25**

**No. 380**—Best grade saddle leather and neatly stamped with rose bud design. 1½" wide. Each, without buckle set and without tapered ends, fitted with solid nickel buckle and leather loops..............**$5.50**
Belt as pictured, complete with horseshoe buckle set No. 22. Sterling silver, hand engraved, and with gold overlays; 6 rubies in buckle. Each..................................................................**$16.25**

**No. 378**—Another new hand stamped design on a high quality saddle leather belt. 1⅜" wide. Each, without flat silver buckle, but equipped with solid nickel buckle and leather loops.........................**$5.50**
Complete with flat buckle No. 30 as pictured. Buckle is Sterling silver and hand engraved; bucking horse and rider stands out in sharp relief. Each.................................................................**$12.25**

**No. 337**—FOR THE LADIES. Here is a neat 1⅜" belt that is just right for the lady who rides. Each, without silver buckle, but equipped with solid nickel buckle and leather loops.....................**$5.00**
Complete as shown, with flat Sterling silver buckle No. 26. A beautifully engraved buckle, with steerhead in raised GOLD. Steer has ruby eyes. Each.................................................................**$14.25**
**No. 377**—FOR THE LADIES. A neat, light weight belt of solid saddle leather, beautifully hand-stamped in flower design. 1⅜" wide. With tapered ends as on belt No. 380, and equipped with buckle set No. 46X, page 106. Sterling silver, hand-engraved, and overlaid with gold. Four rubies. Each.......................**$18.75**
Without tapered ends, and without silver buckle, but equipped with neat solid nickel buckle and leather loops......................................................................................................**$5.00**

## LOW-PRICED FANCY BELTS—*for Men and Women*

**No. 1710**—Here is a fine new belt for men, with Nickel Silver buckle set as shown on page 116. Buckle set is hand engraved and looks almost like sterling silver. Hand stamped belt in floral design, with long panel of check stamping in back. Belt is 1½" wide with one inch tapered ends. Waist measures 30" to 44". Each, complete with buckle, loop and tip.........................................................................................**$7.00**
Buckle set alone **$2.25**; Belt alone with plain nickel buckle and leather loop **$4.75**.

**No. 1720**—Same as No. 1710, but made in slightly smaller size for ladies. Belt is 1¼" wide with ends tapered to ¾" to fit the buckle set which is made for ¾" strap, and full flower stamped except for neat hand check stamp on ends as pictured. Waist measures 24 to 36. Each, complete with buckle, loop and tip.....**$5.75**

**No. X324-1T**—For a LADY on her skirt, or a MAN on his slacks; this little belt has really got class. Medium weight Hazel Pigskin 1" wide tapered to ½". Mounted with No. 223-½ sterling buckle set. **$5.85**
Each, complete as shown. ............................................................................
**No. X324-1**—Belt not tapered, bronze buckle.......................................................**$1.75**
**No. X321-1T**—Same belt as above but leather is Light London Tan color. Complete..............**$5.85**
**No. X321-1**—Light London Tan belt, not tapered, bronze buckle..............................**1.75**

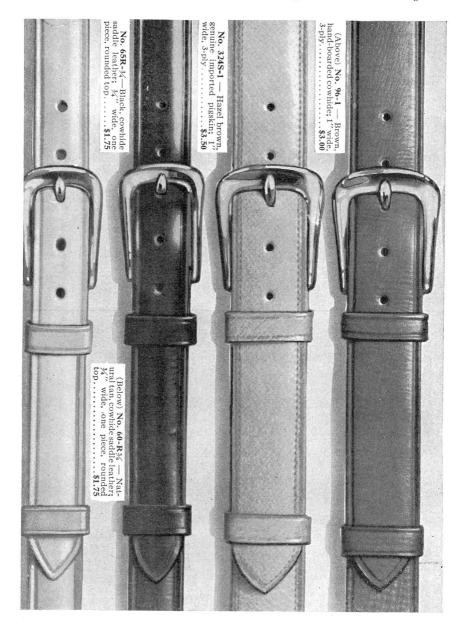

No. 65R-¾ — Black, cowhide saddle leather; ¾" wide, one piece, rounded top......$1.75

No. 324S-1 — Hazel brown, genuine imported pigskin; 1" wide, 3-ply.........$3.50

(Above) No. 96-1 — Brown, hand-boarded cowhide; 1" wide, 3-ply.........$3.00

(Below) No. 60-R¾ — Natural tan, cowhide saddle leather; ¾" wide, one piece, rounded top.........$1.75

# EXAMINE A HAMLEY BELT
## MADE BY WESTERN SADDLE CRAFTSMEN
### *SEE THE DIFFERENCE—AND FEEL IT*

The Hamley Belt is made by craftsmen who "cut their teeth" on Western saddles. For many years, they have been experts in the fine art of hand-working durable, solid leathers. That experience, and the preeminent reputation earned with the Hamley saddle, is inherited by your Hamley belt. That's why there is real satisfaction in wearing a genuine Hamley

Hamley Hand-Made Dress Belts are sold by leading Men's Shops and Department Stores all over the country, and we would like to have you drop in at your dealer's and "feel" a good belt. If he cannot supply you, send direct to us for catalog.

# THE GREATEST
# TOILET KIT
# IN THE WORLD

Here's the handiest toilet kit you ever owned . . . a simple, saddle leather box that conveniently and compactly holds all your favorite toilet articles without fuss or bother in packing. The Hamley Kit is made in five sizes to serve a multitude of uses.

If your dealer cannot supply you, send direct to us for complete catalog.

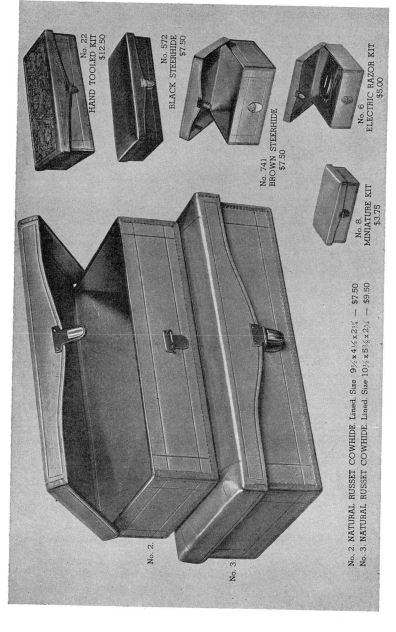

No. 22 HAND TOOLED KIT $12.50

No. 572 BLACK STEERHIDE $7.50

No. 741 BROWN STEERHIDE $7.50

No. 6 ELECTRIC RAZOR KIT $5.00

No. 8 MINIATURE KIT $3.75

No. 2. NATURAL RUSSET COWHIDE. Lined. Size 9½ x 4½ x 2¼ — $7.50
No. 3. NATURAL RUSSET COWHIDE. Lined. Size 10½ x 5⅜ x 2¾ — $9.50

No. 2.

No. 3.

# HAMLEY *Saddle Leather* KIT . . . A HAMLEY INVENTION
. . . A HAMLEY PRODUCT

# High Grade Solid Leather Bill Folds

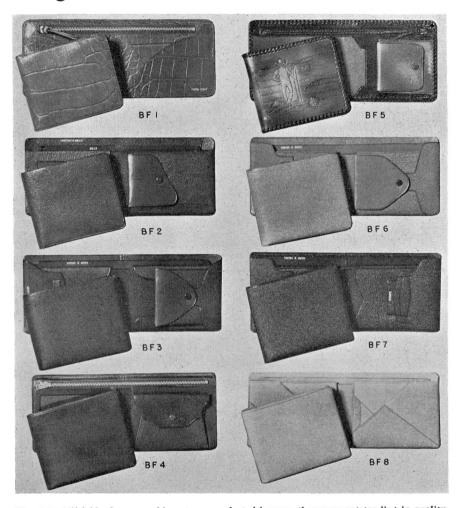

The eight bill folds shown on this page were selected because they were outstanding in quality, construction, beauty and price. Order the style you like best. If, upon arrival, it isn't the finest article of its kind you have ever seen at the price, you may return for full refund.

**No. BF1**—Genuine India Goat finished with alligator grain and antique brown color. Zipper currency pocket. Size 4½" x 3½" folded. 4 card pockets. Each, postpaid............................**$3.00**

**No. BF2**—Dark brown grain cowhide. Two currency pockets with close-in flap on large one. "Patented Paymaster" removable change or card pocket which holds $3.50 and up in ordinary change. Can be used with billfold or separately. Transparent window. Size 4⅜" x 3½" folded. Each, postpaid **$3.50**

**No. BF3**—Black, genuine Pin Seal. Large and small currency pockets, two card pockets, and gusseted change pocket. Size 4½" x 3½" folded. No stitching. You can feel the quality in this bill fold. Each, postpaid............................**$3.50**

**No. BF4**—Brownish red Russia Calf. Zipper currency pocket, and open currency pocket. Gusseted change pocket, card pocket and transparent window. Size 4¼" x 3½" folded. Soft beautiful finish. Each, postpaid............................**$1.50**

**No. BF5**—Real Calf, mottled color—light and dark brown with some black on inside. "Cowboy looking over his range land" embossed on outside. Soft, smooth finish. One zipper and one open currency pocket. Roomy coin pocket attached. Three card pockets. Size 4⅜" x 3¾". Each, postpaid....**$3.50**

**No. BF6**—Genuine English Pigskin, light hazel color. Beautiful finish; no stitching. Two currency pockets and three card pockets, one of which slides out but does not detach—makes cards easy to find. Size 4½" x 3½" folded. Each, postpaid......**$3.50**

**No. BF7**—Genuine black English Morocco, and one of the neatest yet. Stamp pocket with folder, and two card pockets. Inside currency pocket may be reversed for secrecy—this "inner billfold" also has two more card pockets. No stitching. Size 4½" x 3⅝" folded. Each, postpaid....................**$3.50**

**No. BF8**—Real calf, saddle leather color. Four card pockets, one of which has separate card folder. Two currency pockets. No stitching. Size 4½" x 3½" folded. Each, postpaid....................**$3.00**

**NAME OR INITIALS EMBOSSED ON ANY OF ABOVE BILL FOLDS, 25c EXTRA.**

# HAMLEY GLOVES

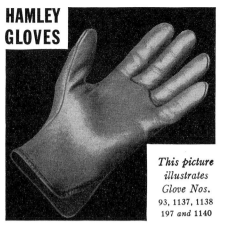

*This picture illustrates Glove Nos. 93, 1137, 1138 197 and 1140*

**No. 93**—Open wrist type glove that is soft and pliable, yet made for service and hard wear. Considering the low price, it is one of the best service gloves we have seen. Usually a good glove costs much more than this one. Fit guaranteed.
Tan color. Pair, delivered........... **$1.65**

### SAME STYLE—BETTER QUALITY

**No. 1137**—A picture of this glove looks just like No. 93 described above. However, No. 1137 glove is made of a more select grade of leather, is full welted, and has moccasin fingers. Soft, **$1.95** pliable. Tan color. Pair, delivered.....

### LADIES' OPEN WRIST SLIP-ON GLOVE

**No. 1138**—Same appearance as shown at left except open wrist is slightly longer. Soft as chamois, yet sturdy, this is the ideal glove for the lady who rides. Color is tan. Size 6½ to 8½. Pair, **$1.65** delivered: return if you don't like them.

### BOYS' OPEN WRIST GLOVE

**No. 1140**—Cadet style, incorporating all of the features of No. 93 Glove described above and made especially for boys. Tan color, short cuff, nice soft leather. Size 6 to 8½.
Pair, delivered.................... **$1.00**

## Popular Roping Glove

**No. 323**—The most glove money can buy. Made of high grade buckskin; almost white. Soft and tough. Strong loop fastener holds cuff snugly to wrist. Pair, delivered............. **$3.25**

## Hamley "All-Around"

**No. 561** — All around gloves for riding, roping, driving and working. Made of top quality smoked horsehide, thick and strong, yet pliable as cloth. Sizes 7 to 11, including half sizes.
Pair, delivered........ **$1.90**

**No. 562,** FLEECE LINED—Same glove exactly as No. 561, except is fleece lined for warmth on those cold winter days. Be comfortable!
Get a pair; delivered................. **$2.15**

## Ladies' Gauntlet

**No. 72**—(Above). A classy looking fringed gauntlet for women. Fine, soft, heavyweight kid. Color is beige-tan. Horseshoe and whip decoration. Ladies' sizes 6 to 8½. Pair, delivered.......**$2.65**

**No. 345**—A popular gauntlet with the ladies. Made of soft, drab, Siberian colt—almost as soft as chamois. Will stand the wear, and has fringed cuff as shown on No. 72
Pair, delivered..................... **$2.25**

**No. 932**—White, soft, light weight doeskin, fringed gauntlet similar to No. 72, but blue brocade trimming on back of hand.
Pair, delivered..................... **$3.95**

*Slip-on Style Patented "Moccasin" Fingers*

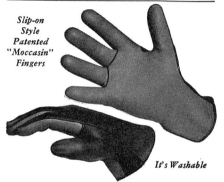

*It's Washable*

Here are some nice fitting, good looking gloves. Can be washed successfully with castile soap and water.
**No. 1001**— Two-tone soft velvety washable brown calfskin backs with "bucklike" cream color Kango-Buck fronts. (This glove is a great favorite with the Oregon State police—you'll like it too.)
Pair, delivered..................... **$2.50**

**No. 2002**—Same style as above but solid color—washable Kango-Buck—cream color.
Pair, delivered..................... **$2.50**

*Double thick here*

## New Double Duty Roper

**No. 68**—A great new service glove made of washable kangaroo. Soft and comfortable, made to give double service to ropers because it's double thick in palm under the thumbs as pictured; double strength where the rope wears.
Pair, delivered... **$1.75**

## OREGON DEERSKIN GLOVE

**No. 197**—Illustrated by picture in upper left hand corner of this page. About the neatest real deerskin glove yet. Made in the open wrist style of genuine Oregon deerskin. Medium heavy weight; extremely soft and comfortable. Price per pair, **$2.25** delivered to you is only..............

# SQUAW GLOVES *...made by the Umatilla Indians*

**No. 18**—No gloves made by white men, at even higher prices, will wear as long as will Squaw Gloves. The leather will never harden; and while they may seem too big or too small for you when you first put them on, they soon shape to your hand. Not made in definite sizes, but give glove size in ordering. Two grades: Grade A, **$1.60**; Grade B, **$1.35**.

# Full Color Prints of C. M. Russell Oil Paintings
### Suitable for Framing

Here are some of the most famous pictures of the West ever painted. C. M. Russell loved the West and being a great artist he captured the spirit and action of the times in a series of spectacular oil paintings. Printed in full colors, with margin for framing. Horizontal unless otherwise specified. Sizes given are to the paper edge. Select the titles you like best—we're sure you will be delighted with them.
Your choice of any picture listed, postpaid.............................35c each. 3 for $1.00

**No. 1—The Wagon Boss,** 16½x11. A hardy leader looks back down the valley toward the settlement watching the ox-drawn wagons lumber up the hill.

**No. 2—Sun Worshippers,** 16½x11¼. The Red Man raises his arms to the setting sun.

**No. 3—When Horseflesh Comes High,** 15½x9. Horse rustlers overtaken by legal owners . . they shoot it out.

**No. 4—The Queen's War Hounds,** 14¼x9¾. A "Mountie" talks the situation over with several Red Men.

**No. 5—Caught with the Goods,** 14½x 10. In the light of a setting desert sun, with Rimrock Ridges as background, two Mounties get their men.

**No. 6—In the Wake of the Buffalo Runners.** 10¼x8¾. Indian women, and older members of the tribe watch the younger braves run buffalo down. The spectators are on a hill . . . there is a late afternoon sun.

**No. 7—Signal Fire,** 10½x14¼ (vertical). Indian braves on the Rimrock Point of the mesa, build their signal fire.

**No. 8—Sagebrush Sport,** 10x14½. On flat plains, with Russell's favorite Rimrock horizon, cowboys chase a coyote, using lariats.

**No. 9—Carson's Men,** 15x10½. A setting sun on a dry-land-river, the bones of an ox in the foreground, and Carson, his two assistants, and their pack train move westward

**No. 10—When Sioux and Blackfeet Meet,** 15½x9. Scouts of enemy tribes meet on the plains and the skirmish is enthusiastic.

**No. 11—Single Handed,** 14½x10. A "Mountie" rides into the Indian village *alone* during a tribal war dance, and tells the chief to halt . . . the Mounties could handle the Red Man.

**No. 12—In Without Knocking,** 14½x10½. Descriptive of the early small town days in the West, when it was not unusual for one man, or several men, to ride right into the bar room on their horses, shooting and yelling.

**No. 13, The First Wagon Tracks,** 15½x9. A setting sun, a mountain top, and in the foreground a group of Indian braves seem to be discussing by sign language, their next move . . . the Pale Faces have entered their land.

**No. 14—The Cinch Ring,** 15½x9. While branding on the desert, two top hands are ambushed by rustlers. The calf is tied . the horse is pulling . . . one man is down . . .

**No. 15—On the Trail,** 11x7½. Colorfully dressed Indian braves search for buffalo. The leaders have sighted the herd.

**No. 16—The Red Man's Wireless,** 14x7. Brave signals with white lady's mirror. Rays of August sunset strike his companions . . vivid color.

**No. 17—The Hold Up,** 13x8¼. Bandits . . . stagecoach . . . victims lined up, their valuables strewn on the ground . . . funny, but true.

There are several books of authentic Cowboy Songs, but we believe this to be the first one published with the songs set to music. Contains songs exclusively—29 of the best. Each, delivered..$1.00

**"COWBOY SONGS"**

Collected by John A. and Alan Lomax. A large book—6½" x 9", 428 pages— filled with hundreds of Cowboy and Folk Songs. Just off the press and the greatest book of its kind ever published. Each, delivered.....$3.75

**COWBOY "LORE"**

By Jules Verne Allen, the singing cowboy of NBC. 169 illustrations; 36 cowboy songs complete with music. Cowboy dictionary, brands, customs, pranks, stories, etc. Each, postpaid.....$1.65

Full color Original Bronco Picture; margin for framing. 15½" x 20". Stippled paper; solid red background. Each, postpaid..................50c

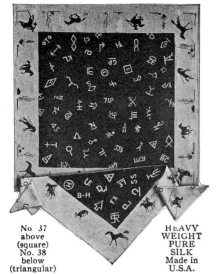

No 37
above
(square)
No. 38
below
(triangular)

HEAVY
WEIGHT
PURE
SILK
Made in
U.S.A.

# "RANCH SQUARES"

Here are just the scarfs for folks who ride, ideal for sports wear, perfect gifts for boys and girls. Triangular ones made double thickness, and square ones single of real silk, soft and lustrous. Solid area in center shows actual brands now in use on cattle ranches from Montana to Mexican border. Made in two styles.

In ordering, please specify which of the following color combinations you want: BROWN and TAN, RED and WHITE, BLUE and WHITE, ORANGE and BROWN, TURQUOISE BLUE and BROWN, GREEN and WHITE.

No. 37—28 inches square. Each, postpaid. .**$1.50**
No. 38—Triangular, made to conveniently tie about the throat. Each, postpaid............**$1.00**

## Picture Muffler

No. 889—A new extra heavy Rayon Satin Muffler, made in U.S.A. About 25″ square, decorated with an inset 1½″ border filled with pictures of riding scenes, steer heads, covered wagons, Indians on the march, stage coaches, etc., and decorated across a large part of one corner with a corral scene showing bucking horses, etc. Choice of three background colors: Orange, green, or blue. Each, delivered........**75c**

Slightly smaller size, lighter material, but similar designs............**50c**

## BINOCULARS

### . . . *real value!*

No. 34A—These glasses will really give you your money's worth. Have 4-power, ground and polished 40 mm. Achromatic objective lenses entirely free from color fringing, and 20 mm. double concave ocular lenses. Complete with leather carrying case. Each

# $10.00

Postage & packing, 25c.

# Hat Bands

### Narrow Black or White Leather Bands

No. 40—Narrow white leather hat bands, flat with nickel buckle, each........................**$0.25**
No. 45—Very narrow rounded leather hat band, black or white, small nickel buckle. Price each. .**$0.35**
Black, White or Tan

## Hair Hat Bands

Each of the hat bands in this line is hand braided from full length hair. No short and spliced hairs. This method of manufacture produces articles of utter smoothness. None of the ends sticking out. Smooth as can be and made to last.

No. 521—Hat band about 1″ wide, silver mounted, white and black and assorted colors. Price, each **$2.00**
No. 522—Same as No. 521, but without mountings, price, each...........................**$1.50**
No. 525—Hat band, about ⅝″ wide, mounted with pure silver, white and black and assorted colors. Price, each................................**$1.75**
No. 526—Same as No. 525, but without mountings. Price, each........................**$1.00**

## Saddle Watch Fob

No. 75—Saddle Watch Fob, made of non-corrosive metal, gray silver, green gold, and rose gold. Your choice. Each, postpaid.............. 30c

## SPUR ASH TRAY

It has the appearance of a genuine cowboy spur and serves as either ash tray or paper weight. A most unique gift item, in two finishes.

112BP—Bronze plate, each, postpaid......**$1.25**
112SP—Silver plate, each, postpaid........**$1.50**

# CATTARAUGUS
## KNIVES... *best we've seen*

"The best we've seen"—that is as good a thing as we can say about these knives because we haven't seen all the knives in the world. These are finer than any others we've looked at and we've looked at some knives. We're just anxious for you to see them. Order the style you think you'd like and return it if you can tear yourself away from it—we dare you to—we'll return your money immediately if the knife comes back.

Materials and workmanship guaranteed.

**No. 249**—Over-all length 3¹³⁄₁₆". 2⅞" Clip blade. Sheepfoot and Punch blades. Weight, 2¾ ounces. Milled silver lining. Nickel silver bolsters. Stag handle. Full polish.
Each, delivered..................... **$2.00**

**No. 479**—Over-all length 3⅞". 2⅞" Sabatier blade. 2¾" long Spey, Sheepfoot and Punch blades. Weight 3½ ounces. Milled silver lining. Nickel silver bolsters. Stag handle. Full polish Shielded.
Each, delivered..................... **$2.50**

**No. 209**—Over-all length 3¹³⁄₁₆". 2⅞" Sabatier blade. long Spry and Punch blades. Weight, 2½ ounces. Milled silver lining. Nickel silver bolsters. Stag handle. Full polish. Shielded.
Each, delivered..................... **$2.25**

---

## "DIAMOND EDGE" KNIVES
### ... *you know their reputation*

Diamond Edge is a known dependable name in cutlery. That good name is here backed up by Hamley service and fair dealing. Every knife guaranteed.

**No. 447**—A neat 3-blade knife, with punch and flesh blades. Length 4". Nickel silver bolsters and shield; brass lined. Handle is nice shape stag. Each, delivered........... **$1.75**

**No. 311**—Three blades, including punch and flesh blades. This knife is 3½" in length, has stag handle; brass lined, with nickel silver bolsters and shield. Each, delivered.... **$1.75**

**No. 201**—A four blade, 4" knife with stag handle. Notice that both flesh and punch blades are included. Brass lined, nickel silver bolsters and shield. Each, delivered............... **$2.35**

# CHAPS

There is a reason for the fact that Hamley Chaps enjoy the same reputation for service as do Hamley Saddles. Our saddles have been brought to a high degree of perfection through the years of study and experimenting which have been put into the trees upon which they are built and the patterns to which the materials are cut.

Hamley Chaps are made on patterns which result in proper fit and each pair is made-to-order. Few people, who have never attempted to make a pair of chaps, can understand the reason they cost as much as they do. We want to give those folks a little information:

*First:* How many cows or steers do you see without a brand or blemish? Chap leather in large sides must come from the few animals with clear hides, (this is costly selection).

*Second:* The best chaps are made from two of these selected sides— one leg only being cut from the *butt* of each side—this leaves a lot of waste leather which must be worked up in some way in other products and figures at a lower base cost, (another costly procedure in the production of good chaps).

Notwithstanding the fact that good chaps are of fairly high original cost it pays in the long run to buy them because the slight extra cost of good ones over cheap ones is in *material* and that is where the wear comes from—the labor cost is about the same in producing chaps from poorly selected material as it is from carefully selected, clear butts— the wise course to follow when buying chaps is obvious.

*Shoulder Chaps:* As explained above, our best chaps are made from selected butts of sides. This leaves on hand a supply of shoulders. These shoulders are used in making our cheaper chaps and when reading the specifications on different styles you will notice that usually the lower priced chaps are described as being made from shoulders, shoulder leather is slightly lighter in weight and somewhat softer than the butts.

### CHEYENNE LEG

Most leather chaps are now made with the back of legs cut as shown here. Someone named this the "Cheyenne Leg."

If you want your chaps made this way please mention it in your order unless the chaps are described that way in the catalog.

**Style No. 8**
It fits snug as a bug in a rug. Notice how these chaps fit in front. The No. 8 belt does it. If you want this belt on your chaps just say so.

Prices include belts all made up with buckles and billets and ready to put on chaps.

Prices on Chap Belts, either style 1, 2, or 3:
Plain....$2.75
Check Stamped
.........$3.00
Flower Stamped
.........$3.75
Extra Fancy
Flower Stamped
.........$4.25

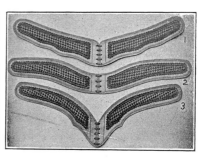

Here are three good chap belts. You may have one of these shapes on your chaps or any other shape you prefer—send your own belt pattern, if you wish. Other good shapes are shown on the chaps pictured on following pages.

**Short Waist** If you want short-waisted chaps— to come well down in front and fit over hip—order No. 8 or No. 3 belt.

**Long Waist** If you want long-waisted chaps—to fit well up in front and above hips —order No. 2 or No. 1 belt.

## For Taking Measurements

### PLEASE GIVE:

Your height.........................feet.........................inches.

Your weight.........................pounds.
Thigh measure: Large part of one leg just below crotch................inches.
(Dotted line "C" in picture.)

Waist measure....................inches. (Dotted line "D").
Leg length (dotted line "A-B" in picture); measure from crotch down to bottom of chap leg—usually about to your ankle or a little above.

Inches............................
Do you like long or short-waisted chaps?............................

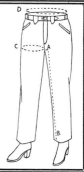

# NOTICE THE BELT ON THIS CHAP

*It is a Hamley feature that makes this chap hang better and last longer*

The belt on this chap is "a part of the chap"—not a separate piece. Notice the length of leather that extends down from the belt to the top concha. No more ripping off the belt with an arrangement like this. What's more, you can easily see that with support of this kind the chaps "hang" better and will stay that way.

## The 'WINNER'

### No. 6316

A top grade fine-fitting chap —selected chap butts are used and the chap is made from start to finish to really fit the wearer and give him real service.

The belt shown is our No. 8 shape shown on page 119, but you may have some other style or shape if you prefer.

The weakest point on any chap is at the top where the front joins to the belt. This weakness is overcome by the extended points of leather projecting as a part of the belt itself down onto the front body of the leg.

Contrasting leather buttons are used for decoration instead of metal conchas or buttons.

Will be made in combinations of Black or Brown body and pearl trim; Golden West (rich yellow) body with brown, black or pearl trim; or in fact any other color combination of Pearl, Black, Brown or Golden West. Wings are 7″ wide at fourth button from bottom and 10½″ at bottom. Pair (leg length to 31 inches), delivered

## $26.50

(If wanted with legs longer than 31″ add 50c for each extra inch.)

For inside swinging pockets, add $1.50.

●

There may be some small detail about these chaps which you do not like. They will be made-to-order for you so tell us about the changes you would like made.

# The Finest Chaps Money Can Buy

**No. 6455**—Top quality and expert workmanship clear through. Black, Pearl, Smoke, Cream or Brown chap leather butts with contrasting trimmings. Fancy "cut out" belt and wing trim. Wings and pockets have scalloped edges. Pockets have hand made leather buttons for fastening. Conchas are solid nickel silver plated. Cheyenne style legs. Reinforced backs.

If you want a real fancy show chap of high quality here it is. If you prefer swinging pockets to those shown just so state in order. Pair, delivered in U. S.......... **$36.50**

(For each inch of leg length over 32-in. add 50c)

---

**No. 6459**—Finest quality selected cowhide chap leather butts with full hand flowered belt. Fancy contrasting border and cut out ornaments. Solid white nickel tie conchas on strings. Backs reinforced where snaps attach. A real quality chap for the fellow who likes good things. Pocket Flap fastens with snap button, Cheyenne legs, swinging pockets may be had instead of outside pockets if wanted. Price, delivered in U. S. ......... **$32.50**

(Deduct $1.25 if pockets not wanted)
(For legs longer than 32-in. inseam add 50c for each extra inch)

Chaps shown on this page made with snap and dee backs regularly. Laced backs will be furnished if you request them.

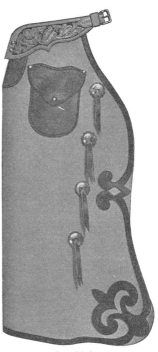

No. 6455

No. 6459

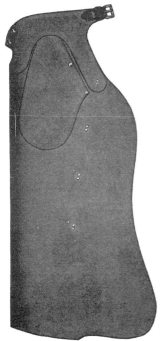

## LOW PRICED
# SERVICE CHAPS

**No. 5460**—Heavy weight buffed cowhide. Chrome tanned Black or Pearl color or bark tanned Saddle color (slightly heavier). Wings 5" wide at lower end of pocket opening and 9" at bottom of leg. Double head rivets used throughout. Fronts reinforced at both ends of belt. Cheyenne style legs. A real good chap for hard service and only— Pair, delivered in U.S........... **$14.75**

---

**No. 6458**—Here is a real fine chap at a price. Your choice of black, brown, pearl or yellow. Reinforced backs where snaps fasten. All rivets have double heads. Hand flowered belt. Wings 9" at bottom. Cheyenne legs. Leg lengths to 32". Pair, delivered in the United States.......... **$19.85**

No. 5460

No. 6458

# Hamley & Co. *is "Chap headquarters"*

No. 620

No. 601 and No. 602

**No. 620**—Here's a fine all leather chap, no nickel or silver mountings of any kind, made with full flower stamped belt, either shaped as pictured or as shown on any other chap in the catalog. The body of the chap is brown, black or pearl, with contrasting trimmings. Snap and dee or laced backs. The wing is 6½" at concha next to top and 11" at bottom. Pair, delivered.....**$28.50**

Your initials or brand in place of lower circle on wing if so ordered. Plain belt, no trimmings on wings. Pair, delivered............**$24.50**

If leg measure longer than 31" is wanted add 50c for each extra inch.

**No. 601 and 602 Chap**—A plain, all-leather style for service. Made of brown, pearl or black, soft chap leather. Leather pocket thonged in with buckskin string, or leather swinging pocket. Wings 6 inches at bottom, 4 inches at the top. No tie conchas. Snap and dee backs and Cheyenne leg. If you do not want Cheyenne leg—say so in your order. If wanted with conchas and tie strings or laced, add $1.75 to price. For each inch over 31 inches leg measure, add 50 cents to price.

**No. 601** — Seams are double-stitched with waxed linen thread, pair, delivered............**$23.50**

**No. 602** — Seams hand buck sewed as pictured. Pair, delivered............**$25.75**

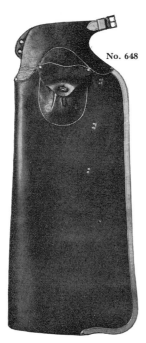

No. 648

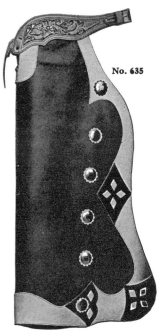

No. 635

## Wings Stand Straight on This Chap

**No. 648**—The trim on the edge of the wing in this chap is saddle leather, which gives a mighty neat appearance and a stiffness to the wing that makes it stand straight, yet flexible enough to make for comfort. A good idea we know you will like. Body of the chap may be had in brown, black or pearl service weight chap leather. New style chap belt that makes this number hang straight and look neat day in and day out. Roomy pocket as pictured. Snap and dee backs and Cheyenne leg. For each inch over 31 inches leg measure add 50c to price. Pair, delivered...... **$22.50**

**No. 635**—This one has been given a lot of thought in making and designing. We have selected the good points from several chaps and combined them here. The pattern for cutting the shape of the leg to assure proper fit; the style of belt; shape of the wings; and the contrasting leather buttons are all features which make this chap a good one. Made with black, brown, pearl or Golden West body with contrasting color trimmings—be sure to specify the color combination you desire when sending order. Wings 5½" wide at concha next to top and 10½" wide at bottom. Solid nickel conchas, will not turn brassy.

Price includes leg length to 31 inches. Add 50c for each inch of leg over 31 inches. Pair, delivered....**$31.50**

## Ring Fastening for Bronc Chaps

This fastener has proved popular particularly among bronc riders who want their chaps to fit tight around the legs. Gives absolute freedom in adjustment, because the fasteners are composed of two rings through which straps are fitted. A man with nearly any size legs can wear your chaps if you have this fastener. Holds perfectly if drawn up snugly. May be had at no extra cost on any of the chaps you order from us. If wanted, please so specify in your order.

# THESE TWO CHAPS HAVE PLENTY OF CLASS

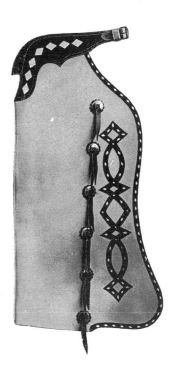

No. 131—Just the slickest service chap for which one could wish. Made of finest full grain chap leather. Can be had in combination of black, brown, pearl and yellow. Use your imagination in deciding just how you want yours made. Pearl body and brown trim looks fine or fix up any other combination you think you would like. Careful workmanship throughout. Snap and dee backs, Cheyenne legs. Leg length to 31 inches.
Pair, delivered.............................$26.50

No. 944—A fine pattern chap made entirely of leather except for six solid nickel conchas on each leg. Even these nickel conchas will be omitted and leather conchas put on if so ordered.

For a person who does not care for the combination of pearl and black as shown in the picture, the chap is also furnished in the darker leathers. For instance, a black chap with brown trimming., which would have brown diamond insets instead of the white diamond insets as shown here, makes a mighty fine looking article. Wing 5 inches at concha, next to top, and 10 inches at bottom.

These chaps are made with snap and dee backs, and the price includes leg lengths up to 31 inches. For longer lengths add 50 cents for each additional inch. For laced backs add $1.00. Price as described and shown, pair, delivered $33.50

## Notice the Prices

**No. 803**—At left. If you want a pair of chaps at a price—a pair that will give you good service—then here you are. Well made, of chap leather shoulders and in our most popular style. The fact that there are no decorations on this number, with the exception of the horseshoe on the wing, makes it cost less to produce. Your choice of brown, black or pearl colors. Wing is 6″ wide at second from top snap, and 9″ wide at bottom snap. Cheyenne style leg. Price includes leg lengths up to 30″. Add 50c per inch for leg length over 30″. Pair, delivered. . **$17.95**

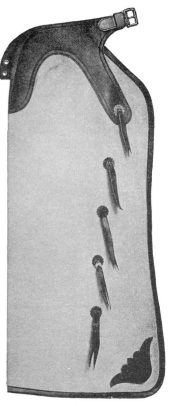

**No. 97**—At right. This chap was first listed in a folder quite a few years ago. It has been a favorite ever since, and many, many pairs have been shipped all over the country. It is ideal for bronc riders, and can be made light as 3½ pounds in black or brown color. Golden yellow or beaver brown body with black trimmings; Cheyenne leg style. Price includes leg lengths up to 30″. Add $1.00 per inch for leg length over 30″. Price, pair, delivered. . . . . . **$19.85**

Some of the materials used in this chap have brand scars and scratches. These imperfections, however, do not in any way detract from the wearing quality and it's a great chap for the money. The best ever.

### No. 803

# $17.95

### No. 97

# $19.85

---

# BOYS' CHAPS

No. 1500

**No. 105**—A dandy pair of play chaps, and good enough for the youngster who rides occasionally. They are not for large boys—inseam leg measures are from 16″ to 22″. Fronts are split chrome, soft chap leather, and the backs are of 8-oz. khaki canvas. Made in black, gray or tan colors with suitable contrasting trimmings.
Pair, delivered. . . . . . . . . . . . . . . **$4.95**

**No. 1500**—A nifty little chap for boys, light weight, good looking buffed chrome leather (cowhide). Pearl body and black trim or black body and pearl trim. Nickel ornaments, snap and ring backs. Cheyenne style leg cut up to second concha from bottom—(see page 120).

Not made with inseam leg measure greater than 24″ nor thigh measure greater than 22″. These chaps are made for boys who really ride a horse and want chaps which will fit and give real service.
Pair, delivered. . . . . . . . . . . . . **$12.50**

### No. 105

# THE 4 ACES . . . *every one a winner*

No. 720

No. 888

**No. 888**—It is hard to show in a picture or to explain in print just how good looking this chap is. Imagine changing the fronts to brown—a pearl wing and then on top of the pearl wing the "Fleur-de-lis" design in black. You may work out your own combination of colors, either two or three, from black, pearl, brown, yellow.

Wings 5½" wide at concha next to top and 10½" at bottom. Nickel conchas as pictured or large leather buttons of contrasting color. Made with Cheyenne leg unless ordered otherwise. Pair, delivered....................$23.50

(Add 50c for each extra inch if wanted with legs longer than 30" inseam).

**No. 720**—Some people do not like button ornaments and still prefer a rather fancy chap to a plain pair. Here is one all leather except the conchas. Diamond shape insets on belt and all around edge of wing. Insets same color as body, border in contrast. Body may be had in pearl as shown, or black or brown. If black or brown body, the wing trimming as well as belt and top of fronts will be pearl. Wings are 10" wide at bottom. If wanted longer than 30" leg measure, add 65c for each extra inch. Made of selected chap shoulders. Pair, delivered.........$26.75

No. 715

No. 8290

**No. 715**—A good grade all leather chap, not extra fancy but made to deliver service and sell at a reasonable price. The leather is regular full grain chap, black, pearl, or chocolate, cut from shoulders of full sides. Snap and ring backs. Wings 3½" wide at snap next to top, and 8" wide at bottom. Cheyenne legs to second snap from bottom. Pair, delivered...........$18.75

(For leg lengths over 30 inches, add 50c for each additional inch.)

**No. 8290**—A fine little chap made of good quality split leather. Shown here with chrome tanned pearl body and black trim. Belt is made similar to the regular No. 8 style. Has Cheyenne leg and plain nickel conchas 1¼" in diameter. A combination of any of the following colors may be had: Chrome tanned Pearl, Black; bark tanned Saddle color.

Pair, delivered ......................$12.75

# WIDE LEATHER SUPPORT BELTS

**No. 45**—A soft leather belt, 6-in. wide, shaped to fit. Brown, pearl or black, (specify the two colors you wish). Each...........................$3.95 Add 10c for each inch over 34-in. waist measure.

**No. 40**—Width, 8½-in. in center, 8-in. in front. Each, (buckles and billets attached with double head rivets)..............................$4.50 Each (sewed buckle and billet pieces).......$5.00

**No. 41**—Same shape as pictured but made of saddle leather, creased border, 6-in. wide, 28-in. to 34-in. waist measure. Each.................$2.95 Full basket or check stamp. Each...........$4.00

**No. 42**—Same as No. 41, but has stay in center and is spliced under stay. Just as good as No. 41. Each......................................$2.65

Add 10c per inch for lengths longer than 34-in. Sewed billets and buckle pieces, 50c extra. Postage 20c.

# *Made for a Queen*

## *Suits of This Type Made To Order Only*

During the year we make a considerable number of fancy leather riding suits for women. The suit shown here is pure white throughout and made of pure white leather. The fringe from the pocket reaches to the extreme bottom of the skirt; the fringe around the bottom of the skirt itself is double, and the top row, which is about eight inches long at the front, graduates to a length of about 18 inches on the sides.

The bolero jacket is fringed around the collar, down the front, around the bottom, and is lined with white silk.

This suit complete................................$62.50
Skirt alone........................................ 50.00
Jacket alone....................................... 12.50

When ordering bolero jacket specify measurement across the back between the arm hole openings, width desired on top of the shoulders, length down back, also give waist measurement and bust measurement. In addition to this tell us your height and weight.

### HOW TO ORDER RIDING SKIRTS

Every jacket and skirt we produce is made to order fresh and clean after the order is received. When ordering skirts give the following measurements:

1. Measurement around waist.

2. Around hips at largest place.

3. Length from top of waist band to bottom of skirt.

4. Crotch measurement. Measure from top of waist band in front, between legs, and up to top of waist band in back.

(In measuring length, measure from the waist line to extreme bottom of skirt.)

If the exact style you want is not shown here, we shall be glad to make changes as desired and price same accordingly.

Model is wearing a Stetson hat, Pendleton shirt, Cowboy silk 'kerchief and special Nocona boots.

## *Regular Styles*

Below are shown two of our regular style skirts which have proven popular.

No. 66

No. 86

**No. 66**—Six-gore pattern skirt made of soft brown, black, or white sheep leather. Pockets will be made as on No. 86 unless wanted as pictured.

Price, made of high quality Glove Leather.............$26.50

This same skirt made of fine heavy weight corduroy to your measurement with leather faced bottom leather, trimmed pockets..................$15.00

If leather fringe is wanted around bottom and on pockets, add **$3.00** to price.

**No. 86**—This is a full cut six-gore shirt with special long fringe on pockets and graduated fringe around bottom as shown. Can be had of the same fine leathers as described above for No. 66 skirt, and both this and No. 66 can be had in two color combination if so ordered— that is, body of skirt in one color of leather, and fringe of another color. The combination of colors does not change price.

Price, made of sheep leather **$32.50**

For skirt length longer than 37" add **50c** for each extra inch in sheep leather, **$1.00** for each extra inch in calfskin. For hip measurement over 39" add **25c** for each extra inch.

# JUSTIN BOOTS Standard of the West Since 1879

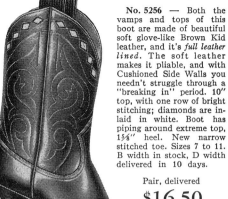

This feature is exclusive in Justin Boots. In the drawing you will notice how a soft felt cushion lies snugly between the vamp and the leather lining at the Inside and Outside Ball where there is the greatest pressure. This feature is your assurance of genuine foot comfort; it is used in all Justin *full leather lined* boots.

**No. 5256** — Both the vamps and tops of this boot are made of beautiful soft glove-like Brown Kid leather, and it's *full leather lined*. The soft leather makes it pliable, and with Cushioned Side Walls you needn't struggle through a "breaking in" period. 10" top, with one row of bright stitching; diamonds are inlaid in white. Boot has piping around extreme top, 1⅝" heel. New narrow stitched toe. Sizes 7 to 11. B width in stock, D width delivered in 10 days.

Pair, delivered

## $16.50

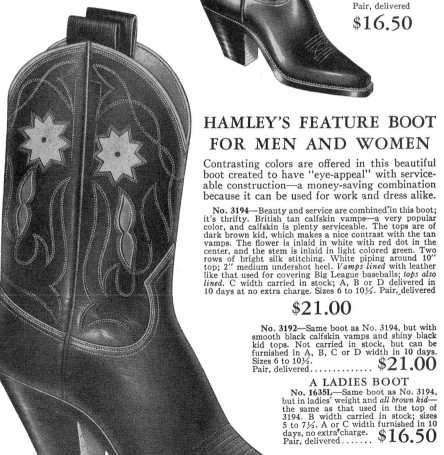

## HAMLEY'S FEATURE BOOT FOR MEN AND WOMEN

Contrasting colors are offered in this beautiful boot created to have "eye-appeal" with serviceable construction—a money-saving combination because it can be used for work and dress alike.

**No. 3194**—Beauty and service are combined in this boot; it's thrifty. British tan calfskin vamps—a very popular color, and calfskin is plenty serviceable. The tops are of dark brown kid, which makes a nice contrast with the tan vamps. The flower is inlaid in white with red dot in the center, and the stem is inlaid in light colored green. Two rows of bright silk stitching. White piping around 10" top; 2" medium undershot heel. *Vamps lined* with leather like that used for covering Big League baseballs; *tops also lined*. C width carried in stock; A, B or D delivered in 10 days at no extra charge. Sizes 6 to 10½. Pair, delivered

### $21.00

**No. 3192**—Same boot as No. 3194, but with smooth black calfskin vamps and shiny black kid tops. Not carried in stock, but can be furnished in A, B, C or D width in 10 days. Sizes 6 to 10½.
Pair, delivered..............   **$21.00**

#### A LADIES BOOT
**No. 1635L**—Same boot as No. 3194, but in ladies' weight and *all brown kid*— the same as that used in the top of 3194. B width carried in stock; sizes 5 to 7½. A or C width furnished in 10 days, no extra charge.
Pair, delivered......   **$16.50**

No. 3194
No. 3192
No. 1635L

**NEW
NARROW
SQUARE TOE**

# JUSTIN'S "BOOTMAKER"

**No. 3880**—Called the "Bootmaker" because it is the result of experience gained through generations of fine boot makers. Our customers have asked us to show a truly elegant boot, and here it is. Color is medium tan calf, finished by hand with an "antique" stain that gives the boot its unusual and attractive tone. Pinking around top, vamp, foxing, and wing tip; top is piped. Inlaid panels are lighter tan kip tooled in a flower design adding distinction and richness to the appearance of the boot. 10″ top, 2″ regular western heel, *full leather lined*, medium square toe. D width, sizes 6½ to 9½. (May be had in black with light inlays on special order— six weeks.) Pair, delivered

## $35.00

**No. 3664**—A Brown Justin Dress Boot with the new narrow square toe, and 1¾″ underslung heel. *Full leather lined* from top to toe, steel reinforced, rounded, hand-pegged shank; Goodyear welt sole; calf vamps, and 10″ kid tops with 4 rows of fancy silk stitching. White piping and white inlays decorate the top. Sizes 5½ to 10½ in D width.

Pair, delivered

### $22.50

**No. 5346** — Justin Longhorn design for combination service and dress. Two-tone color scheme. Vamps of soft and pliable tan elk; tops of brown kid, 10″ high. Has the popular narrow square toe. Diamonds are inlaid in white, and tops have white piping. 2″ standard western heel. 2 rows bright silk stitching. D width, 5½ to 10½. Pair, delivered

### $17.50

# YOU CAN'T MISS WITH THESE!

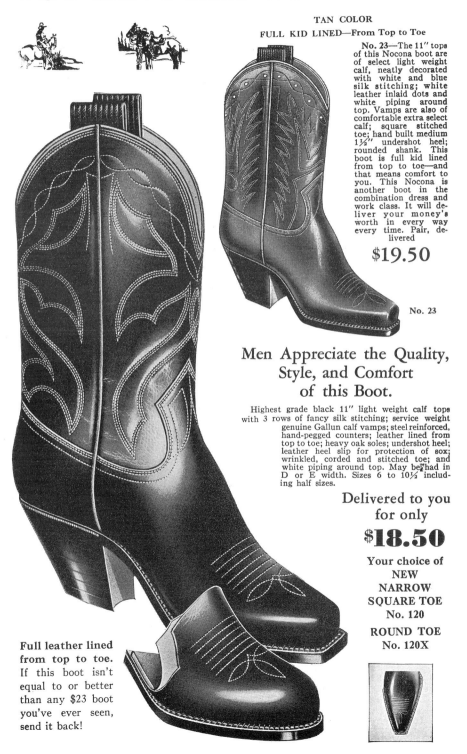

**TAN COLOR**
**FULL KID LINED—From Top to Toe**

**No. 23**—The 11″ tops of this Nocona boot are of select light weight calf, neatly decorated with white and blue silk stitching; white leather inlaid dots and white piping around top. Vamps are also of comfortable extra select calf; square stitched toe; hand built medium 1½″ undershot heel; rounded shank. This boot is full kid lined from top to toe—and that means comfort to you. This Nocona is another boot in the combination dress and work class. It will deliver your money's worth in every way every time. Pair, delivered

## $19.50

No. 23

## Men Appreciate the Quality, Style, and Comfort of this Boot.

Highest grade black 11″ light weight calf tops with 3 rows of fancy silk stitching; service weight genuine Gallun calf vamps; steel reinforced, hand-pegged counters; leather lined from top to toe; heavy oak soles; undershot heel; leather heel slip for protection of sox; wrinkled, corded and stitched toe; and white piping around top. May be had in D or E width. Sizes 6 to 10½ including half sizes.

### Delivered to you for only

## $18.50

**Your choice of**
**NEW**
**NARROW**
**SQUARE TOE**
**No. 120**

**ROUND TOE**
**No. 120X**

**Full leather lined from top to toe.** If this boot isn't equal to or better than any $23 boot you've ever seen, send it back!

# KANGAROO, KID AND CALF LEATHERS
# FEATURED IN THESE JUSTINS

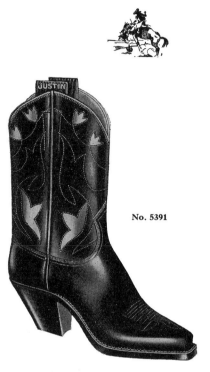

No. 5391

## BLACK
## KANGAROO
## and KID

No. 3535—A Black Justin with genuine Kangaroo vamp. The finest in dress boots. Has underslung heel, and rounded, hand-pegged shank. Medium weight. Goodyear welt oak soles. 10" kid top with 4 rows of blue and gold silk stitching; and white inlays. White piping around top. New narrow stitched tow. Sizes 5½ to 10½ in D width.

Pair, delivered

## $23.50

## BEAUTIFUL RED KID

### No. 5391 (Above)

A new number in the Justin line, developed as a result of the increasing demand for good colored boots. Vamps and tops are made of best Red Kid with insets in Yellow and Green. The boot is very well designed and indeed beautiful. Tops are 10" high; heels are undershot; toe is the popular wrinkled and stitched narrow square style. Tops have one row of colored silk stitching. This one will give you real comfort. Sizes 5½ to 10½ in D width.
Pair, postpaid.................... **$18.85**

## BLACK CALF and KID

### No. 474 (At Right)

Notice the undershot heel! This hand-shaped heel has made this boot one of the most popular in the line, and besides that the boot itself is an unusually good value! Smooth, glossy black calf vamps; black kid tops decorated with 4 rows of fine silk stitching. Wrinkled and stitched narrow square toe. Black piping around the tops. Actually you'll find that it's one of the best fitting boots you ever put on. Made on a combination last—fits everywhere. E width, sizes 5 to 10½. Pair, safely delivered to you................... **$22.50**

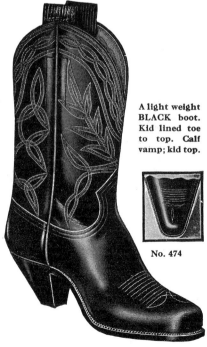

A light weight BLACK boot. Kid lined toe to top. Calf vamp; kid top.

No. 474

# POPULAR SERVICE BOOT

## Square Toe—
### Black

**No. 181**—Square toe combination last pleasing hundreds of riders. Vamps and tops of good chrome calf; tops lined and 11½" high with one row of fancy silk stitching. 1½" undershot heel. Sole leather counters; inside leather supports; rounded shank, pegged and sewed; Goodyear welt solid oak soles. You'll enjoy the fit. E width, Sizes 5 to 10.

Pair, postpaid

### $12.50

## *Dressy Black and White*
### *Nocona*

**No. 296N**—Light and dark contrast makes this a very striking boot. Black kid 10" tops. Three rows of orange and yellow stitching. Black kangaroo double lined vamps, oak soles. 2" undershot heel. New, narrow, wrinkled and stitched square toe. Best construction. C width; sizes 5 to 10. Pair, postpaid... **$22.50**

(May be had in D width on special order. Delivery 15 days.)

**No. 296N**

# BLACK NOCONA
## *Square Toe*

**No. 51**—A dress or work boot. It's genuinely comfortable, and what's the use of living if you're feet aren't happy? 11" tops with white piping as shown; 2 rows of silk stitching; welted legs. Oak counters, veal vamps, stitched medium square toe; rounded shank, oak soles, 1½" medium undershot heel. E width, sizes 5 to 10.

Delivered to you

### $17.85

## *Beautiful Tan Nocona*

**No. 284N**—A neat looking number for all around wear. Made of smooth, best quality tan calf with two rows of gold and blue stitching and white piping around tops. Double lined vamp, 10" tops, wrinkled and stitched medium narrow square toe. 2" undershot heel, oak soles. D width; sizes 5 to 10½. Pair, post paid... **$21.50**

(Above boot available in A, B, or C widths or in Black color on special order. Delivery 15 days.)

**No. 284N**

## Cowboy Boot
## Overshoe

**No. 434**—In the overshoe pictured, notice that the top of the vamp or tongue joins to the side of the shoe. This high grade "snow excluder" is not to be confused with the ordinary kind of boot overshoe. Fits boots or boot shoes. Heavy pure gum soles. Give boot size when ordering.
Pair, postpaid...................... **$2.95**
**No. 436**—High top, 4 buckle style........**$3.95**

**NEWEST OVERSHOE IS ALL RUBBER**
**No. 373**—This one never listed before. About 1" higher than illustration and *all rubber*. 2 buckle style. Closed bellows tongue. Full flannel lined. Pair, postpaid................. **$3.95**

# "Whistle While You Work"

### The "Husky"

**A long-lasting Service Boot if there ever was one!**

**No. 5104**

**No. 53**—Made in every detail to give honest-to-goodness service. It's comfortable like your favorite slippers, and after the hardest abuse will remain neat looking. Tops and vamps are of black veal, thoroughly reinforced throughout. 12" tops are leather lined. Genuine Goodyear welt oak soles. Steel reinforced shanks. Medium round toe; 1⅞" heel. E width; sizes 5 to 10½. If you're tough on boots just try this one. Pair, postpaid, only

## $11.95

**No. 5104**—A dressy looking Black Work Boot by Justin. It has "strength and good form" like any good athlete. 1¾" underslung heel, and the same shank as on No. 3664, page 129. Extra fine, medium heavy Goodyear welted oak soles, narrow square toe. Fancy silk stitched 10" top; and the boot is of fine grade cowhide that can stand the gaff! Top is leather lined. Sizes 5½ to 10½ in D width. Pair, delivered........ **$12.50**

No. 53

---

## FOR MEN AND BOYS

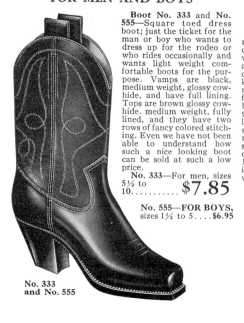

**Boot No. 333 and No. 555**—Square toed dress boot; just the ticket for the man or boy who wants to dress up for the rodeo or who rides occasionally and wants light weight comfortable boots for the purpose. Vamps are black, medium weight, glossy cowhide, and have full lining. Tops are brown glossy cowhide. medium weight, fully lined, and they have two rows of fancy colored stitching. Even we have not been able to understand how such a nice looking boot can be sold at such a low price.

**No. 333**—For men, sizes 5½ to 10.......... **$7.85**

**No. 555—FOR BOYS,** sizes 1½ to 5....**$6.95**

No. 333 and No. 555

## *The* Famous "41"

**No. 41** — We believe more riders have purchased this boot than any we have ever shown. It's a *real* service boot, doesn't cost much and gives the kind of satisfaction that makes wearers come back for more. Good weight black cowhide with 10½" tops that are full leather lined. Goodyear welt stitched, full oak soles; rounded shanks with steel supports; sole leather counters. Medium toe, 1¾" heel. Sizes 5 to 10 including half sizes. E width only.

Pair, delivered

## $10.95

No. 41

# LADIES' *Cowboy Style* BOOTS

No. 274

No. 626L

JUSTIN
"WESTERN
GYPSIES"
For Ladies
and Girls.

No. 514

### FANCY BLACK BOOTS

No. 274—A ladies' fancy, black cowboy style boot. Fine black calfskin vamps with fancy green silk stitched black kid tops. Boot heels 1½″ high. Rounded shanks. Goodyear welt soles. Reinforced counters. A real quality article. Sizes 3 to 7, with half sizes, C width. Pair, delivered to you.. **$13.50**

### BROWN BEAUTY

No. 626L—A ladies' boot that is really beautiful. Made of soft brown kid; stitched with colored silk thread as pictured. As comfortable as a glove, and made to give long service. Oak counter and sole. Soft kid lined vamp. Medium round toe. C width, sizes 3 to 7. Pair, delivered ...... **$15.00**

No. 514—Ladies' brown kid leather boot. Swanky 10″ top; new narrow square toe and close fitting heels; light weight soles. White inlays around top. Bright silk stitching. C width. Sizes 3 to 7. A or B width del. in 10 days.
Pair, postpaid..... **$12.85**

No. 512—As above but round toe, 12″ top. B width. A or C width del. 10 days. Pair, postpaid, **$12.85**

No. 502—Same as No. 512 only *black* kid. B width. A or C width del. 10 days. Pair, postpaid, **$12.85**

For more decorative Ladies' Boots, see No. 1635L, page 127.

---

## COWGIRL CONGRESS

No. 397

No. 028—Select quality Tan Kid. Medium narrow square toe. Satin goring. Full kid lined. 2″ undershot heel with rubber cap. Sizes 3 to 7, C width only. Pair, postpaid...... **$9.50**

No. 397 — Gore side Jodhpurs not stocked but delivered in about 15 days.
Brown color calf, full lined. D width. For men, pair **$8.85**

No. 397L — For ladies. Sizes 3 to 7, B and C widths.
Pair......**$7.85**

## COWBOY CONGRESS

No. 026—The best Tan Kid. Satin goring. Medium narrow square toe. Full kid lined. 2″ undershot heel with rubber cap. Corded and stitched vamp. Sizes 5 to 12, D width only. Pair, postpaid... **$10.50**

No. 027 — Same shoe as No. 026, but slick looking Black Kid. Special order only—10 days. Pair, postpaid....**$10.50**

### BOOT JACK

No. 2—A fine hardwood jack with rubber tread and leather lined throat. Each, delivered........**$1.25**

### BOOT HOOK

No. 117 — Polished handle—strong nickel plated hook. Pair..**25c**

**No. 700**—BLACK. A beautiful smooth, glossy, full grain black calf leather with twill lining throughout. A long protecting counter that permits the wearing of spurs without injury to the heel. Leather heels made of solid lifts; oak leather soles; wrinkled and stitched square toe as pictured. Comfortable, classy. D width; sizes 5 to 10½.
Pair, delivered................... **$12.00**

**No. 827**—TAN. Made of nice soft tan kid and fits like a glove. Wrinkled and stitched square toe. Goodyear welt oak inner and outer soles. Full leather lined; 1¾" rubber tip heels. Nicely wing and dot decorated. D width; sizes 5 to 10½. Pair, delivered......... **$10.95**

No. 700 Pictured

No. 664X

**No. 664X**—A real quality shoe made of good, serviceable black leather. Heavy weight. Wrinkled, medium toes, heavy sewed oak soles, boot heels and rounded shanks. Reinforced counters. Sizes 5 to 10 (half sizes) E width. Per pair, delivered.......................... **$7.45**

## "Hardy Hank"

*A Trusty Servant at a Low Wage*

**No. 704**—FULL COVERED COUNTER. For the man who wants a good, hard-working boot shoe, we offer this as one of the sturdiest yet designed, and at a very inviting price. A medium heavy, black shoe with reinforced counters, Goodyear welt oak soles; half bellowed tongue, 1¾" heel. "Hardy Hank" will do your work, and he'll give you no discomfort. Sizes 5 to 10½, E width (half sizes).
Pair, delivered to you............... **$6.50**

**MEDIUM SQUARE TOE**

No. 435

**No. 435**—BLACK. A remarkable boot shoe for the money. Full lined, comfortable, serviceable and good looking. Rounded, steel reinforced shanks. Leather heels; wrinkled and stitched medium square toe. Blucher type construction. E width, sizes 5 to 10, in half sizes.
Pair, postpaid...................... **$5.95**

## "Dressy Dick"

*and a Worker, Too!*

**No. 237**—A Black Nocona, very high grade medium weight boot shoe suitable both for dress and work. One of the finest fitting boot shoes we have ever listed. It really looks and feels like a made-to-measure job. Rounded shanks, undershot heel. Goodyear welt, and every other feature essential in making a real shoe. Sizes 6 to 10½, D width. Pair, delivered to you....... **$9.95**

# Pendleton "Tepee" Blanket

*A rich brown, with tan, green, red and white design* (at right)

**No. 27**—The original Pendleton Indian blanket, and the most popular pattern ever produced. Just thousands of them are in use today and will continue to be for years to come—because Pendleton blankets are so well-made that it is practically impossible to wear them out. The pattern listed here is in a dark brown body color, with the "tepees" in tan. The center and end designs are in green, red and white. One of the most practical and beautiful blankets you can buy—will not become soiled easily.
BLANKET—size 62x78, felt bound. Each postpaid ...........................$16.50
SHAWL—size 64x66, yarn fringe. Each, postpaid ...........................$17.50

# *Soft!*
# PENDLETON MOTOR ROBES

The Pendleton Woolen Mills is now producing an exceptionally fine robe at a remarkably low price. 100% pure wool, and woven as only the Pendleton Mill knows how to weave a blanket—soft to the touch, warm and comfy, yet nearly as sturdy as canvas. Perfect for use in the home, out of doors, and in the car. Available in *through* plaids (show the same on both sides), in the body colors listed below. In ordering, specify size wanted and color number preferred.

List of colors:

| | |
|---|---|
| 1—Tan Heather combination | 5—Brown combination |
| 2—Dark Green combination | 6—Maroon combination |
| 4—Navy Blue combination | 7—Maroon Heather |
| | 8—Grey |

**No. 220**—Driver's Robe. Size 44x56, fringed ends, Each, postpaid......................**$4.25**

**No. 220X**—Same blanket exactly as No. 220, but larger. Size 56x76, fringed ends.
Each, delivered..........................**$6.50**

# THE MT. HOOD
## *Guaranteed Moth Proof for Five Years*

**No. 7503**—Here is one of the best blanket values we have seen in many a day. "Hudson Bay Type," with solid body color (White, Gold, Tan, or Cedar) and wide stripes on ends in White, Gold and Red. Full size—72"x90". Lifetime wool binding. 100% wool, soft and fluffy, and woven to wear for years. Made by one of the leading woolen mills in the West. We are so enthusiastic about this blanket that we know you can't help liking it too—and especially at this remarkably low price.
Each, postpaid, only..................... **$9.95**

# *Finest Frontier Pants Money Can Buy*

## MADE BY THE PENDLETON WOOLEN MILLS

*100% Virgin Wool Fabric . . . tailored as only Pendleton can tailor riding pants.*

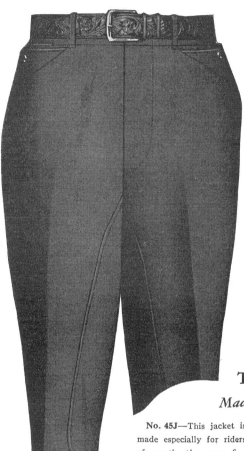

The fabric in these pants is the finest we have ever seen for the purpose. It is an elastic weave, near serge, which has that silky feel known only in quality wool garments of this type. It is exactly the same fabric (but different color) as that used by Pendleton in making the uniforms for the Oregon State Police. It is woven to withstand day after day of hard wear in all kinds of weather, and still look like the wearer had just stepped out of a band-box. Those who appreciate the fit, feel and service of genuine quality articles will find these pants in exactly the same class as Hamley Saddles! Guaranteed to please you on arrival or your money will be refunded.

Cut and tailored especially for the man who rides, these pants have double reinforced knees and seat; have button flap front and hip pockets; wide belt loops.

**19-oz. quality—choice of 2 colors.**

**No. 46**—TAUPE COLOR (dark brown), and the color which we believe you will like best. Pair,
delivered................... **$16.50**

**No. 45**—LIGHT BROWN, near tan. Pair,
delivered................... **$16.50**

(Samples of material sent on request)

In ordering, be sure to give waist measure and inseam leg length.

## A JACKET
## TO MATCH No. 45 PANTS

### *Made of exactly the same material*

**No. 45J**—This jacket is made especially for riders of exactly the same fine material and same color as the No. 45 Pendleton Pants described above. Read that description. 100% pure virgin fleece fabric of a heavy, silky, serge-like weave. Quality to the $n$th degree. Adjustable belt in back. Zipper front to keep out every bit of wind and cold. Waterproof. Pleated back. Fits snug, yet allows plenty of arm freedom. Two slash pockets. Sizes 34 to 46. Length down back is 23″.
Each,
delivered... **$16.50**

# PENDLETON PANTS
## *2 Qualities*

**No. 57**—PENDLETON CALIFORNIA STYLE. 26-oz. Texas Cashmere—the heaviest, longest wearing, most comfortable riding pants money can buy. See the illustration and description of the material below. For riding and general ranch work, and for neat appearance, there is no better garment made. Thousands of pairs have been sold. If you'd like a sample swatch, we'll send it promptly.
Pair, delivered.................... **$14.50**

**No. 58**—PENDLETON CHEYENNE PANTS. 22-oz. 100% wool fabric very tightly woven. Rain, wind and cold resistant. Mouse color, with tan and brown checks—very similar to the regular California Style pattern and color. Made exactly like No. 57 but material is a little lighter in weight, not quite so tightly woven, and slightly different in color. If you want to see the material, write for sample swatch. Pair, delivered......... **$9.75**

**Be sure to give waist measure and inseam leg measure when ordering**

No. 57 and 58

This close-up picture illustrates the tightly woven material used in the No. 57 California Style Pants. It's 100% pure virgin wool. Rain, wind and cold resistant. Dark brown plaid color. Extremely durable.

# PENDLETON *Buckaroo* SHIRT
## to match your Pendleton Pants

See page 139 for Pendleton Blazer

**No. 543**—BUCKAROO SHIRT. Exactly the same material as used in the No. 57 Pendleton Pants but of lighter weight. At the same time it is heavy weight for a shirt. So tightly woven that the texture closely resembles buckskin. Resists wind, cold and rain. Literally thousands of Hamley customers are wearing these shirts. Rancher friends in and around Pendleton tell us they would wear no other kind—they have found that this shirt pays dividends in comfort and economy. Sizes 14½ to 17½. (Sizes over 17½, 10% extra.) Each, delivered..... **$7.50**

## RIDER JACKET
### to match Pendleton Pants

**No. 194**—A neat looking, comfortable riding jacket. Made of exactly the same cloth as Pendleton California Style Pants No. 57—widely famous for its wearing and protective qualities. Fits snugly at belt line. (Back view of jacket No. 45J, page 136, is just the same as on this one). Zipper front, slash pockets. Sizes 34 to 46.
Each, delivered.................. **$15.50**

# Frontier Twill Riding Pants

## TAILORED ESPECIALLY FOR THE MAN WHO RIDES

The pants listed on this page are made in the style pictured. They are tailored to fit snugly about the seat and thighs and are cut in back to allow perfect comfort in the saddle.

### Rich Seal Brown or Light Brown Twill

**No. 319F**—Rich Seal Brown Color. 100% wool cavalry twill; buttoned pockets front and back. A very soft, but firm and tough material for long wear and continuous good appearance. Pair, postpaid........ **$16.50**

**No. 368F**—Light Brown Color. Same pant as No. 319F but beautiful light brown color. Pair, postpaid........ **$16.50**

### Fawn Grey or Dark Green

**No. 840F**—These shapely pants are of wool cavalry twill, and they are comfortable against the skin. They will hold their shape and give you plenty of good hard service Pair, delivered.... **$12.95**

### Dark Green or Cocoa Tan

**No. 406F**—A new pant of wool mix gabardine that you'll really like. It will hold a press indefinitely, and give you plenty of wear. It's medium light in weight. The colors are smooth, and the fabric is smoother. Pair, postpaid.... **$10.85**

### Oxford Grey Herringbone

**No. 485F**—A very finely woven, all wool oxford grey herringbone with narrow black stripe. An extremely dressy pair of pants, and yet not so flashy that they stand out as being too extreme. They'll hold a press, and they can take it! Pair, delivered........ **$15.50**

### Light Tan Bedford Cord

**No. 208F**—Fairly heavy weight wool mixture of the best quality. Made to look nice yet give the utmost in service and comfort. This new fabric is built to give satisfaction. Pair, postpaid.... **$10.85**

**Notice special reinforced seat and legs.**

### Dark Brown or Fawn Grey

**No. 602F**—Finest quality, wool mixture. The weave of the fabric is just the same as in the higher priced pants and we know from experience that for the average man this number is just right. The fabric holds its shape, gives you more than your money's worth of wear. Pair, delivered........ **$10.85**

In ordering be sure to give waist measure and inseam leg measure.

### Black and White Check

**No. 600F**—These pants have class. Small black and white check. Fine wool mix fabric, light weight. This material will hold its shape better than the average light wool pant of this kind. Just what you've been looking for. Pair, postpaid...... **$9.50**

### Sand Color

**No. 500F**—Fine, light weight genuine Whitman cotton gabardine. Made as pictured. Pair, delivered.......... **$5.85**

### Bark Brown Color

**No. 701F**—Brown color. Some pants selling at $12.50 will not compare with this number in quality and appearance. It is absolutely one of the best values we've seen! Pair, delivered.... **$10.50**

### Fawn or Brown Cavalry Twill

**No. 977F**—Fawn Color. Made of the very finest grade cotton cavalry twill. Will wear well and look neat—all features embodied—buttoned pockets, reinforced seat and legs. Pair, postpaid...... **$5.75**

**No. 983F**—Brown Color. Same pant exactly as No. 977F but dark brown color. Pair, postpaid...... **$5.75**

## RIDING JACKETS TO MATCH

Riding jackets made of same material and to match riding pants described above can be had. We carry a number of them in stock, and on these, deliveries can be made immediately. Other styles are made special and require 12 to 18 days for delivery.

Prices average about $1.50 above prices quoted for the different styles of pants. When ordering, just give size and number of pant you want matched.

### *English Riding Breeches on Special Order*

# PENDLETON BLAZER

## Matches No. 57 Pants

## on Page 137

**No. 944**—The perfect garment for the rider. Made of exactly the same material as the famous Pendleton California Style Pants. Wear this blazer with the pants and you have a complete suit. Just turn to page 137 for a minute, and read about this wonderful material—it will pay you. Color is dark brown plaid. Two slash button pockets. Button wrists to keep out cold wind. Convertible collar that looks neat buttoned up close or worn open. Sizes 34 to 46. Each, delivered..... **$14.50**

### Pendleton "ZIPPO" Jacket

A light-weight, 100% pure virgin wool jacket of closely woven covert cloth waterproofed by a special Pendleton process. Tailored yoke shoulder; inverted box pleat in center of back. All the body freedom in the world, and it's dressy. Keeps out rain, wind, cold; wears like leather. Tabs for easy adjustment on bottom of jacket, and also on sleeves. Sizes 34 to 48. Your choice of 4 colors. Order by number:

**No. 2500—Oxford Gray.**
**No. 2501—Light Beaver Tan.**
**No. 2524—Dark Blue-Grey Mix.**

No. 2516—**Steel Blue**, with 1" dark blue overplaid. Each, postpaid...... **$12.50**

---

For fifty years the products of Hamley & Co. have been distributed throughout the country to particular people. We mean by this people who "are tired of the extravagance of buying cheap things." Every article shown in this book has been selected for quality and the real service and satisfaction it will give its owner. There is a pride of possession in good things which often outweighs even the price paid for them. A staff of trained people are here to serve you, and to see that your wants are cared for in the right way. Give us a chance to prove these statements.

---

# Saddle Slicker

**No. 205**—Famous Tower's Yellow Saddle Slicker. For many years this has been the most satisfactory waterproof riding slicker on the market. Used by cattlemen and cowboys throughout the nation. Made with extension front and gusset in the back, covering the entire saddle—both fork and cantle. For walking, the extension fronts may be overlapped and buttoned. Double construction throughout.

Each, delivered.............. **$5.50**

| Size | 0 | 1 | 2 | 3 |
|---|---|---|---|---|
| Chest | 44"-46" | 41"-43" | 38"-40" | 35"-37" |
| Length | 62" | 61" | 59" | 57" |

# WHITE STAG Riding and Ranch Togs

No. 7700    No. 7800    No. 7602    No. 7802    No. 290L    No. 653

Every line of these trim togs smacks of the West . . . every feature adds to the pleasure of the wearer . . . *White Stag* designers are famous for their Western styling.

**No. 7700—Cowgirl Shirt.** Western plaids in shrunk cotton twill. Attached fringed neckerchief of same plaid at neck running through hand-plaited leather thong. Two pockets. Tan Plaid, Blue Plaid, Red Plaid. Sizes 12 to 20.................**$2.95**

**No. 7800—Rodeo Skirt.** 8-oz. Sanforized-shrunk Blue denim. Pockets copper riveted as on Cowgirl Overalls. Split skirt for riding ease. Sizes 12 to 20.............................**$4.95**

**No. 7602—Saddle Cord Coat.** Hip-length, full lined. Loose half-belt and saddle-vent in back. Frontier Tan. Sizes 12 to 20.................**$12.95**

**No. 7802—Saddle Cord Frontier Pants.** Snugtex patented waist band lining to prevent shirt from slipping out. Button-top pockets, double seat, double knees. Frontier Tan. Sizes 12 to 20....**$9.95**

**No. 290L—Frontier Shirt.** 100% wool Gabardine tailored true "Gambler" style with plain top, smoked pearl buttons, 3-button cuffs. Four extra buttons with each shirt. Zelan perspiration treated arm shields. For hunting, fishing, ranching, skiing, etc. White, Beige, Marine Blue, Old Rose and Scarlet. Sizes 12 to 20...........................**$7.95**

**No. 653—"Bronco Betty" Cowgirl Overalls.** 9-oz. sanforized-shrunk Blue Denim. Zipper opening at left hip. Copper riveted at all strain points. Narrow riding leg. Sizes 10 to 22, with leg inseams 29", 31", and 33"..............................**$1.95**

# *White Stag* FOUR SEASON *Sport Jackets*

## FOR YEAR 'ROUND

### ACTIVE SPORTS

Wind and water repellent Adirondack poplin. Free-swing back; double shoulders; zipper front; zipper pockets; elastic shirring at hips.

**No. 958—Ladies' Jacket** in Natural, Sand, Steel Blue, Dark Green. Sizes 12 to 22...**$6.95**

**No. 959—Men's Jacket** in Sand, Grey, Dark Green. Sizes 34 to 46. (48, 50, 52 add 10 per cent).........................**$6.95**

**No. 998—Men's Four Season Jacket** in wool covert, plaid lined. Green, Tan, Heather Blue. Sizes 34 to 46...................**$7.95**

# LADIES WESTERN STYLE
# RIDING PANTS

Please Give
Your Waist
and Inseam
Leg Measure
When Order-
ing Pants

### *Tailored for Fit and Comfort*

**No. 509D**—POWDER BLUE CAVALRY TWILL. The material in this pant is an excellent *pure virgin wool* cavalry twill. This particular shade of blue is fast becoming popular for women's riding pants. For supreme quality, nice fit, lasting shape, and all around satisfaction, this number will fill the bill. Pair, postpaid...... **$14.95**

**No. 208D**—LIGHT TAN BEDFORD CORD. A heavier weight women's riding pant which will give years of service, and yet retain its shape and good looks. A number of our lady customers have asked for this pant, so here it is. Material is best quality wool mixture.
Pair, postpaid.......................... **$10.75**

**No. 406D**—LIGHT WEIGHT WOOL GABARDINE; CHOICE OF FOUR COLORS: Rich dark brown, dark green, black or new chamois color. The material is an extremely fine grade of light weight wool gabardine. Will hold a press, and they're dressy. Pair, postpaid **$10.75**

**No. 602D**—BROWN OR FAWN GREY CAVALRY TWILL. A wool mixture with plenty of endurance. They will hold their shape (or yours, as you wish).
Pair, postpaid.......................... **$10.75**

**No. 404D**—DARK GREEN CAVALRY TWILL. Good quality wool mix cavalry twill. The appearance of an all wool pant without the extra cost. Serviceable. Available in tan, brown, or black on special order; delivery 15 days. Pair, postpaid........................ **$8.75**

**No. 977D**—SUN TAN COLOR COTTON TWILL. Just a little darker color than sand. Nicely tailored pant made to give service. *Without reinforced seat and knee.* **$5.75**
Pair, postpaid............................

**No. 050D**—SUMMER WEIGHT WHITMAN COTTON GABARDINE; CHOICE OF THREE COLORS: Sand, dark brown or black. Discreetly tailored. An ideal everyday riding pant. Pair, postpaid.... **$5.25**

All women's pants listed on this page made in the style illustrated with left side zipper opening, button pockets, and reinforced seat and legs unless otherwise noted. Carefully tailored to fit.

# PENDLETON
# SHIRTS
# FOR THE LADIES

## Soft Wool Fabric

Made of 10-oz. pure virgin fleece, mill-shrunk and tailored to a queen's taste. Button-flap pockets pleated as pictured. Sateen-lined neck band. Material insulates against heat and cold. Sizes 14, 16, 18. (20 and 22 on special order.)

CHOOSE FROM THESE TWO SOLID COLORS
**No. 1550—Royal Blue.**

**No. 1510—Maroon.**
Each, delivered.................... **$6.00**

## "Soft-as-Silk" Gabardine

Finest quality, 8-oz., 100% virgin wool gabardine. "Western Gambler" style. Pleated sleeves. Three-button cuff. Inverted pleat back. Diagonal pockets and flaps. Sizes 14, 16, 18. (20 and 22 on special order.)

**No. 2290—Turf Tan**       **No. 2295—Sage Green**

**No. 2299—Teal Blue**
Each, delivered.................... **$8.50**

# PENDLETON *SHIRTS*

Here's a hand-picked assortment of famous Pendleton shirts—a choice that's guaranteed to please. You're sure to be right with a Pendleton.
*"Since the Winning of the West."*

**No. 658—TAN AND BROWN SHADOW PLAID.** Here is a beautiful pattern of soft shadow tones, heavy and light, that harmonize to make a distinctive fabric. Two button-flap pockets; harmonizing buttons; sateen lined neck band. Sizes 14½ to 17¼. Each, postpaid............$7.00

**No. 659—MAROON SHADow PLAID.** Same as above, but different color. Sizes 14½ to 17¼. Each, delivered.....$7.00

**No. 445—RED AND BLACK PLAID.** Truly a beautiful pattern; the large checks are outlined in red and the plaid background is somewhat like the *shadow plaid* in the No. 658 shirt. Has two button-flap pockets; harmonizing buttons; sateen lined neck band. Sizes 14½ to 17½. Each, postpaid........$5.00

**No. 447—GREEN AND GREY PLAID.** Same as above; green color dominates the shadow plaid. Sizes 14½ to 17½.
Each, postpaid............$5.00

**No. 567—SCOTCH TARTAN PLAID.** *Gray body, Cardinal and Oxford over-plaid.* If you want a colorful shirt, here it is. Authentic Scotch Tartan design. Two button-flap pockets. 11-oz. pure virgin wool. Sateen lined neck band. Sizes 14½ to 17¼. Each, delivered..............$7.00
**No. 569—**Similar to above, but this one has MAROON body with HUNTER'S GREEN and WHITE OVERPLAID. A real beauty. Sizes 14½ to 17¼. Each.............$7.00

**No. 1301—TAN AND WHITE HONEYCOMB PATTERN.** One of the finest grade Pendletons in a neat pattern. 12-oz. pure virgin wool. Two-button flap pockets; sateen lined neck band. Buttons harmonize with the color of the shirt. Mill shrunk. Sizes 14½ to 17¼. Each, postpaid........$7.50

**No. 564 — NAVY BLUE** body, DARK GREEN and CARDINAL OVERPLAID.
This is another authentic Scotch Tartan design of outstanding beauty. 11-oz. pure virgin wool fabric; harmonizing buttons; sateen lined neck band; two button flap pockets. Sizes 14½ to 17½. Each, postpaid ...$7.00

**No. 546 — BLACK AND WHITE CHECK.** If you want a shirt that is really distinctive in appearance, you will like this one. Checks are about ⅛" square. Two button flap pockets; sateen lined neck band; harmonizing buttons. Made of 10-oz. pure virgin wool fabric. Sizes 14½ to 17½. Each, postpaid...............$6.00

For shirts to match Pendleton Pants see Page 137

# WOOL GABARDINE
# SERGE SHIRT

### *Choose From Five Colors*

Outdoor men everywhere are coming more and more to appreciate the fine wearing qualities and appearance of serge shirts. We present here an exceptional value in that type of garment. It is a fine grade of all wool gabardine serge; two button-flap breast pockets and three-button cuffs. Buttons are made to harmonize with the solid colors of the shirts and are of the smooth type as pictured. Sizes 14½ to 17½. We stock the following 6 solid colors:

| | |
|---|---|
| Light Tan—No. 107-7 | Royal Blue—No. 107-2 |
| Brown—No. 107-12 | Wine—No. 107-10 |
| | Slate Green—No. 107-3 |

Your choice.
Each, delivered.................................. $7.50

## HAMLEY SPECIAL SHIRT

### *A Real Value*
### Choose From Four Colors

No. LS84—WASHABLE GABARDINE GAMBLER STYLE SHIRT. The material used in this shirt is a special fabric that has been *Crown Tested and approved for durability, color fastness and general wearing qualities.* Choice of 4 colors: Tan, Light Blue, Green, and Wine. (As illustrated at right.) Sizes 14 to 17.
Each, postpaid.................................. $3.50

# *Genuine* PENDLETON
## "Soft as Silk" Gabardine Shirt

The finest quality, 8½-oz. weight, 100% virgin wool gabardine. This shirt, when you see it, will surpass your highest expectation. It's soft; holds its shape. It's tailored to fit correctly, and believe us you are properly dressed when you wear one of these comfortable, classy shirts. The "Western Gambler" has three button cuff, hand-sewn pearl stud buttons to match body color of shirt, and open pleat back. Diagonal pockets and pocket flaps. Sizes 14½ to 17½.

No. 1090—Turf Tan.
No. 1092—Dark Brown.
No. 1094—Maroon.
No. 1095—Sage Green.
No. 1096—Wheat.
No. 1099—Light Blue.
Each, delivered..................... $7.50

# Broadcloth & *Genuine*
# Irish Poplin Shirts

"Sportsman" style in both these shirts (illustrated at left). They will wear indefinitely—especially the Poplin. Special vat colors—guaranteed against sun and perspiration as well as washing; fully preshrunk throughout. Two button-down flap pockets—lined flaps. Full length with square military tails. Ocean pearl buttons. Pleated sleeves; pencil stitch on left pocket. Sizes 14½ to 17.

No. 810—Broadcloth; Suntan, Steel Grey, or Green Olive color. Each, delivered.................. $1.45

No. 865—Poplin; Suntan, Nickel Grey, or Green Olive color. Each, delivered................. $2.65

## *The Celebrated*
# LEVI STRAUSS
## OVERALLS and JACKETS

**No. L501** — OVERALLS. The original copper riveted waist overall, made especially for men who ride—a favorite among hard working cowboys for over 50 years. Heavy 9-oz. specially woven denim. Tailored like a pair of tailor-made pants—they fit everywhere! Five roomy pockets. These overalls stay up without use of belt or suspenders; they have special belt loops, however, and an adjustable strap at the back of the waist. Ask any rider what he thinks of LEVI'S—he'll tell you. A new pair free if they rip. 30" to 46" waist; please give your inseam length.
Pair, postpaid................**$1.90**

**No. L503**—BOYS' LEVIS. Just like the men's but in smaller sizes. 24" to 29" waist; please give your inseam length. Pair, postpaid.........**$1.70**

**No. L506**—JACKET. Look at the picture. Have you ever seen a better work and riding jacket? Made of the same fine material as No. L501 overalls listed above. Roomy at the shoulders and snug at the bottom. Gusseted front so you can let it out if you want to. One big breast pocket. Can be worn open at throat or closed, as pictured.
Sizes 34 to 44. Each, postpaid... **$1.95**

## *"Lady Jeans"*

# LEVIS FOR THE LADIES

**No. L401**—LADY LEVIS. Patterned especially for the lady who rides. Copper riveted, and constructed of heavy 9-oz. specially woven denim just as are the regular Levi's for men. Neat in appearance because they are tailored right—they fit everywhere. 25" to 33" waist; please give inseam length. Pair, postpaid............................**$1.80**

**No. R528**—LADIES' SANFORIZED DENIM FRONTIERS. A new garment same color as No. L401, but softer because it's *sanforized*. Double seat and knee, nice fit, and zipper side opening. 24" to 36" waist; please give your inseam length. Pair, postpaid................................**$2.95**

**No. RJ92**—LADIES' SANFORIZED DENIM JACKET. Styled similar to No. L506. Zipper front. Matches No. R528, or No. L401, but softer than No. L401. Sizes 12 to 20. Each, postpaid................................**$2.95**

## STETSON'S *"La Vista"*

## Now An Established Leader

### Real Nutria Beaver Quality

**No. 288**—Here is a hat that has won the most discriminating westerners. It's quality through and through, and looks it. Crown is 6 inches high, and brim is 3¾" wide. Braid crown band in a color to harmonize with the Buckskin color of the hat. Order your size, and if, upon arrival, you don't agree that this is one of the finest hats you have ever seen, just send it back for full refund. Each, postpaid............$17.00

## STETSON'S "TOPPER"
### Chocolate Brown Color

**No. 494**—The last word in a fine looking hat for shape, color and appearance all around. Crown is 6" high; brim is 3¼ inches wide. Narrow braid binding on under side of brim, and narrow braid crown band. Color is the new Chocolate Brown. Stetson's No. 1 quality. Each, postpaid....$10.00

## STETSON'S SOUTHERN
### Sudan Brown Color

**No. 334**—Here is another Stetson in such a style, color and quality to make it one of the most popular hats of the year. Order this one, and we believe you'll be wearing "the hat of the year." Color is rich tobacco brown. Stetson's No. 1 quality. 3¾" brim has neat narrow braid binding on under side. Crown is 6" high with braid band. Each, postpaid............$11.00

**Prices on Stetson Hats subject to change without notice.**

# STETSON'S
# *San Luis*

Your choice of 3 colors:

**BLACK, BISQUE, BELGIAN BELLY**

No. 145—Black
No. 140—Bisque
No. 144—Belly
(gray)

Here is a Stetson No. 1 quality hat that is sure to please. The crown is 6½″ high, and the medium flat set brim is 4″ wide. Brim has slight curl as pictured. Notice the neat 3-cord silk braid crown band. Brim is full bound. This is the kind of hat that will give you long wear and keep looking like a million all the time. Choose the color you like best: Your choice of BLACK or BELGIAN BELLY.
Each, postpaid.................................................................. **$11.50**
BISQUE COLOR, a light tannish white shade........................................**$12.50**

**No. 887**—BISQUE COLOR. Same quality hat as above picture. Has the same 3-cord band and bound brim. Difference is in the size—6″ crown, 3½″ brim. Each, postpaid... **$11.50**

**No. 887X**—BELGIAN BELLY COLOR. Same as No. 887, just the difference in color......................... **$10.50**

No. 622

# STETSON'S STERLING

### SILVER BELLY COLOR
#### Very Light Shade

**No. 622**—We believe that this Stetson is one of the finest service hats, yet one of the nicest appearing that we have ever presented at the price. It is a No. 1 quality Stetson, and the crown is 6″ high; brim 3½″ wide. Notice that the brim is full bound, and that the crown has a 6-cord band. A real hat if there ever was one.
Each, delivered.......... **$11.50**

# STETSON'S
# DEL REY

### SILVER BELLY or BLACK COLOR

**No. 508**—SILVER BELLY COLOR. Beautiful Stetson as shown. A rejuvenation of one of the most popular shapes ever made. 6″ crown with 1-cord band. 3″ raw edge brim curled on the sides.
Each, postpaid............ **$10.50**

**No. 507**—BLACK COLOR, otherwise the same as No. 508 ............. **$10.00**

No. 507
No. 508

Prices on Stetson Hats subject to change without notice.

# STETSON'S "LA JOLLA"

**No. 142X—**
**Sudan Brown**

**No. 141X—**
**Silver Belly**

Choose
from
2 colors:

**SILVER BELLY**

**SUDAN BROWN**

The picture really doesn't do this particular hat justice. Really, it's one of the nicest we've ever seen and that's no foolin'. Has 5¾" crown with 2-cord band, and 3¾" bound brim. It's Stetson's No. 1 quality. If you like these dimensions, and this quality, choose your color and order today. We'll ship promptly.
No. 142X—SUDAN BROWN COLOR.
Each, postpaid.................................................................... **$11.00**
No. 141X—SILVER BELLY COLOR.................................................**$12.00**

# STETSON'S
## "San Diego"

### 3X Beaver Quality. Buckskin Color.

NOTICE: Our supply of this hat in the Buckskin color is limited, and Stetson has discontinued it. If we cannot furnish Buckskin for you, we will send Silver Belly color.

No. 650—Small shape hats are becoming increasingly popular, and for that reason we feel that more of our catalog space should be devoted to outstanding numbers such as this one. Has 5½" crown with 1-cord band, and 2⅝" bound brim. You'll like it. Each, postpaid................... **$14.00**

# STETSON'S
## "Monte Vista"

### No. 1 Quality Bisque Color

No. 410—If you want a medium large hat along the lines of the one illustrated, and one that won't show the dust, you need look no further. This one has 5¾" crown with 1-cord band, and 3½" raw edge brim with very slight curl on the sides. Each, postpaid...... **$11.50**

**Prices on Stetson Hats subject to change without notice.**

# STETSON'S "SOUTH AFRICA"

## BLACK COLOR

**No. 280**—*This Black Stetson is really a darb!*
No. 1 quality; 6" crown, 2⅞" brim. Has a neat,
narrow braid crown band, and a
braid under-brim binding. For
service and good looks, this one
can't miss.
Each, postpaid.....**$10.00**

No. 280

## ONCE YOU TRY A STETSON
## YOU'LL WEAR NO OTHER!

**3X BEAVER
QUALITY**

### Stetson's "*La Prima*"

**Buckskin Color**

**No. 1886**—If you want a *real good*
hat—one that is right in style, and is
made in every way to give lasting
service—then here is the hat you want.
Stetson's 3X Beaver Quality. Crown is
6" high; brim 2⅞" wide. Neat 3-cord
crown band, and brim has a single cord
binding on under side
only. Can be reblocked
time and again .. made
to last for years! Each,
postpaid... **$15.50**
With silk
lined
crown.. **$16.50**

### STETSON'S
### SAN MATEO

**BISQUE COLOR (Very light
shade, almost like buckskin)**

**No. 1180**—A fine Stetson in
No. 1 quality that has proved
one of the most popular ever
shown. It is a good looking,
practical hat. Crown is 6" high,
with 3-cord
silk braid
crown band.
Brim is 3"
wide, silk
bound. Each
postpaid

**$10.50**

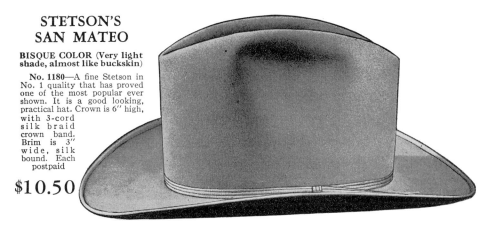

Prices on Stetson Hats subject to change without notice.

# STETSON'S *"VAQUERO"*
## SUDAN BROWN COLOR

No. 273

No. 273—The "Vaquero" was a new number in 1940, and it'll probably be right in there pitching for a good many years to come, at least that's our prediction. This Sudan Brown color is a rich shade just a little darker than the popular Chocolate Brown already being featured so strongly. The "Vaquero" is Stetson No. 1 quality, has a 6-in. crown with a slick 2-cord crown band, 3½-in. raw edge brim slightly curled, and an appearance that'll "knock 'em dead." Each, delivered safely..................... **$10.50**

## DENT YOUR STETSON AS YOU PLEASE

No. 188
No. 180
No. 588

## STETSON'S TAOS
### 3 Colors: Bisque, Chocolate Brown and Black

A mighty neat little hat that catches the eye. It is a No. 1 quality Stetson with a 6-in. crown and 2⅞-in. brim. Braid under binding around the brim; exceptionally neat narrow crown band. This number is shown in the picture dented in a manner popular at the present time—you can of course crush it to suit your own tastes. Two cord silk crown band and under brim binding same color as hat.

No. 188—Bisque Color, safe delivery guaranteed........... **$10.50**

No. 180—Brown color........ **$10.00**
No. 588—Black color.......... 10.00

## STETSON'S TETON
### Silver Belly Color

No. 1100S—The Teton is a Real Nutria quality Stetson. It is right in style in every way, including the new silver belly color that gives this fine hat the appearance for "dress-up". Can be cleaned time after time at the factory and each time look like a new hat. This is true of all Stetsons. The dimensions are neat —6-in. crown and 3-in. brim. The brim is full bound; three cord crown band—trimmings same color as the hat. Price, postpaid..... **$14.00**

No. 1100S

Prices on Stetson Hats subject to change without notice.

## Stetson's "*LaMar*"

**Your Choice of 2 Colors: BISQUE or CHOCOLATE BROWN**

**No. 885**—No. 1 quality Stetson with raw edge brim and neat, single-cord crown band. Crown is 5¾" high, and brim is 3¼" wide—proportions that make this one of the nicest looking hats we have ever seen. In ordering be sure to specify whether you want *Bisque* or *Chocolate brown color.*

Chocolate Brown color, post-paid... **$10.00**

Bisque color.. **$11.00**

## Stetson's "*La Mesa*"

**A beautiful hat with a low crown.**

**Belgian Belly Color No. 884**

**No. 884**—Here is a Stetson No. 1 quality hat that will please you right down to the ground. The crown is only 5½" high, and the brim 3½" wide. Beautiful Belgian Belly color. Brim has raw edge. The only decoration on this hat is a neat single-cord crown band in harmonizing color. A hat that's made for service and neat appearance. Each, postpaid........................................ **$10.50**

The same hat, No. 680 crushed in a different way, is shown above.

No. 680

## STETSON'S "*Francisco*"

**Belgian Belly Color**

**No. 680**—This hat is another in the service and fine appearance class. It is up to date in style, and yet has those extra features that mean long satisfactory wear. The quality is Stetson's No. 1. The crown is 6¼" high; brim 3½" wide. Full narrow brim binding with three cord silk braid crown band in color to match. Price, safe delivery guaranteed..... **$10.50**

Prices on Stetson Hats subject to change without notice.

**Choice of
2 colors:**

SUDAN BROWN
SILVER BELLY

# STETSON'S
## *Don Juan*

The most discriminating hat buyer could not pass up this beautiful number. In either of the two colors, it's a knockout, and we know you will agree when you see it. Has 5¾" crown, and 3¾" bound brim. Crown has 2-cord band. Quality is Stetson's No. 1.

**No. 412**—SUDAN BROWN COLOR. Each, postpaid................................. **$11.00**
**No. 411**—SILVER BELLY COLOR.................................................**$12.00**

## STETSON'S
## BLACK CROW

**No. 616**—Here is a mighty neat black Stetson. The proportions are just right to make it a fine looking hat— 6¼" crown and 3½" brim. It is made for exceptionally good service in addition to fine appearance—notice the silk brim binding and the 6-cord crown band. Made in Stetson's famous No. 1 quality. Each, safe delivery guaranteed... **$10.50**

No. 616

## STETSON'S "FIESTA"
### *Pure White Color*

**No. 1222**—Looking for a good show hat? Then consider this one—it will stand out in any crowd. The crown is 6" high and the brim 3¾" wide. The braid brim under binding and crown band are of pure white silk. This is a No. 1 quality Stetson—and the kind of show hat that will last you for a good long time because it will stand repeated cleaning and blocking. Each, delivered safely............... **$11.00**

NOTE: Hat No. 1222 is pictured with No. 13 braided hat band. This band is available in either black and white or brown and white combination. If you want one sent with your hat, just specify the color, and add 60c to the price.

No. 1222

Prices on Stetson Hats subject to change without notice.

## STETSON'S SAN FRAT

### *Bisque Color*

**No. 882**—A snappy looking Stetson with 6″ crown and 3″ brim. Raw edge brim, and neat 6-cord crown band. No. 1 quality. This hat has *everything* to make it one of the most popular we have ever shown —style, quality and price.

Each postpaid... **$10.50**

## STETSON'S TEXAS

Bisque Color—about like buckskin

**No. 613**—We wish you had the opportunity to pick up this Stetson, put it on your head and look at yourself in the mirror. Because it is one of the finest appearing hats we have ever seen. The color is Bisque—sort of a whitish gray. The only trimming is a very neat narrow silk braid band around the crown; the brim is raw edged. No. 1 quality; dimensions 5½-in. crown, 3-in. brim.

Each, delivered safely...................................................................**$10.50**

NOTE: In the illustration above hat band No. 13 is shown on the hat. If you want one of these attractive new braid bands in brown and white or black and white please just specify color, and add 60c to the price.

## STETSON'S SIERRA

### Silver Belly Color

**No. 4202X**—Here's a hat for wear on rare occasions. Appearance which will top off any good outfit. Only slight roll to the brim and crown is of such shape and proportion that it looks well with various kinds of dents and creases. Will more than please if you want a high grade light color hat. Real Nutria quality Stetson. The under brim braid binding and the silk braid crown band are of a greenish brown color and harmonize nicely with the body color. The crown is 7-in. high and the brim 4½-in. wide. Each, safe delivery guaranteed..... **$21.00**

**No. 4202**—*Belgian Belly color.* Identically the same hat in appearance as shown here, except for the difference in color. No. 1 quality. Each, postpaid...........**$14.00**

No. 4202X

Prices on Stetson Hats subject to change without notice.

# STETSON'S *"DON JOSE"*
## *A Killer for Looks!*

**No. 136**
**BLACK**

**No. 136**—This is the hat they've all been asking for. It is a Black Stetson, No. 1 quality and takes your eye the minute you see it. Has a medium flat, raw edge brim 3½-in. wide. The crown is fairly low—5¾-in. high, and notice the silk 3-cord crown band. This hat is different, and will appeal tó the type of individual **$10.50** who selects his hats with the utmost care. Each, postpaid...............................

## STETSON'S SAN SOUCI
### BISQUE COLOR
*About like buckskin*

**No. 200B**—It doesn't take a lot of imagination to visualize what a really fine appearing hat this is. While all Stetsons are invariably "top-notch"— we frequently receive a style which has that something extra that makes it really outstanding. This is one of them. Made in the popular bisque color. No. 1 quality, 6″ crown, 3¼″ brim. Each, delivered safely... **$11.00**

**No. 200B**

**No. 420**—BELGIAN BELLY COLOR, otherwise exactly like No. 200B. Each, safe delivery guaranteed.............................................................**$10.50**

## STETSON'S PALOMAR
### *Available in three colors*

**No. 883**—*Belgian Back Color*, a brownish gray, slightly darker than ordinary belly color. It's a neat Stetson, No. 1 quality, for the man who likes a hat of comparatively small proportions. Crown 5¾-in. high; brim 2¾-in. wide and full bound. Neat 3-cord crown band. Each, postpaid............ **$10.00**

**No. 1150S**—Black color.............**$10.00**
**No. 1160S**—Belgian Belly (tannish gray)....**$10.00**

**Prices on Stetson Hats subject to change without notice.**

# Take your choice if you want a BIG hat

## STETSON'S CAREYHURST

### PURE WHITE
*Light tan color trimmings*

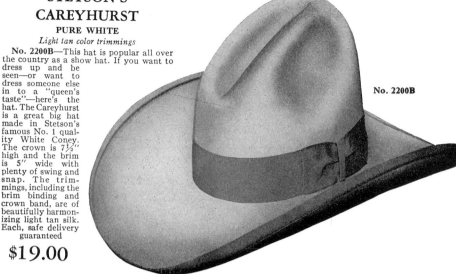

No. 2200B

**No. 2200B**—This hat is popular all over the country as a show hat. If you want to dress up and be seen—or want to dress someone else in to a "queen's taste"—here's the hat. The Careyhurst is a great big hat made in Stetson's famous No. 1 quality White Coney. The crown is 7½" high and the brim is 5" wide with plenty of swing and snap. The trimmings, including the brim binding and crown band, are of beautifully harmonizing light tan silk. Each, safe delivery guaranteed

## $19.00

No. 1600B

## STETSON'S CALGARY
### BISQUE COLOR

**No. 1600B**—The Calgary is the most popular hat in its class that we have ever shown. Probably this is because one friend sees another wearing this hat, asks him where he got it and what kind it is—then sends to Hamley for one for himself. It's that kind of a hat—it takes the eye and at the same time stands up under plenty of hard wear. The Calgary is a No. 1 quality Stetson with 7" crown and 4½" brim. Plenty of swing to the big curl brim. Each, delivered.

*Bisque Color*

## $15.00

**No. 600B**—BELGIAN BELLY COLOR. You'll like this excellent color. It's a tannish grey shade that will not show the dirt. Except for color it's the same as No. 1600B. Each, postpaid....... **$14.00**

---

No. 062

## *The* KIT CARSON . . . *Boy's Hat*

**No. 062**—The little fellows like western hats, too, but their heads grow so fast that high grade hats for them are not advisable. Here's a little light colored "Western Gentleman's" hat which the small boys like and it will give more service than you would expect at the price. Each, delivered...... **$1.85**

Sizes 6⅜ to 7¼

**No. 063**—Identically the same hat as above except this one is *solid BLACK* color. Each, postpaid.... **$1.85**

Prices on Stetson Hats subject to change without notice.

## STETSON'S KINGSTON
**Choose From Three Colors**

**3 Colors**
BISQUE,
BLACK,
CHOCOLATE
BROWN

| No. 620<br>Bisque color (about like buckskin) | No. 625<br>Black | No. 626<br>Chocolate Brown |

This hat is light weight and has that "something" about it which appeals to westerners who follow the trend of western hat styles. You'll like the Kingston if you prefer real western atmosphere in a small bundle. Notice the bound brim and the narrow harmonizing crown band. The brim is 2½" wide and the crown 5½" high.

Take particular note that this hat is available in 3 different colors: *bisque, black* and *chocolate brown*. It is a toss-up as to which color is most popular—so just send for the one that appeals to you most from the description and if it does not more than please you just return it for exchange or full refund.
Price, safe delivery guaranteed...................................................**$8.50**
Be sure to specify color and size.

**No. 627**—Same style as above, a good grade fur felt hat, not a Stetson, tobacco brown color only. Each, delivered ........................................................ **$3.95**

## STETSON'S "BLACKIE"

**Available also in Chocolate or Bisque**

No. 1820
No. 1822
No. 1824

The picture of this hat shows the crown dented in a manner which has become very popular; of course, you can dent it to suit yourself. This hat is a fine No. 1 quality Stetson with practical dimensions—6-in. crown and 2⅞-in. brim, with braid binding on its under edge. Neat 2-cord crown band and under-brim binding are same color as hat.

No. 1820—Black color, postpaid...............**$10.00**
No. 1822—Chocolate brown color...............$10.00
No. 1824—Bisque color........ 10.50

---

# NOT A STETSON—BUT A BEAUTY!

*Real Fur Felt*

### BEAUTIFUL TAUPE COLOR

**No. 119**—The color of this hat is its biggest asset. It will not show the dust; at least not before it becomes thoroughly coated with it. 5¾" crown with braided band and leather button; 3" brim with lock-stitched binding—a dressy feature.
Each, postpaid.................**$6.00**

Prices on Stetson Hats subject to change without notice.

# KENSINGTON ... *Quality Hats*

"Kensington" is a fine quality of hat being produced by one of the world's leading manufacturers of fine hats. The styles offered are authentic in every way. The quality and finish is the finest we have seen outside the Stetson line. If you are not pleased you may return for refund.

### THE KING PIN
*Sudan Brown Color*

**No. 722**—A service hat that looks like a million. Crown is 5½" high, and brim is 2¾" wide. Notice the 3-cord crown band. Brim has neat single cord binding on under side. A new color you'll like. A hat that's made to give you long service and has plenty of what it takes to be a real dress hat, too. Each, postpaid...... **$6.50**

### "LA LANDE" STYLE
*Belgian Belly Color*

**No. 811**—Here's a fine hat in the most popular style. Crown is 5½" high and brim is 3" wide. Notice the neat single-cord crown band. That's all the decoration on this hat; the brim is raw edge. This is a fine little hat that we know you'll like Each, postpaid..... **$7.00**

Silk lined crown

### KENSINGTON HATS *are high grade,* *"up-to-the-minute," serviceable*

### THE DONNER
*Black Color*

**No. 908**—One of the slickest little black hats we've ever shown in our catalog. Crown is 5½" high, and brim is 2¾" wide. Notice the neat manner in which it crushes. And notice the one-cord silk braid crown band. Brim has raw edge. Order your size, if you want a black hat in this quality, and if this one does not please you upon arrival, just return for full refund. Each, delivered..... **$6.50**

# 3 Popular Low-Priced Hats... *Not Kensington's*
## *"The Texan"*

No. 318

### FAVORITE SAND COLOR

**No. 318**—A new edition of the old "Carlsbad" shape, and it really has the lines. When you see this up-to-the-minute hat we know you'll say it's one of the best hats you ever saw for the money. 7″ crown, 4¼″ brim with 5 cord crown band, and ¼″ brim binding. Each, postpaid................... **$6.95**

No. 712C

## THE HOTTENTOT
### BEAVER BELLY COLOR

**No. 712C**—A hat that is right up to the minute in style, made in a good dependable quality—worth the price asked in any man's money. The crown is 6″ high and the brim 3″ wide. Trimmed with narrow 3-cord crown band and under brim binding in harmonizing color. Silk lined. Each, delivered safely.... **$3.95**

**No. 204**—Same hat as No. 712C, but 2-cord crown band, 5½″ crown and 3½″ brim. Each, postpaid.. **$3.95**

**Real Fur Felt**
**NOT Wool Felt**

## THE BLACK BEAUTY
### BLACK

**No. 730C**—This is identically the same hat as the 712C except it is made in solid black. One of the nicest looking hats for the price you can find anywhere—it has style, class and wear. Silk lined. Under brim braid binding and crown band in shiny black silk. Each delivered safely...... **$3.95**

No. 730C

# The New
## *San Felipe*

**No. 655
Light Beaver
Belly Color**

**No. 655**—The San Felipe is made in a style that is rapidly becoming popular in many sections of the country. Although it is very low in price, it is made from REAL FUR FELT, and not wool felt. This uniquely styled hat has a low 5½" crown, a 4½" raw edge brim, and a single cord crown band. It's recommended for service and appearance. Each, delivered safely.................................... **$3.95**

**No. 195**

## THE STOCKMAN
### Light Gray Color

**No. 195**—Fine Real Fur Felt hat. We know that you'll like it because it's a real value for the money. It's built for service and yet it's soft and shapely. 5¾" crown, 2⅞" bound brim, and 5-cord crown band. Each, postpaid................... **$3.95**

## SMALL SHAPE for MEN

**No. 154**—The ALAMO. One of the neatest little hats we have ever seen at the price. A nice Belly color. Silk lined crown. Raw edge 2⅝" brim. Crown is 5½ inches high. Comes complete with new braided leather band and leather band button. Folks who want a fine-looking, good quality hat at a low price will find the Alamo exactly to their liking. Each, postpaid... **$3.95**

**No. 627**—Same style as Stetson's "Kingston" pictured on page 152, but not of Stetson make. Tobacco brown color only. Each, delivered...... **$3.95**

**No. 922
and
923**

## "STRAWBOSS"

**No. 922**—Here's that Genuine, Original Mexican Hand Woven PALM BRAID HAT everyone's talking about. Has a guaranteed sweat-proof band inside for extra comfort and service. 6¼" crown, 3¾" brim. Each, postpaid................... **$1.25**

**No. 923**—Same hat, but 6" crown and 3" brim, postpaid..................**$1.25**

## LADIES' "WESTERN"

*Stetson's*
## PLAYGIRL

**No. 227**—A fine western hat for the ladies—a real Stetson in three colors—Brown, Bisque (buckskin), and Black—eyelets in brim through which is fastened a neat calfskin chin strap.
Each............................ **$9.00**

**No. 228**—Same hat, not a Stetson—Brown only (with strap).
Each................................ **$4.45**

Any hat in catalog available with calfskin chin strap—black, brown, tan, or white—**50c** extra.

May be had in **Navy Blue, Medium Tan,** or **Black.**

**No. 32**—This is one of Stetson's most popular models, and is featured in smart stores throughout America. A fine felt, trimmed with grosgrain and bright feather flicker. Sizes 21½, 22, 22½, 23. Be sure to specify color and size in ordering. Each, postpaid............. **$5.95**

**No. 32X**—The "Canter". Somewhat like the "Playgirl", and a good grade of felt, but not of Stetson make. Your choice of 3 colors: Hunter's Green, Dark Brown, Black. Sizes 21½, 22, 22½, 23. Each, postpaid......... **$3.85**

# Print Blouses and Head Scarfs

### Western Scenes on Rayon

### Hunting Scenes on American Shantung

These beautiful blouses are available in two background colors—all soft tones; white, and red, with designs in harmonizing shades. Blouses and scarfs match perfectly. Scenes are all very horsey, and they're hand prints! Specify whether you want pictures of the English Hunt, or of the Western Rodeo.

**No. 13**—Blouse, with red or white background. Sizes 32, 34, 36, 38, 40.
Each, delivered..................... **$2.25**

**No. 13S**—Scarf to match No. 13 blouse.
20″ square, each........................$0.60
27″ square, each........................ 1.10

If ordered in sets, deduct 15c when small scarf is wanted, 25c when large one is wanted.

The Blouse and Scarf set pictured above and described above left has become very popular among sports minded young women. The blouse is cool and allows much freedom; the scarf is practical either as pictured, or for neck wear.

*See Index for other women's apparel*

Prices on Stetson Hats subject to change without notice.

# INDEX

**"QUALITY ARTICLES
ARE MADE FOR MEN WHO
ARE TIRED OF
THE EXTRAVAGANCE
OF BUYING
CHEAP THINGS"**

●

A CATALOG OF SELECTED
# DOVER BOOKS
IN ALL FIELDS OF INTEREST

# A CATALOG OF SELECTED DOVER
# BOOKS IN ALL FIELDS OF INTEREST

CONCERNING THE SPIRITUAL IN ART, Wassily Kandinsky. Pioneering work by father of abstract art. Thoughts on color theory, nature of art. Analysis of earlier masters. 12 illustrations. 80pp. of text. 5⅜ x 8½. 23411-8

ANIMALS: 1,419 Copyright-Free Illustrations of Mammals, Birds, Fish, Insects, etc., Jim Harter (ed.). Clear wood engravings present, in extremely lifelike poses, over 1,000 species of animals. One of the most extensive pictorial sourcebooks of its kind. Captions. Index. 284pp. 9 x 12. 23766-4

CELTIC ART: The Methods of Construction, George Bain. Simple geometric techniques for making Celtic interlacements, spirals, Kells-type initials, animals, humans, etc. Over 500 illustrations. 160pp. 9 x 12. (Available in U.S. only.) 22923-8

AN ATLAS OF ANATOMY FOR ARTISTS, Fritz Schider. Most thorough reference work on art anatomy in the world. Hundreds of illustrations, including selections from works by Vesalius, Leonardo, Goya, Ingres, Michelangelo, others. 593 illustrations. 192pp. 7⅛ x 10¼. 20241-0

CELTIC HAND STROKE-BY-STROKE (Irish Half-Uncial from "The Book of Kells"): An Arthur Baker Calligraphy Manual, Arthur Baker. Complete guide to creating each letter of the alphabet in distinctive Celtic manner. Covers hand position, strokes, pens, inks, paper, more. Illustrated. 48pp. 8¼ x 11. 24336-2

EASY ORIGAMI, John Montroll. Charming collection of 32 projects (hat, cup, pelican, piano, swan, many more) specially designed for the novice origami hobbyist. Clearly illustrated easy-to-follow instructions insure that even beginning papercrafters will achieve successful results. 48pp. 8¼ x 11. 27298-2

THE COMPLETE BOOK OF BIRDHOUSE CONSTRUCTION FOR WOODWORKERS, Scott D. Campbell. Detailed instructions, illustrations, tables. Also data on bird habitat and instinct patterns. Bibliography. 3 tables. 63 illustrations in 15 figures. 48pp. 5¼ x 8½. 24407-5

BLOOMINGDALE'S ILLUSTRATED 1886 CATALOG: Fashions, Dry Goods and Housewares, Bloomingdale Brothers. Famed merchants' extremely rare catalog depicting about 1,700 products: clothing, housewares, firearms, dry goods, jewelry, more. Invaluable for dating, identifying vintage items. Also, copyright-free graphics for artists, designers. Co-published with Henry Ford Museum & Greenfield Village. 160pp. 8¼ x 11. 25780-0

HISTORIC COSTUME IN PICTURES, Braun & Schneider. Over 1,450 costumed figures in clearly detailed engravings–from dawn of civilization to end of 19th century. Captions. Many folk costumes. 256pp. 8⅜ x 11¾. 23150-X

PERSPECTIVE FOR ARTISTS, Rex Vicat Cole. Depth, perspective of sky and sea, shadows, much more, not usually covered. 391 diagrams, 81 reproductions of drawings and paintings. 279pp. 5⅜ x 8½. 22487-2

DRAWING THE LIVING FIGURE, Joseph Sheppard. Innovative approach to artistic anatomy focuses on specifics of surface anatomy, rather than muscles and bones. Over 170 drawings of live models in front, back and side views, and in widely varying poses. Accompanying diagrams. 177 illustrations. Introduction. Index. 144pp. 8⅜ x11¼. 26723-7

GOTHIC AND OLD ENGLISH ALPHABETS: 100 Complete Fonts, Dan X. Solo. Add power, elegance to posters, signs, other graphics with 100 stunning copyright-free alphabets: Blackstone, Dolbey, Germania, 97 more–including many lower-case, numerals, punctuation marks. 104pp. 8⅛ x 11. 24695-7

HOW TO DO BEADWORK, Mary White. Fundamental book on craft from simple projects to five-bead chains and woven works. 106 illustrations. 142pp. 5⅜ x 8. 20697-1

THE BOOK OF WOOD CARVING, Charles Marshall Sayers. Finest book for beginners discusses fundamentals and offers 34 designs. "Absolutely first rate . . . well thought out and well executed."–E. J. Tangerman. 118pp. 7¾ x 10⅝. 23654-4

ILLUSTRATED CATALOG OF CIVIL WAR MILITARY GOODS: Union Army Weapons, Insignia, Uniform Accessories, and Other Equipment, Schuyler, Hartley, and Graham. Rare, profusely illustrated 1846 catalog includes Union Army uniform and dress regulations, arms and ammunition, coats, insignia, flags, swords, rifles, etc. 226 illustrations. 160pp. 9 x 12. 24939-5

WOMEN'S FASHIONS OF THE EARLY 1900s: An Unabridged Republication of "New York Fashions, 1909," National Cloak & Suit Co. Rare catalog of mail-order fashions documents women's and children's clothing styles shortly after the turn of the century. Captions offer full descriptions, prices. Invaluable resource for fashion, costume historians. Approximately 725 illustrations. 128pp. 8⅜ x 11¼. 27276-1

THE 1912 AND 1915 GUSTAV STICKLEY FURNITURE CATALOGS, Gustav Stickley. With over 200 detailed illustrations and descriptions, these two catalogs are essential reading and reference materials and identification guides for Stickley furniture. Captions cite materials, dimensions and prices. 112pp. 6½ x 9¼. 26676-1

EARLY AMERICAN LOCOMOTIVES, John H. White, Jr. Finest locomotive engravings from early 19th century: historical (1804–74), main-line (after 1870), special, foreign, etc. 147 plates. 142pp. 11⅜ x 8¼. 22772-3

THE TALL SHIPS OF TODAY IN PHOTOGRAPHS, Frank O. Braynard. Lavishly illustrated tribute to nearly 100 majestic contemporary sailing vessels: Amerigo Vespucci, Clearwater, Constitution, Eagle, Mayflower, Sea Cloud, Victory, many more. Authoritative captions provide statistics, background on each ship. 190 black-and-white photographs and illustrations. Introduction. 128pp. 8⅞ x 11¾. 27163-3

PIANO TUNING, J. Cree Fischer. Clearest, best book for beginner, amateur. Simple repairs, raising dropped notes, tuning by easy method of flattened fifths. No previous skills needed. 4 illustrations. 201pp. 5⅜ x 8½. 23267-0

HINTS TO SINGERS, Lillian Nordica. Selecting the right teacher, developing confidence, overcoming stage fright, and many other important skills receive thoughtful discussion in this indispensible guide, written by a world-famous diva of four decades' experience. 96pp. 5⅜ x 8½. 40094-8

THE COMPLETE NONSENSE OF EDWARD LEAR, Edward Lear. All nonsense limericks, zany alphabets, Owl and Pussycat, songs, nonsense botany, etc., illustrated by Lear. Total of 320pp. 5⅜ x 8½. (Available in U.S. only.) 20167-8

VICTORIAN PARLOUR POETRY: An Annotated Anthology, Michael R. Turner. 117 gems by Longfellow, Tennyson, Browning, many lesser-known poets. "The Village Blacksmith," "Curfew Must Not Ring Tonight," "Only a Baby Small," dozens more, often difficult to find elsewhere. Index of poets, titles, first lines. xxiii + 325pp. 5⅝ x 8¼. 27044-0

DUBLINERS, James Joyce. Fifteen stories offer vivid, tightly focused observations of the lives of Dublin's poorer classes. At least one, "The Dead," is considered a masterpiece. Reprinted complete and unabridged from standard edition. 160pp. 5³⁄₁₆ x 8¼. 26870-5

GREAT WEIRD TALES: 14 Stories by Lovecraft, Blackwood, Machen and Others, S. T. Joshi (ed.). 14 spellbinding tales, including "The Sin Eater," by Fiona McLeod, "The Eye Above the Mantel," by Frank Belknap Long, as well as renowned works by R. H. Barlow, Lord Dunsany, Arthur Machen, W. C. Morrow and eight other masters of the genre. 256pp. 5⅜ x 8½. (Available in U.S. only.) 40436-6

THE BOOK OF THE SACRED MAGIC OF ABRAMELIN THE MAGE, translated by S. MacGregor Mathers. Medieval manuscript of ceremonial magic. Basic document in Aleister Crowley, Golden Dawn groups. 268pp. 5⅜ x 8½. 23211-5

NEW RUSSIAN-ENGLISH AND ENGLISH-RUSSIAN DICTIONARY, M. A. O'Brien. This is a remarkably handy Russian dictionary, containing a surprising amount of information, including over 70,000 entries. 366pp. 4½ x 6⅛. 20208-9

HISTORIC HOMES OF THE AMERICAN PRESIDENTS, Second, Revised Edition, Irvin Haas. A traveler's guide to American Presidential homes, most open to the public, depicting and describing homes occupied by every American President from George Washington to George Bush. With visiting hours, admission charges, travel routes. 175 photographs. Index. 160pp. 8¼ x 11. 26751-2

NEW YORK IN THE FORTIES, Andreas Feininger. 162 brilliant photographs by the well-known photographer, formerly with *Life* magazine. Commuters, shoppers, Times Square at night, much else from city at its peak. Captions by John von Hartz. 181pp. 9¼ x 10¾. 23585-8

INDIAN SIGN LANGUAGE, William Tomkins. Over 525 signs developed by Sioux and other tribes. Written instructions and diagrams. Also 290 pictographs. 111pp. 6⅛ x 9¼. 22029-X

# CATALOG OF DOVER BOOKS

THE STORY OF THE TITANIC AS TOLD BY ITS SURVIVORS, Jack Winocour (ed.). What it was really like. Panic, despair, shocking inefficiency, and a little heroism. More thrilling than any fictional account. 26 illustrations. 320pp. 5⅜ x 8½.
20610-6

FAIRY AND FOLK TALES OF THE IRISH PEASANTRY, William Butler Yeats (ed.). Treasury of 64 tales from the twilight world of Celtic myth and legend: "The Soul Cages," "The Kildare Pooka," "King O'Toole and his Goose," many more. Introduction and Notes by W. B. Yeats. 352pp. 5⅜ x 8½.
26941-8

BUDDHIST MAHAYANA TEXTS, E. B. Cowell and others (eds.). Superb, accurate translations of basic documents in Mahayana Buddhism, highly important in history of religions. The Buddha-karita of Asvaghosha, Larger Sukhavativyuha, more. 448pp. 5⅜ x 8½.
25552-2

ONE TWO THREE . . . INFINITY: Facts and Speculations of Science, George Gamow. Great physicist's fascinating, readable overview of contemporary science: number theory, relativity, fourth dimension, entropy, genes, atomic structure, much more. 128 illustrations. Index. 352pp. 5⅜ x 8½.
25664-2

EXPERIMENTATION AND MEASUREMENT, W. J. Youden. Introductory manual explains laws of measurement in simple terms and offers tips for achieving accuracy and minimizing errors. Mathematics of measurement, use of instruments, experimenting with machines. 1994 edition. Foreword. Preface. Introduction. Epilogue. Selected Readings. Glossary. Index. Tables and figures. 128pp. 5⅜ x 8½.   40451-X

DALÍ ON MODERN ART: The Cuckolds of Antiquated Modern Art, Salvador Dalí. Influential painter skewers modern art and its practitioners. Outrageous evaluations of Picasso, Cézanne, Turner, more. 15 renderings of paintings discussed. 44 calligraphic decorations by Dalí. 96pp. 5⅜ x 8½. (Available in U.S. only.)
29220-7

ANTIQUE PLAYING CARDS: A Pictorial History, Henry René D'Allemagne. Over 900 elaborate, decorative images from rare playing cards (14th–20th centuries): Bacchus, death, dancing dogs, hunting scenes, royal coats of arms, players cheating, much more. 96pp. 9¼ x 12¼.
29265-7

MAKING FURNITURE MASTERPIECES: 30 Projects with Measured Drawings, Franklin H. Gottshall. Step-by-step instructions, illustrations for constructing handsome, useful pieces, among them a Sheraton desk, Chippendale chair, Spanish desk, Queen Anne table and a William and Mary dressing mirror. 224pp. 8⅛ x 11¼.
29338-6

THE FOSSIL BOOK: A Record of Prehistoric Life, Patricia V. Rich et al. Profusely illustrated definitive guide covers everything from single-celled organisms and dinosaurs to birds and mammals and the interplay between climate and man. Over 1,500 illustrations. 760pp. 7½ x 10⅛.
29371-8

Paperbound unless otherwise indicated. Available at your book dealer, online at **www.doverpublications.com**, or by writing to Dept. GI, Dover Publications, Inc., 31 East 2nd Street, Mineola, NY 11501. For current price information or for free catalogues (please indicate field of interest), write to Dover Publications or log on to **www.doverpublications.com** and see every Dover book in print. Dover publishes more than 500 books each year on science, elementary and advanced mathematics, biology, music, art, literary history, social sciences, and other areas.